EXPLORING ADA
VOLUME 2

Geoffrey O. Mendal
Systems Engineering Research Corporation

Douglas L. Bryan
Stanford University

Prentice Hall
Englewood Cliffs, New Jersey 07632

Library of Congress Cataloging-in-Publishing Data

(Revised for vol. 2)

Bryan, Douglas L.
  Exploring Ada.

  Includes bibliographical references and indexes.
  1. Ada (Computer program language)   I. Mendal,
Geoffrey O.   II. Title.
QA76.73.A35B79 1990 vol. 2 005.13'3   89-4014
    ISBN 0-13-295684-5 (v. 1)
    ISBN 0-13-297227-1 (v. 2)

Acquisitions editor: Marcia Horton
Production editors: Kathleen Schiaparelli and Irwin Zucker
Copy editor: Brian Baker
Prepress buyer: Linda Behrens
Manufacturing buyer: David Dickey
Editorial assistant: Diana Penha

To my family, who still will not comprehend one word of this.

G. O. M.

To those who teach.

D. L. B.

ⓒ1992 by Prentice-Hall, Inc.
A Simon & Schuster Company
Englewood Cliffs, New Jersey 07632

50 BAL·C   MCS-C   6/8/92

Printed in the United States of America

10 9 8 7 6 5 4 3 2 1

ISBN   0-13-297227-1

Prentice-Hall International (UK) Limited, *London*
Prentice-Hall of Australia Pty. Limited, *Sydney*
Prentice-Hall Canada Inc., *Toronto*
Prentice-Hall Hispanoamericana, S. A., *Mexico*
Prentice-Hall of India Private Limited, *New Delhi*
Prentice-Hall of Japan, Inc., *Tokyo*
Simon & Schuster Asia Pte. Ltd., *Singapore*
Editora Prentice-Hall do Brasil, Ltda., *Rio de Janeiro*

Contents

List of Figures   x

Foreword   xi

Preface   xii

Introduction to Volume 1   xv

      Method of Presentation   xvi

      Goals   xvii

16 Derived Types   1

   16.1   Declaration of Derived Types 2

      16.1.1   Derived Booleans, 2
      16.1.2   Static versus Nonstatic Derived Types, 3
      16.1.3   Base Type versus Derived Type versus Subtype, 4
      16.1.4   Derived Attributes, 5
      16.1.5   Type Conversions, 6

16.2   Derived Subprograms   7

      16.2.1   Emulating the Derivation of a Package, 8
      16.2.2   The Parent Type, 9
      16.2.3   Derivable versus Derived, 11
      16.2.4   Calling Derived Subprograms, 14
      16.2.5   Deriving Generic Units, 17

17 The Tasking Model   **19**

17.1   Declaration of Task Types and Objects   20

      17.1.1   It's a Program Unit, Too, 20
      17.1.2   Task Specifications, 20
      17.1.3   Discriminated and Generic Tasks, 22
      17.1.4   Task Objects as Parameters, 24
      17.1.5   Anonymous Task Types, 25
      17.1.6   Task Bodies, 26

17.2   Operations and Attributes of Task Types   27

      17.2.1   Membership Tests, 28
      17.2.2   Callable and Terminated, 29
      17.2.3   The Count Attribute, 30

17.3   Activation and Execution   31

      17.3.1   Exceptions during Activation, 31
      17.3.2   Activation by Allocation, 34
      17.3.3   Spawning Siblings, 35
      17.3.4   Activation and Execution Order, 36

17.4   The Rendezvous   40

      17.4.1   Brief Encounters, 41
      17.4.2   Where to Accept, 42
      17.4.3   Calling Families, 45
      17.4.4   Raising Exceptions, 46
      17.4.5   Minimalist Accept Statements, 48

17.5   The Multitalented Select Statement   49

      17.5.1   Selecting among More than One Accept, 49
      17.5.2   Inherent Nature of Indeterminism, 50
      17.5.3   Guard Expressions, 52
      17.5.4   Count, Families, and Priorities, 54
      17.5.5   The Delay Alternative, 56
      17.5.6   The Meaning of "Immediately", 57
      17.5.7   Timed versus Conditional Calls, 59
      17.5.8   The Impatient Callee Task, 61
      17.5.9   The Terminate Alternative, 62

Contents

17.6   Completion and Termination   64

    17.6.1   Impatient Masters, 64
    17.6.2   Death by Exception, 66
    17.6.3   Naming Terminated Tasks, 67
    17.6.4   Library Tasks, 68

17.7   The Task State Model   70

    17.7.1   Deadness Errors, 71
    17.7.2   Synchronization Points, 72
    17.7.3   Self-abortion, 75

17.8   Shared Variables   76

    17.8.1   Synchronizing Variables, 77
    17.8.2   Finders Keepers, 80
    17.8.3   Transitivity of Synchronization, 82
    17.8.4   Shared Variables as Parameters, 84

18 Exceptions   87

18.1   Declaration of Exceptions   88

    18.1.1   Exceptions as Objects, 88
    18.1.2   Hiding Exceptions, 89
    18.1.3   Generic Exceptions, 89
    18.1.4   Recursive Exceptions, 90

18.2   Raising, Propagating, and Handling Exceptions   92

    18.2.1   Static Semantic Issues, 92
    18.2.2   Propagation Logs, 93
    18.2.3   Raising Another Exception, 94
    18.2.4   Call Stack Tracing, 95
    18.2.5   Preventing Propagation, 97
    18.2.6   Propagation from Packages, 99
    18.2.7   Handling an Exception outside of Its Scope, 99
    18.2.8   Propagation Styles, 101

18.3   Optimization and Reordering   103

    18.3.1   Eliminating Operations, 103
    18.3.2   Reordering Operations, 105
    18.3.3   Delayed Reactions, 107
    18.3.4   Erroneous Reorderings, 108

19 Generic Units   110

19.1   Declaration of Generic Units   110

    19.1.1   They Are Declarations, 111

19.1.2   Unconstrained Formal Objects, 112

19.1.3   Parameter Modes, 113

19.1.4   Limited Formal Objects, 113

19.1.5   Generic Formal Type Classes, 114

19.1.6   Subtype Indications in Generic Formal Parts, 116

19.1.7   Formal Types with Discriminants, 117

19.1.8   Importing Operations, 118

19.1.9   Binding Time, 120

19.1.10   Empty Parts, 121

19.2   Instantiation   123

19.2.1   Self-instantiation, 123

19.2.2   Discriminants, 125

19.2.3   Type Matching, 127

19.2.4   Generic Actual Subprograms, 129

19.2.5   Default Actual Subprograms, 130

19.2.6   Overload Resolution, 132

19.2.7   Program_Error, 133

19.3   Instances   134

19.3.1   Predefined Exported Operations, 135

19.3.2   Types Are Types, 136

19.3.3   Constraints Are Constraints, 137

19.3.4   Constraints on Formal Objects, 138

19.3.5   Homographs in Instances, 140

19.3.6   Importing Static Properties, 140

19.3.7   Breaking the Contract Model, 142

19.3.8   Exceptions in Instances, 142

20 The Program Library   **145**

20.1   Package Standard   145

20.1.1   Homographs, 147

20.1.2   Hiding the Predefined Package Standard, 148

20.2   Package Calendar   148

20.2.1   Midnight Caller, 148

20.2.2   Running Out of Time, 149

20.2.3   Subtype Assumptions, 150

20.2.4   Time Warps, 150

20.2.5   Unsupported Date, 151

20.2.6   Clock Resolution, 152

20.2.7   Multiple Clocks, 153

20.3   The With-Clause   155

20.3.1   Imported Unit Names, 155

20.3.2   Inheriting Visibility, 156

20.3.3   *Circular Dependency, 157*
20.3.4   *Redundant Visibility, 159*

20.4   Compilation and the Main Program   160

20.4.1   *Compilation versus Compilation Unit, 160*
20.4.2   *What Can Be a Compilation Unit?, 161*
20.4.3   *Recompiling a Unit, 162*
20.4.4   *Library Unit versus Secondary Unit, 163*
20.4.5   *What Can Be a Main Program?, 165*
20.4.6   *The Return of the Main Program, 166*

20.5   Body Stubs and Subunits   166

20.5.1   *Specifying Subunits, 167*
20.5.2   *The Parent Unit, 168*
20.5.3   *Conformance, 169*
20.5.4   *Family Trees, 170*

20.6   Compilation Dependencies   172

20.6.1   *Forced Recompilations, 172*
20.6.2   *Obsolescence, 174*
20.6.3   *Contract Violation, 175*
20.6.4   *Dependencies for Generic Units, 177*

20.7   Elaboration of Program Units   179

20.7.1   *Order of Elaboration, 179*
20.7.2   *Elaboration of Subunits, 181*
20.7.3   *Handling Elaboration Exceptions, 182*

21 Scope and Visibility   185

21.1   Scope of Declarations   186

21.1.1   *Scope Bindings, 186*
21.1.2   *Kinds of Scope, 187*
21.1.3   *Naming Scopes, 190*
21.1.4   *Subprogram Hiding, 190*
21.1.5   *Homographs, 191*
21.1.6   *Hiding Package Standard, 193*
21.1.7   *Nesting, 194*
21.1.8   *Nested Accept Statements, 194*

21.2   General Visibility Rules   196

21.2.1   *Self-seeing, 196*
21.2.2   *End Game, 197*
21.2.3   *Tricky Expanded Names, 198*
21.2.4   *Visibility of Block Names and Labels, 199*
21.2.5   *Hide-and-seek, 200*

21.2.6   *Names in Operations, 202*
21.2.7   *In Search of Character Literals, 203*

21.3   The Use Clause   204

21.3.1   *What to Use, 204*
21.3.2   *Scope of a Use Clause, 204*
21.3.3   *Counterintuitive Semantics, 205*
21.3.4   *Clash of the Clauses, 207*

22 Renaming Declarations   210

22.1   Renaming Objects and Packages   211

22.1.1   *Syntax and Simple Static Semantics, 211*
22.1.2   *Transitivity, 212*
22.1.3   *Subtype Constraints, 213*
22.1.4   *Components and Slices, 214*
22.1.5   *Dynamically Created Objects, 215*
22.1.6   *Subprogram Formal Parameters, 217*
22.1.7   *Evaluating Names, 218*
22.1.8   *Implicit Importation, 219*
22.1.9   *Prefixes of Expanded Names, 220*
22.1.10   *Renamable, 222*

22.2   Renaming Operations and Exceptions   225

22.2.1   *Changing Subprogram Formal Parameters, 225*
22.2.2   *Renaming Entries, 228*
22.2.3   *Attributes, 229*
22.2.4   *Equality, 230*
22.2.5   *Name versus Entity, 231*
22.2.6   *Overload Resolution, 232*
22.2.7   *On Being Static, 232*
22.2.8   *Type Conversions, 233*

23 The Predefined I/O Packages   235

23.1   File Management   236

23.1.1   *Roses, 236*
23.1.2   *Name Dropping, 238*
23.1.3   *Reset, 239*
23.1.4   *Temporary Files, 240*
23.1.5   *Side Effects Associated with Files, 241*
23.1.6   *Exception Pecking Order, 242*
23.1.7   *Propagation of Predefined Exceptions, 243*

23.2   Binary Input and Output   244

23.2.1   *Random Access, 244*

23.2.2   *Access Values, 245*
23.2.3   *Heterogeneous Files, 247*

23.3   Text Input and Output   250

23.3.1   *Extensions, 251*
23.3.2   *Buffering Output, 251*
23.3.3   *Resetting Default Streams, 252*
23.3.4   *Closed Default Files, 254*
23.3.5   *Nonexistent Default Files, 254*
23.3.6   *Parsing with Enumeration_Io, 255*
23.3.7   *Nongraphic I/O, 257*
23.3.8   *Invalid Data, 258*
23.3.9   *Parsing Integer Literals, 260*
23.3.10   *Real Imaging, 261*
23.3.11   *Skipping Lines, 263*
23.3.12   *Turn the Page, 265*
23.3.13   *The Disappearing Line Trick, 266*

24 Machine Representations   **269**

24.1   Scalar Types   271

24.1.1   *Internal Codes versus Position Numbers, 271*
24.1.2   *The Predefined Type Character, 272*
24.1.3   *The Cost of Internal Codes, 272*
24.1.4   *Changing Model Numbers, 273*
24.1.5   *Conflicting Representations, 275*
24.1.6   *Dynamic Sizes, 276*
24.1.7   *Biased Types, 277*

24.2   Composite Types   278

24.2.1   *Packing Records, 278*
24.2.2   *Odd Record Representations, 280*
24.2.3   *Biased Components, 281*
24.2.4   *Record Component Attributes, 282*
24.2.5   *Minimizing Array Sizes, 283*

24.3   Access and Task Types   284

24.3.1   *Dynamic Collection Sizes, 284*
24.3.2   *Two Sizes of Tasks, 286*

24.4   Addresses and Interrupts   287

24.4.1   *Visibility of the Address Attribute, 287*
24.4.2   *Address Clause Static Semantics, 288*
24.4.3   *Component Addresses, 290*
24.4.4   *Overlaying Objects, 291*
24.4.5   *Termination of Interrupt Handlers, 293*
24.4.6   *Multiple Accepts for One Handler, 294*

24.5   Positioning of Clauses   296

    24.5.1   The Force, 296
    24.5.2   Declarative Parts, 298
    24.5.3   Type versus Subtype, 299
    24.5.4   Parent and Derived Type Representations, 300
    24.5.5   Derived Sizes, 301

24.6   Machine Code Insertions   302

    24.6.1   Static Semantic Issues, 302
    24.6.2   Programming with Code Statements, 303

24.7   Unchecked Programming   305

    24.7.1   Unchecked Conversion, 306
    24.7.2   Unconstrained Conversions, 308
    24.7.3   Deallocating Tasks, 309

Bibliography   **313**

Index   **314**

List of Figures

17.1   Ordered and concurrent calls to *Note*   38

17.2   Task state diagram   70

17.3   Order of access of shared variables   79

19.1   Generic formal type classes   115

20.1   Illegal secondary unit hierarchy   171

20.2   Illegal overloaded subunits   172

21.1   Simple example of scope and visibility   186

21.2   Immediate and extended scopes   188

24.1   Categories of representation clauses with attributes   270

Foreword

The expressiveness and complexity of programming languages has increased markedly over several generations. The Ada programming language covers many areas of system and software behavior which have traditionally been absent from programming languages. The number and types of features within the Ada programming language make it difficult for the beginner to grasp the totality of Ada. This book serves as an excellent second book about Ada by which one may progress from a novice or casual user of Ada to a much higher degree of proficiency about understanding Ada.

This is not a "how-to" book. This is more of a "how-come" book. Extensive thought has been given to non-trivial explanations of Ada features and semantics by words, examples, and related problems to solve. The reader will obtain great satisfaction in having his or her degree of in-depth understanding of the capabilities as well as the limitations of the Ada language grow significantly as a result of mastering the material in this book.

The Socratic style of posing questions, exposing technical foundations, use of examples, and citing references is a style which appears in few books about programming and software engineering today. The possible bounds of Ada proficiency are explicitly set forth as Novice, Programmer, Designer, and Language Lawyer levels. This unknowingly sets new standards of expectations for the reader to progress beyond the traditional definition of programmer which is prevalent in the software industry today. It is a most welcome change.

The book promotes understanding of the entire Ada culture. This not only includes the language definition, but insight into the thought process and rationale which underlies the Ada language. This book fills a void between introductory level Ada material and the formal ANSI/ISO Ada Reference Manual. It encourages the reader to be proactive in the process of mastering Ada. Upon completion of the book, the reader will have fulfilled two goals: (1) becoming a sophisticated Ada user, and (2) becoming a knowledge source about rationale and interpretation issues which must be dealt with as use of Ada becomes more sophisticated over time. These skills will also help address future software issues which include comparison and interaction of Ada with other languages, as well as any future migration and change to the Ada language itself.

Mark S. Gerhardt

Mountain View, California

Preface

*In computer science it is not polite to say, "I don't like your
language." Instead you say, "Your language is too complex."*
Jean Ichbiah, October 7, 1986, at a Bay
Area SIGAda meeting, Sunnyvale, California
(in response to a question concerning some reviewers'
negative comments regarding the language design)

*I hold no quarter with those who say Ada is too complex to learn. Just
the opposite is true. It is the problem space which is too complex
to not use features as in Ada. Ada is a vastly simplifying tool.*
Professor Charles McKay, November 20, 1985, at the
National SIGAda meeting, Boston, Massachusetts

In 1974, the United States Department of Defense concluded that a new, more powerful
high-order programming language was needed for their software development. The
language would have to increase program reliability, decrease maintenance costs, and
increase the productivity of the human programmer. A study was performed by the
High Order Language Working Group within the Department of Defense in which it was
found that none of the programming languages available at that time satisfied all of those
requirements. Thus began the design of Ada.

On December 10, 1980, Ada was approved as the U. S. Department of Defense
MIL-STD-1815, and on January 22, 1983, Ada was accepted by the American National
Standards Institute (ANSI) and became ANSI/MIL-STD-1815A. Ada has been adopted
as a French standard as well (AFNOR Standard NF Z 65-700). Thus, Ada became an
international standard. On March 12, 1987, the central secretariat of the International
Standards Organization (ISO) announced the approval of ISO/8652-1987; this one-page
endorsement names the American and French Ada standards.

Ada contains many programming features that directly support modern software
engineering principles. For instance, strong typing, information hiding, data abstraction,
distributed computing, facilities to model parallel tasks, handling of exceptional conditions, software reuse, and consistency across separate compilations are directly supported

by the semantics of the language. Because of these features and the strong support from the U. S. Department of Defense and the European Economic Community, Ada will continue to be an important programming language well into the 21st century.

This book is designed to teach the reader the full semantics of Ada. Because Ada is a large language and might initially appear too cumbersome for the novice to learn, we have adopted a novel approach to presenting the language: Hundreds of small, isolated issues are presented and discussed that collectively cover the entire language.

We have made an effort to maintain the viewpoint of the programmer: The book is for programmers, by programmers. To the Ada student, the book walks the reader through Ada's detailed semantics, one concept at a time. To the programmer, the book presents examples of the features of Ada in a direct and concise format. To the software designer, the book presents concepts and illustrates their use with examples. To the maintenance programmer, the book is presented in the same format in which one works: A small program or program fragment is presented, and one is asked to explain its semantics and resolve any problems it may have. To the evaluation and testing programmer, the book presents Ada features and common problems or pitfalls associated with their use.

The text should not be read as one long test: It is not a goal of this book simply to evaluate the reader's current competency in Ada. There are many problems presented that will foil even the most knowledgeable Ada programmers. The reader should not consider these problems as material to be memorized. One cannot fully understand Ada and use its features properly by memorizing a number of special cases. The reader's goal should be to understand *how* and *why* the problems are solved. With this goal, the reader will acquire an understanding of the rationale behind the language and how it forms a cohesive programming mind-set.

This method of learning is based on the Socratic method. In applying the Socratic method, the student solves a large number of problems that collectively address all concepts in the domain of study; a more traditional approach is to study the concepts directly, perhaps memorizing them, and then apply them to many problems. The goal of the Socratic method is to lead the student in achieving a deeper understanding of the domain by allowing one to derive one's own conceptually complete model of the domain. This method allows the reader implicitly (maybe even subconsciously) to derive the concepts from the problems. It is this self-realization of the underlying concepts which reenforces the student's understanding of the domain so that it may be applied to future problems.

At first, the reader may feel intimidated by the difficulty of the problems. It may appear as though one is making no progress at all. Do not despair! Through the Socratic method, the reader is learning a discipline—a philosophy in which to *address* Ada problems, and not simply solve them. Once this discipline has been acquired, the programmer will find it enjoyable to develop software using the Ada programming language.

This volume is the second of two. It expands upon the larger language issues and issues dealing with Ada's more advanced features. Chapter 1 of Volume 1 follows and provides an introduction to the method of presentation used in this text.

ACKNOWLEDGMENTS

We would like to thank the many people who have contributed to the five-year effort of developing this text. We thank the following people for their technical review of the manuscript: Bryce M. Bardin of the University of Colorado, John J. Cupak of Rivier College, Jorge Diaz-Herrera of George Mason University, David Emery of The MITRE Corporation, Anthony Gargaro of Computer Sciences Corporation, Narain Gehani of AT&T Bell Laboratories, Lars Inge Helgeland of the University of Bergen, Norway, Richard N. Henault of Systems Engineering Research Corporation, Jon Mauney of North Carolina State University, Sigurd Meldal of the University of Bergen, Norway, A. Spencer Peterson of the Software Engineering Institute, Patrick Sebrechts of National University, Sissel M. Syvertsen of the University of Bergen, Norway, Mark Temte of Purdue University, Steve Wampler of Northern Arizona University, and Sigve Henning Zachariassen of the University of Bergen, Norway.

Although they were not technical reviewers, we thank the following people who provided much support in getting the text in print: Dr. David Luckham of Stanford University; Paul Saffo, our advisor on publishing law matters; our Prentice Hall editors, Marcia Horton and Patrice Fraccio; and Sriram Sankar, the person who wrote (and rewrote) the TEX macro used to format all of our program examples.

We would like to give special thanks and recognition to John Goodenough of the Software Engineering Institute, who reviewed a few chapters of *Exploring Ada, Volume 1*. In addition, his years of effort on the Ada program have greatly benefited the community as a whole. The book would not have nearly the technical detail it does if it were not for his work in developing the Ada Rapporteur Group Notes and the *The Ada Compiler Validation Capability Implementers' Guide* [Goodenough86].

Special thanks also go to Tom Arkwright of Lockheed Missiles & Space Company, Inc. who reviewed a few chapters of this book. Dr. Arkwright was the one who initially conceived of presenting the detailed semantics of Ada in the format used here. He was also the catalyst for inspiring us to embark on this adventure.

Finally, we would like to give special recognition to Dr. David Rosenblum of AT&T Bell Laboratories. David has been our most valuable technical reviewer. Chapter 17, for example, would be a mess if it were not for David's honesty and technical excellence.

Geoffrey O. Mendal

Mountain View, California

Douglas L. Bryan

Stanford, California

Introduction to Volume 1

> *Though this be madness, yet there is method in't.*
> William Shakespeare, 1600, from *Hamlet*, Act II

> *Example is the school of mankind, and they will learn at no other.*
> Edmund Burke, 1796, from *Letters on a Regicade Peace*

This book is a collection of problems and corresponding solutions primarily addressing intermediate and advanced Ada topics. The book addresses every feature of the Ada language.

Anyone who has had an introduction to the Ada programming language and has a working knowledge of at least one procedural programming language should be ready to tackle most of the problems presented. Since the most difficult problems are marked as such, the Ada novice will not become discouraged when spending a good amount of time on their solutions. A programmer who wants to learn about the "deep dark corners" of Ada, or who wants to learn Ada on one's own time at one's own pace, will enjoy this book.

At first glance, the book might appear to be nothing more than a collection of Ada trivia. However, each set of problems fully presents and explains an Ada feature and thus teaches the reader Ada from the viewpoint of dealing with problems. The reader will find the book a handy reference aid while writing and debugging Ada software. The book is for the professional Ada programmer and the academic student, and is applicable as a supplemental reference or recommended reading in any Ada curriculum.

The problems in the book should be taken in the context of the Ada standard, not from any one particular implementation. Any implementation dependencies that may arise are carefully noted. Many of the problems were adapted from actual problems encountered by the authors, their colleagues, and their students when they were learning Ada. Hence, it is likely that many other Ada programmers will encounter the same problems while learning the language. The book should thus make the reader's learning process more productive, since many of the problems one is bound to encounter are included, explained, and solved. A reader who simply reads the problems and then immediately reads the solutions will learn aspects of the language, but not in the detail that might be desired. We encourage the reader to attempt to solve each problem before looking at its solution.

METHOD OF PRESENTATION

Unlike many programming texts, this book is organized from the programmer's viewpoint rather than from a language designer's viewpoint. A common problem with using the *Reference Manual for the Ada Programming Language* ([Ada83]) as a text or even as a reference during one's education or during program development is that it is organized from the viewpoint of the language designer. In most programming texts, a problem is designed to test the reader's comprehension of the material previously presented. In this book, the problems *are* the material. Each problem is a means of expressing an Ada feature in a way the programmer can easily understand. In most cases, this means presenting source code in the problem, the solution, or both. All program examples have been fully tested.

Each chapter and section is prefaced by a short discussion of the features examined. These discussions are used to further qualify the domain of the problems presented.

Associated with each problem is a *difficulty level*—in ascending order, *novice*, *programmer*, *designer*, and *language lawyer*. The difficulty levels represent an estimate of the Ada experience required by a programmer to solve the problems correctly. However, by attempting difficult problems, readers at all levels of Ada competency will gain experience. Following is a description of the levels:

Novice. Problems at this level are solvable by a programmer who has little more than an overview knowledge of the language. Such problems are primarily for an introductory student.

Programmer. These problems are solvable by a programmer who has been working in Ada for some time but still finds some of its detailed semantics confusing. It is assumed that such a programmer has been exposed to, but has not yet used, the advanced features of the language.

Designer. These problems are solvable by a programmer who often is asked to design system or unit interfaces. Such a programmer has an understanding of the *spirit* of Ada and how best to use its capabilities.

Language Lawyer. Problems at this level are solvable by a programmer who fully understands both the *spirit* and the *letter* of the Ada standard. Furthermore, such a programmer will be able to solve problems where the spirit and the letter of the standard seem to be in contradiction.

Many problems simply present a program, and the reader is asked, *Is the following program legal?* The term *legal* means that a program is both syntactically and semantically correct. Legality has nothing to do with run time behavior; it is concerned only with the static semantics of a program. If a program fragment is presented, the reader should assume that any complete context would preserve the semantics of the fragment. Furthermore, the use of ellipsis (...) does not affect the semantics of the fragment; it only serves as a placeholder. Unless explicitly noted in a problem, the use of an Ada term means exactly what it does in the *Reference Manual for the Ada Programming Language*.

Immediately after each problem statement is a solution. The first sentence or paragraph of this solution is a summary, or condensed answer. This sentence or paragraph is intended for the reader who is using this book as a quick reference during program development. The remainder of the solution presents a correct answer, fully explained and defended. Where applicable, a solution also presents alternate methods of solution and a discussion of their respective advantages and disadvantages.

When an Ada entity appears in *italics*, it matches one given in the Ada code segment being discussed. This use of italics is to emphasize the correlation between the discussion and code.

Some solutions are followed by an unanswered question. These questions are designed to aid the reader in drawing inferences between different concepts of the language. The reader should take the time to ponder the questions. Doing so will reenforce the domain of knowledge the reader has acquired at that point.

Associated with each problem are references from the *Reference Manual for the Ada Programming Language*. The references begin with a section number, annex letter, or appendix letter and are optionally followed by numbers in parentheses. Within the given section or subsection, these numbers indicate paragraphs. For example,

[Ada83]   3.5.4; 7.4.4(1, 3 .. 5); C(6)

refers to section 3.5.4 (in its entirety); paragraphs 1, 3, 4, and 5 of section 7.4.4; and paragraph 6 of Annex C of the manual.

Because some problems address issues not specifically answerable by the Ada manual, additional references are given. These references include various published technical reports that the reader might find worthwhile tracking down. Of special interest are the Ada Rapporteur Group Notes, which provide precise interpretations of current Ada language issues not directly addressed by the *Reference Manual for the Ada Programming Language*. (See the bibliography for information on how to obtain these notes.) An example of an Ada Rapporteur Group reference is as follows:

[ARG]   AI-00388/06, 06-13-88

This refers to Approved Interpretation (AI) number 388, revision 6, dated June 13, 1988.

GOALS

It is the primary goal of this book to teach the reader the various features of Ada, one concept at a time. The reader who takes the time to work out the answers will soon realize that the architecture of the book is designed to teach Ada in detail. The book uses the Socratic method to teach Ada; the reader will learn Ada by working out the solutions and then checking them. By observing our limited set of cases, the reader will build an understanding of the language such that one can assimilate and generate an infinite set of combinations of features beyond those presented in this book. Therefore, the design of the book assures that readers at all levels of Ada competency are able to productively *participate* in learning Ada.

The problems presented are intended to parallel those encountered and solved in practice. Since the book exposes many of the finer points of the language—those not discussed in an introductory class—it is an excellent reference for a programmer who is puzzled by Ada's very large and detailed semantics. This book will promote technical discussions of Ada's semantics and experimentation with its many powerful features. In addition, a programmer who has read and solved every problem will have a more complete understanding of Ada and how it forms a cohesive programming mind-set.

chapter 16

Derived Types

Ada doesn't provide inheritance.
Michal Young, April 15, 1988, at the 10th International
Conference on Software Engineering, Singapore

Derived types are a novel and powerful feature of Ada's typing model. They provide a means of defining new base types and subtypes of any class. Like every base type, a derived type is characterized by a set of values and a set of operations. However, what differentiates derived types from other types is the means by which the set of operations is defined. Associated with a derived type are not only basic and predefined operations, but also user-defined operations, called *derived* operations. When incorporated with packages, derived types provide a convenient balance between strong typing and user-defined types.

   Nearly all Ada programmers have used derived types, perhaps unknowingly. The language relies on derived types to neatly model and explain the semantics of user-defined numeric types. Every user-defined numeric type is actually derived from a predefined numeric type. Other languages have also used derivation to explain their typing models. Ada takes the next step by providing the derivation mechanism to the user. This chapter exposes the reader to the more intricate semantics of derived types. The problems included here challenge the reader to produce a more complete, conceptual model of Ada types in general.

16.1 DECLARATION OF DERIVED TYPES

Much of the semantics of a derived type of a given class is similar to the semantics of a base type of the same class. This section illustrates that, like every other base type, a derived type also defines a subtype. In fact, the syntax of a derived type definition is fairly similar to that of a subtype definition.

16.1.1 Derived Booleans

difficulty: programmer

Is the following code legal?

```
procedure Derived_Boolean is
    type Bools is new Boolean;
    type Inverted_Bool is (True, False);
begin
    if not Bools'First then
        ⋮
    elsif Boolean'Last then
        ⋮
    elsif Inverted_Bool'First then
        ⋮
    end if;
end Derived_Boolean;
```

◇◇◇◇◇

The last elsif-part is semantically illegal.

A *Boolean type* is either the predefined type Boolean or a type derived from a Boolean type. The type *Bools* is a Boolean type, as is the type

```
type B is new Bools;
```

The type *Inverted_Bool* defines an enumeration type, but is not a Boolean type.

Expressions appearing as the condition of an if, exit, or while loop statement must be of some Boolean type. (Select statements with *when conditions* also require Boolean expressions.) Usually, the predefined type Boolean is used. The reason why one may need to have two different Boolean types is the same reason why one would need to have two different integer types: in order to enforce strong typing. In order to increase the usability of the aforementioned statements, Ada allows the conditions to be of any Boolean type.

A Related Problem: What differences are there between the set of operations for *Bools* and that for *Inverted_Bools* given in the problem statement?

[Ada83]   3.4(21); 3.5.3; 5.3(2)

16.1.2 Static versus Nonstatic Derived Types

difficulty: programmer

Is the following code legal?

```
package Static is
   Two : Integer := 2;
      type Int_1  is new Integer  range 1 .. Two;
      type Int_2  is new Positive range 5 .. 10;
      type Int_3  is range 1 .. Int_1'Last;
      type Fp_1   is new Float digits Two;
      type Mass   is digits 3;
      type Grams is new Mass;
      type Str_1  is new String (1 .. Two);
   end Static;
```

◇◇◇◇◇

The definitions of *Int_3*, *Fp_1*, and *Grams* are semantically illegal.

A derived type declaration defines an anonymous base type (the derived type) and a named subtype (the derived subtype) of the base type. The subtype may be either static or nonstatic. The syntax of a derived type declaration includes a subtype indication. Thus, the derived subtype may have a constraint different from that of its base type.

The *parent subtype* is given as the subtype indication in the derived type declaration. The *parent type* is simply the base type of the parent subtype. Consider the following table of the types given in the problem statement:

Derived Subtype	Parent Type	Parent Subtype
Int_1	Integer	Integer **range** 1 .. Two
Int_2	Integer	Positive **range** 5 .. 10
Mass	*predefined*	*predefined* **digits** 3
Str_1	String	String (1 .. Two)

In this table, *predefined* denotes some predefined floating point base type.

All of the predefined and basic operations of the parent type are defined for the derived type. Naturally, the class of the derived type is that of its parent type. For example, a type derived from an integer type is an integer type, a type derived from a private type is a private type, and a type derived from a task type is a task type.

The declaration of *Int_1* is semantically equivalent to the following two type declarations:

```
type new_anonymous_type is range
    Integer'Base'First .. Integer'Base'Last;
subtype Int_1 is new_anonymous_type range
    new_anonymous_type (1) .. new_anonymous_type (Two);
```

Int_1 is a nonstatic subtype whose base type is not *Integer*, but rather a new, anonymous, integer type. The anonymous base type, by definition, is static. (All scalar base types are static.) Notice that *Int_3* is not syntactically a derived type declaration. Even though the language states that the declaration of *Int_3* is equivalent to a derived type declaration (and corresponding named subtype), the range constraint must be static. The type *Int_2* is an example of a static subtype defined by a derived type declaration.

Fp_1 is illegal since its accuracy constraint is not static. All accuracy constraints must be static. *Str_1* is legal since composite types are never static, and thus their constraints need not be static.

A derived type declared immediately within the visible part of a package cannot be used as the parent type of another type appearing in the same visible part. Since *Mass* is a derived type, the declaration of *Grams* is illegal.

[Ada83]   3.3.2(2); 3.4(1 .. 3, 11, 15); 3.5.4(3 .. 6); 3.5.7(2, 10 .. 12)

16.1.3 Base Type versus Derived Type versus Subtype

difficulty: designer

Given the type

```
type Contractor is (Lockheed, TRW, Hughes, General_Dynamics);
```

comment on the comparative utility of defining another type in the following three ways:

```
(1) type Supplier is (Lockheed, TRW, Hughes, General_Dynamics);
(2) type Supplier is new Contractor;
(3) subtype Supplier is Contractor;
```

◇◇◇◇◇

The foci of this problem are the advantages of strong typing and the maintainability of type definitions. The first definition defines a separate set of supplier names having no relation to *Contractor*. If the collections of names *Contractor* and *Supplier* are always to contain the same names, then the second definition is more maintainable. This is simply because a change to the set of names requires only one type declaration to be changed. The second definition also defines an operational relationship between *Contractor* and *Supplier*: Names can be explicitly converted between the two sets. The last definition also provides the maintainability advantage, but does not take advantage of strong typing since accidental mixing of *Contractor* and *Supplier* values may occur.

A Related Problem: What is the difference between a type declaration and a type definition?

[Ada83]   3.3.2(1, 3 .. 4); 3.4(1 .. 6); 3.5.1(1, 3); 4.6(8 .. 9)

16.1.4 Derived Attributes

difficulty: programmer

Consider the declaration

      type Uppercase_Letter **is new** Character **range** 'A' .. 'Z';

What are the values of the following attributes?

    (1) Uppercase_Letter'First
    (2) Uppercase_Letter'Last
    (3) Uppercase_Letter'Pos (Uppercase_Letter'First)
    (4) Uppercase_Letter'Base'Last

◇◇◇◇◇

The values are:

    (1) 'A'
    (2) 'Z'
    (3) 65
    (4) *del*

The base type of *Uppercase_Letter* is an anonymous type whose values and operations are copied from those of its parent type, *Character*. Furthermore, the constraints of *Uppercase_Letter* are copied from those of its parent subtype. Since *Uppercase_Letter* is itself a subtype, the *First* and *Last* attributes will yield the constraints of this subtype. Since *Uppercase_Letter* is not a base type, the third expression evaluates to *65* rather than zero. The last expression references the anonymous base type and thus returns the last value of the base type, namely *del* (or Ascii.Del).

[Ada83]   3.3.3(8 .. 9); 3.4(1 .. 6); 3.5(7 .. 9); 3.5.5(6)

16.1.5 Type Conversions

difficulty: designer

Is the following code legal?

```
package Export is
   type Index is range 1 .. 10;
   type Component is range 1 .. 10;
   type Arr is array (Index) of Component;
   type Rec is
      record
         X : Index;
         Y : Component;
      end record;
end Export;

with Export;
package Re_Export is
   type Re_Index      is new Export.Index;
   type Re_Component is new Export.Component;

   type Arr1 is array (Re_Index) of Re_Component;
   A : Export.Arr := Export.Arr (Arr1'(others => 4));

   type Arr2 is array (Re_Index) of Export.Component;
   B : Export.Arr := Export.Arr (Arr2'(others => 4));

   type Arr3 is new Export.Arr;
   C : Export.Arr := Export.Arr (Arr3'(others => 4));

   type Rec1 is new Export.Rec;
   D : Rec1       := (4, 4);
   E : Re_Index   := D.X;
   F : Export.Rec := Export.Rec (D);

   type Rec2 is
      record
         X : Re_Index;
         Y : Re_Component;
      end record;
   G : Export.Rec := Export.Rec (Rec2'(1, 2));
end Re_Export;

with Export, Re_Export;
procedure Import is
   type Arr4 is new Re_Export.Arr3;
   type Arr5 is new Export.Arr;
```

```
   X : Arr4 := (others => 4);
   Y : Arr5 := Arr5 (X);
begin
   X := Arr4 (Y);
end Import;
```

◇◇◇◇◇

The declarations of *A*, *E*, and *G* are semantically illegal.

In deriving a composite type, a new composite base type is defined. However, the index and component types are not affected. Similarly, in deriving an access type, the designated type is not affected. The index type of *Arr3* is *Export.Index*, and its component type is *Export.Component*.

Explicit type conversion is defined between a derived type and its parent type. Explicit type conversions are also defined between any two types directly or indirectly derived from the same parent type. For example, type conversion is defined between the type *Arr3* and its parent type, *Export.Arr*. Type conversion is also defined between the types *Arr4* and *Arr5*: *Arr4* is indirectly derived from the parent type of *Arr5*. In fact, type conversion is defined between any of the types *Arr*, *Arr3*, *Arr4*, and *Arr5*.

The reason that the declaration of *B*, but not that of *A*, is legal has to do more with array types than derived types. The declaration of *A* is illegal simply because the component types of *Arr* and *Arr1* are not of the same base type.

The type of object *E* is *Re_Index*, but the type of *D.X* is *Export.Index*. Although the parent type of *Re_Index* is *Export.Index*, no implicit conversion is defined between these types. The declaration of *E* could be made legal by using explicit type conversion. Type conversion is not defined between the types *Rec* and *Rec2*. These types are not derived, directly or indirectly, from a common parent type. For this reason, the initialization expression in the declaration of *G* is illegal.

The foregoing problem illustrates that derived types are good for some things, but not for others. If one considers the four types in package *Export* to be an abstraction of some sort, then derived types are not well suited for reexportation or importation of this class of abstraction.

A Related Problem: Are derived types well suited for deriving abstractions defined by private types?

[Ada83]   3.4(4 .. 5); 4.6(8 .. 11, 14)
See also   [BT88a] and [BT88b]

16.2 DERIVED SUBPROGRAMS

When a parent type appears within the visible part of a package, the implicitly defined operations of the derived type include a new set of operations, called *derived* subprograms. This section presents the semantics and use of this new set of operations.

16.2.1 Emulating the Derivation of a Package

difficulty: programmer

What will the following program print?

```
with Text_Io;
procedure Testing_1_2_3 is
    type File     is new Text_Io.File_Type;
    type Spacing is new Text_Io.Positive_Count;
begin
    Put (Standard_Output, "Hello");
    New_Line (Standard_Output, Spacing'(2));
    Put ("There");
    New_Line (2);
end Testing_1_2_3;
```

◇◇◇◇◇

The first call to *New_Line* and the second call to *Put* are semantically illegal.

When the parent type is defined in the visible part of a package (or generic package), some of the subprograms defined immediately within this visible part become operations of the derived type. Subprograms declared in the visible part that include a parameter or result type of the parent type are said to be *derivable*. These derivable subprograms are copied and become directly visible operations of the derived type.

Immediately after the derivation of *File*, copies of the operations defined for *Text_Io.File_Type* become directly visible operations of *File*. These new operations include the subprograms from *Text_Io*, with the type *File_Type* replaced by *File*. For example, the following operations are directly visible within *Testing_1_2_3* (among many others):

```
function Standard_Output return File;
procedure Put     (File   : in File;
                   Item   : in String);
procedure New_Line (File   : in File;
                   Spacing : in Text_Io.Positive_Count := 1);
```

(Note that if the last two declarations were given explicitly, they would be semantically illegal: If *File* is the name of a formal parameter, it may not be used in its own declaration for the type mark.) Because of the derivation of *Spacing*, the following operations also become directly visible:

```
procedure New_Line (File    : in Text_Io.File_Type;
                   Spacing : in Spacing := 1);
procedure New_Line (Spacing : in Spacing := 1);
function Line_Length return anonymous_base_of_Spacing;
```

Two overloadings of *New_Line* become directly visible. However, neither of these match the first call to *New_Line* given in the problem statement. (Text_Io.Standard_-Output is not directly visible.) That call specifies a parameter of the type *File* and a parameter of the type *Spacing*. The second call to *Put* is illegal: The Put procedure with one parameter of the type String is not derived in the program and is not directly visible.

When *Spacing* is derived, only the operations defined within the package *Text_Io* are derived, not those previously derived as the result of the declaration of the type *File*. For example, the operation

```
procedure  New_Line  (File      : in  File;
                      Spacing : in  Text_Io.Positive_Count := 1);
```

defined within *Testing_1_2_3* is *not* a derivable operation of the type *Text_Io.Count*.

The power of derived types is best illustrated when the parent type is defined within the visible part of a package. All of the operations (basic, predefined, and user defined) of the parent type are redefined for the derived type. However, when some of the user-defined operations include parameters of other types, the derived operations can be awkward to use. The problem under discussion attempts to illustrate this point. Within *Text_Io* there is an operation (*New_Line*) that takes a parameter of the type *File_Type* and a parameter of the subtype *Positive_Count*. Although both types are used as parent subtypes within *Testing_1_2_3*, no *New Line* operation whose parameter type profile includes both derived types is defined.

Derived types are useful for deriving a type and all its operations, but are inadequate for deriving an entire abstraction. For example, the user of *Text_Io* clearly understands that

```
procedure  Put (Item : in  String);
```

is an operation on some file, viz., *Current_Output*. However, when *File_Type* is derived, this operation is not itself derived. It might be said that derivable operations are defined more systematically than conceptually. Additionally, though exceptions, constants, and objects defined in a visible part are clearly part of the abstraction, they, too, are not derivable. For deriving complete abstractions, one may find generic units a more appropriate vehicle than derived types.

[Ada83]   3.3.3(2); 3.4(4 .. 5, 11 .. 13)
[ARG]   AI-00367/06, 05-23-88

16.2.2 The Parent Type

difficulty: designer

Is the following code legal?

```
generic
   type T is private;
procedure Gp (X : in T);

with Gp;
package P is
   type T is (Alpha, Beta, Gamma);
   procedure A (Thing : in T);
   procedure B (X      : in T) renames A;
   procedure C is new Gp (T);
end P;

with P;
package Q is
   subtype S is P.T;
   procedure D (Thing : in S);
end Q;

with Q;
procedure Derive_Them is
   type N is new Q.S;
   X : N := Alpha;
begin
   A    (X);   -- 1.
   B    (X);   -- 2.
   C    (X);   -- 3.
   D    (X);   -- 4.
   Q.D (X);   -- 5.
end Derive_Them;
```

◇◇◇◇◇

The last two procedure calls are semantically illegal.

In deriving a type, all of the basic, predefined, and user-defined operations of the parent type are redefined (copied) for the new type. Note that a user-defined subprogram can only be an operation of a type if both the subprogram and the type appear immediately within the same visible part. Subprograms declared in any declarative part other than a visible part are never derivable.

The parent type of N is P.T; the parent subtype of N is Q.S. Alpha is a predefined operation of P.T and thus is also an operation of N. Since Alpha becomes directly visible after the declaration of N, the initialization expression for X is legal. It is the user-defined operations of P.T, and not Q.S, which are redefined for N. These user-defined operations are A, B, and C. Note that although B is defined by a renaming declaration, it is still an explicit declaration of a subprogram and thus an operation of P.T. For similar reasons, the instantiation C is an operation of T.

The fourth call is illegal simply because no subprogram D is directly visible. $Q.D$ is not a derivable subprogram of $P.T$, and hence, it is not redefined for N. The last call is illegal because the parameter is of the wrong type. Note that this call could be made legal by means of an explicit type conversion.

[Ada83]   3.4(1 .. 5, 11 .. 14)
[ARG]   AI-00831/00, 08-22-89

16.2.3 Derivable versus Derived

difficulty: designer

Is the following code legal?

```
package P1 is
   type T1 is (Epsilon, Zeta, Eta);
   procedure Q1 (X : in T1);
end P1;

with P1;
package P2 is
   type T2 is new P1.T1;
   package P3 is
      type T3 is (Theta, Iota, Kappa);
      procedure Q3 (X : in T3; Y : in T2);
   end P3;
   type T4 is new P3.T3;
end P2;

with P2;
procedure Pathologia is
   type T5 is new P2.T2;
   type T6 is new P2.T4;
begin
   Q1 (Zeta);
   Q3 (X => P2.Iota, Y => Zeta);
   Q3 (X => Iota,    Y => P2.Zeta);
end Pathologia;
```

◇◇◇◇◇

The first call to $Q3$ is semantically illegal.

The distinction between a *derived subprogram* and a *derivable subprogram* is critical to understanding why the call is illegal. A subprogram whose parameter or result type profile includes a given type is said to be *derivable* if either:

- the type is declared in the visible part of a package and the subprogram is explicitly declared immediately within the same visible part, or
- the type is itself derived and the subprogram is derived by this type.

For the former case, the operations are not derivable until the end of the visible part. This means that if the given type is used as a parent type within the visible part, these operations are not derived. (Note that, in all cases, the predefined and basic operations of the parent type are immediately derivable.) A derived operation is an operation of a derived type, which is defined as the result of a derivation, while derivable operations are always operations of a parent type. All derived subprograms are copies of derivable subprograms.

Consider the following operations of the types *T1* and *T2*:

```
T1: function Epsilon return T1;
    function Zeta    return T1;
    function Eta     return T1;
    procedure Q1 (X : in T1);

T2: function Epsilon return T2;
    function Zeta    return T2;
    function Eta     return T2;
    procedure Q1 (X : in T2);
    procedure Q3 (X : in T4; Y : in T2);
```

Q1 defined for *T1* is derivable. *Q1* defined for *T2* is both derived and derivable. *Q3*, however, is not derivable (see shortly). Similarly, the *Q1* operation and the three literals of *T5* are both derived and derivable as follows:

```
T5: function Epsilon return T5;
    function Zeta    return T5;
    function Eta     return T5;
    procedure Q1 (X : in T5);
```

The operations of *T3* and *T4* include the following:

```
T3: function Theta  return T3;
    function Iota    return T3;
    function Kappa return T3;
    procedure Q3 (X : in T3; Y : in T2);

T4: function Theta  return T4;
    function Iota    return T4;
    function Kappa return T4;
    procedure Q3 (X : in T4; Y : in T2);
```

The operation *Q3* of the type *T3* is derivable at the end of the visible part of *P3*. The operation *Q3* of *T4* is both derived and derivable. Note that this *Q3* operation is also an operation of *T2*, since *T2* appears in its parameter profile. However, it is not a derivable operation of *T2* because:

- although *Q3* is declared immediately within the same visible part as *T2*, it is not explicitly declared, and
- although *Q3* is a derived subprogram, it is derived by *T4*, not *T2*.

In the list of operations of *T5* above, *Q3* does not appear since it is not a derivable operation of the parent type *T2*.

Finally, the operations of *T6* include the following:

```
function Theta   return T6;
function Iota    return T6;
function Kappa return T6;
procedure Q3 (X : in T6; Y : in P2.T2);
```

The *Q3* operation is derived from the corresponding operation of *T4*.

The first procedure call is legal: Only one literal *Zeta* is directly visible. This literal is of the type *T5*, for which the operation *Q1* is defined. The next call is illegal: Although there is a single *Q3* subprogram visible in the scope of *Pathologia*, this subprogram requires parameters of the types *T6* and *P2.T2*. Instead, the call specifies actual parameters of the types *P2.T4* and *T5*. The last call is a legal call to the directly visible operation *Q3* of the type *T6*.

Since derived subprograms are derivable (unless hidden), derived types provide a mechanism for creating levels of abstractions, or extended operations. Consider the following example:

```
package Stacks is
   type Stack is limited private;
   procedure Push (Int : in   Integer; Onto : in out Stack);
   ⋮
end Stacks;

with Stacks;
package Extended_Ops_Stacks is
   type Stack is new Stacks.Stack;
   function Is_Empty (S : in Stack) return Boolean;
   ⋮
end Extended_Ops_Stacks;

with Extended_Ops_Stacks;
procedure Get_Everything is
```

```
   type Stack is new Extended_Ops_Stacks.Stack;
   S : Stack;
   B : Boolean;
begin
   Push (10, S);
   B := Is_Empty (S);
end Get_Everything;
```

This code is legal and illustrates that the operations of *Stacks.Stack* can be extended by another package, *Extended_Ops_Stacks*. The procedure *Get_Everything* then derives the *extended* operations, acquiring the operations from both packages. Such a mechanism could be used to build any number of levels of extended operations and is an example of the transitivity of derivation. However, since all the operations of *Get_Everything.Stack* are implicitly declared, this method may not be very readable or understandable. The method is nevertheless more maintainable than other strategies: The explicit declaration of a given operation appears only once, regardless of the number of levels. Thus, any change to the definition of an operation need be made in only one place.

[Ada83]   3.3.3(2); 3.4(1 .. 6, 11 .. 14, 19)
[ARG]   AI-00393/00, 10-06-85

16.2.4 Calling Derived Subprograms

difficulty: designer

What will the procedure Call_It print?

```
package P is
   type T is range 1 .. 10;
   subtype S is T range 6 .. 10;
   procedure Q (X : in S);
   procedure R (X : in out S);
   function F return T;
end P;

package body P is
   procedure Q (X : in S) is
   begin
      null;
   end Q;

   procedure R (X : in out S) is
   begin
      null;
   end R;
```

```
function F return T is
  begin
    return T'Last;
  end F;
end P;

with P, Text_Io;
procedure Call_It is
  type N is new P.T range 1 .. 5;
  Obj : N := 1;
begin
  begin
    Obj := F;
    Text_Io.Put ("F call worked. ");
  exception
    when Constraint_Error =>
      Text_Io.Put ("F call bombed! ");
  end;

  begin
    Q (3);
    Text_Io.Put ("Q call worked. ");
  exception
    when Constraint_Error =>
      Text_Io.Put ("Q call bombed! ");
  end;

  R (N (Obj));
  Text_Io.Put_Line ("R call worked.");
exception
  when Constraint_Error =>
    Text_Io.Put_Line ("R call bombed!");
end Call_It;
```

◇◇◇◇◇

The call to *R* is illegal. If it and the subsequent call to *Text_Io.Put_Line* were removed, the execution of *Call_It* would print *F call bombed! Q call bombed!*

A call to a derived subprogram is defined simply to be a call to the corresponding subprogram of the parent type, with appropriate type conversions of the parameters and result. The type conversions are performed immediately before and after the call to the corresponding subprogram of the parent type and not within the body of the subprogram itself. These type conversions are always to the parent type or derived (base) type, not the parent subtype or derived subtype. The body of the derived subprogram is exactly that of the corresponding subprogram of the parent type.

The parent type of N is $P.T$; the parent subtype of N is

P.T **range** 1 .. 5

A call to the subprogram F that returns a value of the base type of N is semantically equivalent to

anonymous_base_type_of_N (P.F)

When $P.F$ returns 10, the evaluation of the type conversion will not raise Constraint_Error. However, the assignment of this value to the object *Obj* will raise Constraint_Error. The reason why Constraint_Error is not raised by the type conversion is that the constraints of the derived type are exactly those of the parent type. Note that if the assignment statement were replaced by the statement

Text_Io.Put (N'Image (F));

Constraint_Error would not be raised, since the expressions

N'Image (F)   and   *anonymous_base_type_of_N*'Image (F)

are semantically equivalent. (No constraint check against the derived subtype N is performed.)

Similarly, the call to the derived subprogram Q is equivalent to

P.Q (P.T (3));

Here, the type conversion does not raise Constraint_Error either; however, the association of the actual parameter *3* with the formal parameter X of the subtype S does raise Constraint_Error.

A type conversion, when associated with a formal parameter of mode out or mode in out, must name the type mark used in the parameter declaration. But the type mark used in the parameter declaration of the derived subprogram R is anonymous and thus may not be named. A type mark of a formal parameter of a derived subprogram is anonymous if either of the following conditions is satisfied:

1. The derived type declaration specifies a discriminant, index, range, or accuracy constraint.
2. The type mark of the subtype indication in the derived type declaration is different from that of the corresponding derivable subprogram parameter.

In the case of the type N and the subprogram R, both conditions are satisfied: The declaration of N specifies a range constraint, and the specification of the parameter declaration of the derivable subprogram R names a subtype of T. Thus, the type mark in the derived subprogram declaration is anonymous and equivalent to the following declarations:

```
subtype anon_S is N'Base range 6 .. 10;
procedure R (X : in out anon_S);
```

A Related Problem: Comment on the understandability of defining the type N as in the problem statement versus defining it as follows:

```
type Ns_Base is new P.T;
subtype N is Ns_Base range 1 .. 5;
```

[Ada83]   3.4(13 .. 14, 23); 3.5.5(10 .. 11); 4.6(8 .. 9, 14)
[ARG]   AI-00318/09, 07-06-90

16.2.5 Deriving Generic Units

difficulty: programmer

Is the following code legal?

```
generic
   type Element is private;
package Linked_List_Class is
   type List is private;
   :
   :
   generic
      with procedure Visit (Node : in Element);
   procedure Traverse (The_List : in List);
   :
   :
end Linked_List_Class;

with Linked_List_Class;
procedure Generic_Selector is
   package Vectors is new Linked_List_Class (Element => Float);
   type Vector is new Vectors.List;
   V : Vector;

   procedure Hello (F : in Float) is ... end Hello;
   procedure Say_Hi is new Traverse (Visit => Hello);
```

```
begin
   ⋮
   Say_Hi (V);
end Generic_Selector;
```

◇◇◇◇◇

The instantiation of *Traverse* and the call to *Say_Hi* are semantically illegal.

Generic subprograms are not operations of a type and thus are not derivable. When *Vector* is derived from *Vectors.List*, the generic subprogram *Traverse* is not derived. For this reason, *Traverse* is not directly visible within *Generic_Selector*.

The instantiation *Say_Hi* can be made legal by using the expanded name

```
procedure Say_Hi is new Vectors.Traverse (Visit => Hello);
```

Given this instantiation, the subprogram *Say_Hi* requires a parameter of the type *Vectors.List*. The call to *Say_Hi* could then be made legal by using the explicit type conversion

```
Say_Hi (Vectors.List (V));
```

[Ada83]   3.4(13 .. 14, 20); 4.6(8 .. 9)

chapter 17

The Tasking Model

It's a lot like house hunting in Palo Alto. After a while, you get used to the prices. You forget your initial reaction that it's an outrage.
Professor Robert Dewar, January 13, 1987, at a SIGAda meeting, Hollywood, Florida (response to a question posed about the performance of Ada tasking in early Ada implementations.)

The abort statement was intended to stop a thread of control that has gone awry. Unfortunately, its semantics are ridiculous. It works much like an arrest warrant being issued, but instead of the police actively going out to arrest you, they wait patiently for you to turn yourself in at the police station.
Professor David Luckham, September 18, 1989, Stanford University

The Ada tasking model is often the most difficult part of the language for a programmer to comprehend. One aspect of tasks that should be familiar to all Ada programmers is that they define a type class. Like any other type class, task types define a set of values, have an associated set of predefined operations, and can be used to declare objects and formal parameters.

One major difference between task types and other type classes involves the value of objects of each class. The value of an integer object is an integer, and the value of a floating point object is a floating point number. However, the value of a task object is not a task; instead, a task object designates a task. A task is a thread of control. Each task should be thought of as a logical, independent process, executing concurrently with other tasks. An Ada execution is comprised of at least one task—the environment task—which invokes the main program.

This chapter concentrates on the semantics of a task associated with the concept of a thread of control. Sections 17.1 and 17.2 present aspects of task types common to all other types. The remaining sections address the issues involved with the activation, execution, and synchronization of threads of control.

17.1 DECLARATION OF TASK TYPES AND OBJECTS

Like array types, task types may be declared either explicitly or implicitly. The declaration of a task type includes the definition of *entries* of the type. The entries of a task type can be thought of as user-defined *ports* through which communication with the task may be carried out. Unlike other types, task types have bodies. These bodies define the execution of the threads of control of the task type.

As with any other type class, one may declare named task subtypes. However, since task types cannot be declared with constraints, the only use of a task subtype is to provide a new name for a task type.

17.1.1 It's a Program Unit, Too

difficulty: programmer

As a program unit, is a task more like a procedure or a package?

◇◇◇◇◇

Tasks have more in common with packages than with procedures.

Packages, procedures, and tasks are program units. As such, all are used to modularize and encapsulate parts of a program. Some of the fundamental differences between these three program units are that a task is also a type class and a task specification cannot be a compilation unit.

Conceptually, a procedure defines a single action. A task entry can also be used in this manner. Thus, both packages and tasks can be used to form collections of actions. A package, however, is more capable of defining a complete abstraction, rather than simply a collection of actions. Tasks can be used to define simple abstractions characterized by actions requested of concurrent processes.

The main reason that a task is not a compilation unit has to do with its limited utility in forming abstractions. The package should be considered the main vehicle in Ada for adding modularity and defining abstractions within a program. The restriction disallowing tasks as compilation units reenforces this intent.

[Ada83]   9.1(1 .. 3)

17.1.2 Task Specifications

difficulty: programmer

Is the following code legal?

```
N : Integer := 6;
task type T1;
task type T2 is end T2;
task T3;

task type T4 is
   entry E;
   entry E (X : in Float);
   entry G (1 .. N) (C : in Character);
   entry G (Boolean);
end T4;
```

◇◇◇◇◇

The code is illegal because entry families cannot be overloaded: The second use of the identifier *G* is semantically illegal.

There are two kinds of task types: named and anonymous. The types *T1*, *T2*, and *T4* are named task types. The declaration of *T3* defines an anonymous task type and a single object of this type named *T3*. Objects of anonymous task types are analogous to objects of anonymous array types. The syntax of a task specification is

```
task [type] identifier [is
   {entry_declaration}
   {representation_clause}
end [task_simple_name]];
```

and the syntax of an entry declaration is

```
entry identifier [(discrete_range)] [formal_part];
```

A task type may define any number of entries or no entries at all. Both types *T1* and *T2* define no entries. Note that the syntaxes of these two type declarations differ. The declaration of *T1* is simply a shorthand notation for a task type with no entries (e.g., *T2*). Like other program units, the definition of a task is comprised of a specification and a body. Like a package, the specification of a task is not optional. Unlike a package, however, only entry declarations, representation specifications, and pragmas may appear within a task specification.

An entry declaration may define either a single entry or a *family* of entries. A family of entries defines zero or more entries. The name of a single entry of a family is similar to the name of a single component of an array: Both are formed using an indexed component.

An entry declaration includes an optional formal part, identical to the formal part of a procedure declaration. Like subprograms, entries may be overloaded within a single task type. The rules concerning homographs of subprogram declarations also cover entry declarations. Similarly, the rules governing overload resolution of subprogram calls also govern entry calls.

Entry families may not be overloaded. For this reason, the second use of entry *G* within *T4* is semantically illegal. Suppose such overloadings were allowed, as in the following code:

```
task T is
   entry E (Int : in Integer);
   entry E (Integer);   -- Illegal overloading.
end T;
   :
   :
T.E (Int => 3);
T.E (3);
```

Then the first call could be resolved, but the second call would be ambiguous. In fact, if the entry declarations were legal, it would not be possible to call an entry of the family.

The declaration of an entry family includes a *family index subtype* defined by a discrete range. This family index subtype need not be static but the subtype is determined during elaboration of the task specification rather than at the activation of each task object. Thus, all tasks of the same type would have the same entries. The semantics of the family index subtype are identical to those of an index subtype used in a constrained array definition. Specifically, the family index subtype may define a null range, in which case any execution of a corresponding accept statement or entry call will raise Constraint_Error or Numeric_Error.

A Related Problem: If an accept statement for a null entry family appears as an open alternative of a selective wait statement, will Constraint_Error or Numeric_Error be raised even though this alternative can never be selected?

[Ada83]   9.1(2 .. 3); 9.5(2 .. 3, 5 .. 6)
[ARG]   AI-00287/05, 07-23-86

17.1.3 Discriminated and Generic Tasks

difficulty: novice

Is it possible to declare a task type with discriminants? Is it possible to declare a generic task type?

◇◇◇◇◇

Neither of these declarations is possible; however, it is possible to simulate their effects indirectly.

All tasks of a given type have identical bodies. Yet it is sometimes useful to have tasks of the same type act differently, based on some initialization. One can view the value of a discriminant as a means of classifying record objects. Discriminants can be used, indirectly, to classify task objects as well, as in the following example:

```
type Jobs is (Cashier, Cook, Dishwasher, Manager, Waiter);
task type Restaurant_Staff is
  entry Assignment (My_Job : in Jobs);
    :
    .
end Restaurant_Staff;
type Staff is access Restaurant_Staff;

function Initialize (J : in Jobs) return Staff is
  Result : constant Staff := new Restaurant_Staff;
begin
  Result.Assignment (My_Job => J);
  return Result;
end Initialize;
    :
    .
type Worker (Assignment : Jobs) is
  record
      X : Staff := Initialize (Assignment);
  end record;
Waiters : array (1 .. 5) of Worker (Assignment => Waiter);
```

If the classification of a task cannot (or need not) be assigned during the declaration of a task object, one can always include such initialization in the activation of the task itself:

```
function Job_Assignment return Jobs is ...

task body Restaurant_Staff is
  My_Job : constant Jobs := Job_Assignment;
    :
    .
end Restaurant_Staff;
```

A *generic* task can be implemented simply by nesting a task specification within a generic package specification, as in the following code:

```
generic
   type Id is (<>);
   with function Get_Id return Id;
package Generic_Task_Type is
   task type Worker is ...
end Generic_Task_Type;
```

The intent of the *Get_Id* function is to allow each worker task to obtain a unique identifier for itself.

A Related Problem: Suppose one wants to inform each task of its *name* during initialization, where a name is of the type String. Explain how this can be done.

[Ada83]   9.1(3)

17.1.4 Task Objects as Parameters

difficulty: programmer

Given the declaration

> **task type** T;

is the following code legal?

> **procedure** P (X : **in**   T;
>   Y :   **out** T;
>   Z : **in out** T);

◇◇◇◇◇

The specification of the formal parameter *Y* is illegal: Mode out cannot be used for a formal parameter of a task type.

A task type is a limited type and as such, can never be the type of a formal parameter of mode out. Both modes in and in out are allowed for task types.

The semantic differences between modes in and in out for a formal parameter of a task type are minimal. Conceptually, the value of a task object never changes. Thus, a discussion of which mode to use can be confined to the more subtle differences between the use of these modes. An advantage to using mode in is that a default parameter can be specified; another advantage is that any expression of the appropriate task type can be used as an actual parameter. A disadvantage to using mode in is that such a formal parameter cannot be passed as an actual parameter of mode in out.

The consistent use of mode in provides the flexibility of using default subprogram parameters, as in the code

> **task type** T;
> **function** F **return** Integer;
> A : **array** (1 .. 10) **of** T;
>
> **procedure** P (X : **in** T := A (F)) **is** ...
> :
> :

The consistent use of mode in out allows for the instantiation of generic units with generic formal objects of limited types. An example is where a formal parameter of a subprogram is of a task type, and within the subprogram the parameter is used as a generic actual parameter.

A Related Problem: Can a task object be passed to an entry? Can an entry parameter be of the task type in which the entry is defined?

[Ada83]   7.4.4(4); 9.2(1); 12.1.1(3)

17.1.5 Anonymous Task Types

difficulty: programmer

Explain the semantic differences between the following two sets of declarations:

```
Set 1                  Set 2

task type Named;       task X;
X : Named;
```

◇◇◇◇◇

In general, the two sets should be considered semantically equivalent.

Both sets declare a task type and an object named X of the type. In the left-hand example, the task type is named, whereas in the right-hand example, the task type is anonymous.

Technically, the two sets of declarations are not strictly equivalent. There exists a slight difference concerning the context in which each may appear. The object declaration on the left may appear only where a basic declarative item is allowed. However, the right-hand declaration may appear anyplace within a declarative part. Thus, in the fragment

```
package body Rodney_Dangerfield is
   -- Point A.
   procedure No (Respect : out Boolean) is ... end No;
   -- Point B.
end Rodney_Dangerfield;
```

the *Set 1* declarations may appear only at *Point A*. By contrast, the *Set 2* declaration, an anonymous task declaration, may appear both at *Point A* and *Point B*. This difference is purely syntactical: The right-hand declaration defines a single task, but is not syntactically an object declaration. The situation is similar to that for generic instantiations, which define bodies of program units, but may appear at places where an explicit body declaration cannot.

Another difference between the declarations in the problem statement is common to all anonymous types of any class: The type *Named* can be used to define a number of task objects of the same type, while the task object declared on the right-hand side will be the only object of its type. Furthermore, the right-hand declaration of *X* cannot be passed as a parameter, since its type cannot be named.

Finally, only the *Set 1* declarations can be associated with a length clause representation.

A Related Problem: Arrays whose types are anonymous can be used to form actual parameters. Why is this not true for tasks whose types are anonymous?

[Ada83]   3.1(3); 3.9(2); 9.1(2); 13.2(10)
[ARG]   AI-00359/04, 11-04-88

17.1.6 Task Bodies

difficulty: novice

Is the following code legal?

```
task type T is
   entry E;
end T;

task body T is
   B : Boolean;
   entry F;
begin
   B := T'Callable;
   accept G;
end T;
```

◇◇◇◇◇

The body of *T* is illegal: An entry declaration may appear only within a task specification. Also, an accept statement in the body of a task must be for an entry declared in the specification of the task.

Task bodies are similar to the bodies of other program units. The body of a task begins with a declarative part followed by a sequence of statements and optional exception handlers. Inside, the name of the task always designates a task object. That is, in the expression *T'Callable*, *T* refers to the task executing the body, not the type *T*.

An accept statement may only appear immediately within a task body. (Note, however, that an accept statement can appear within a block statement.) Accept statements need not appear for all entries. The absence of an accept statement for entry *E* is legal.

The effect of calling an entry to a task in which no corresponding accept statement exists in the task's body is to suspend the execution of all callers until the called task is completed, at which time Tasking_Error is raised at the point of each entry call.

An entry should not be considered the counterpart of a procedure. Most of the similarities between procedures and entries have to do with syntax, overload resolution of calls, and parameter passing. The semantics of a procedure call and those of an entry call are vastly different. An entry call can be thought of as a request for service from another thread of control. In its most simple form, an entry call is a request for synchronization. It is considered a request because the service need not be rendered promptly, or in fact, ever. An accept statement is not the *body* of an entry. Indeed, several accept statements may be provided for the same entry. Even if the language required at least one accept statement to appear for each entry, the tasking model still could not guarantee that such entries would be accepted if called. In fact, the semantics of entry families prohibits the static semantic checking of accept statements for all entries. The difficulty of statically checking that just two entries have corresponding accept statements is plain from the following code:

```
task type T is
   entry E (Boolean);
end T;

task body T is

   :

begin
   accept E (Today in Sunday .. Thursday);
   accept E (Today = Saturday);
end T;
```

A Related Problem: If an entry declaration does not require at least one corresponding accept statement, why does a function declaration require at least one corresponding return statement?

[Ada83]   9.1(3 .. 4); 9.5(1, 8, 16)
[ARG]   AI-00373/00, 08-04-85

17.2 OPERATIONS AND ATTRIBUTES OF TASK TYPES

All task types are limited. Thus, the operations predefined for a task type include those predefined for any limited type. This section focuses on the basic operations specific to task types.

17.2.1 Membership Tests

difficulty: designer

The membership test **in** is trivially true for all task types. Why does the language define membership tests for task types?

◇◇◇◇◇

Membership tests are basic operations defined for all types. Even though for task types these tests always return the same value, both tests are defined in order to preserve the consistency of the type model. Not to provide the tests for task types would introduce an unnecessary special case.

A case in point is the use of a task type as a generic actual parameter. Consider the following program fragment:

```
generic
   type T is limited private;
   X : in out T;
package P is
   B : constant Boolean := X in T;
end P;

with P;
package Instance is
   task type T;
   X : T;
   package Np is new P (T, X);
end Instance;
```

If membership tests were not defined for task types, additional complexity would be introduced into the program in the semantic checking of generic units and their instantiations. Suppose that membership was not defined for task types and that such a test appeared in the body of *P* instead of in its specification. Then the specification could be compiled, followed by the instantiation, and then the body. In this case, the instantiation would be legal with respect to the specification, but the body would not be legal with respect to the instantiation. This is an anomalous case, since the body need not be dependent on the instantiation. (Dependency among compilation units is discussed in Chapter 20.)

[Ada83]   3.3.3(2 .. 4); 4.5.2(10); 7.4.2(1); 7.4.4(3); 9.2(1)
[ARG]   AI-00256/23, 06-16-88

17.2.2 Callable and Terminated

difficulty: designer

Consider the following code:

```
task body T is
begin
   :
   :
   if not T'Callable and not T'Terminated then ...
   :
   :
end T;
```

If the Boolean expression evaluates to True, what can the task executing the body infer? Suppose that the state of the task does not change during evaluation of the condition.

◇◇◇◇◇

The task can infer that it has been made abnormal.

The *Callable* attribute yields True, unless the specified task is completed, terminated, or abnormal. (These task states are discussed in Sections 17.6 and 17.7.) The *Terminated* attribute yields False, unless the specified task has terminated. A completed or terminated task can no longer execute. Thus, if a task can evaluate the *Terminated* attribute for itself, the attribute must return False. Similarly, if a task evaluates the *Callable* attribute for itself and the attribute returns False, the task knows that it has been made abnormal.

The following table illustrates the relationship between these two attributes:

Callable	Terminated	Conclusion
True	True	impossible
True	False	normal execution
False	True	terminated
False	False	abnormal or completed

The first case is not possible in any context. The second case indicates that the specified task is executing normally. The third case can be observed only by some task other than the one in question. The last case can be evaluated within any thread of control.

The *Callable* and *Terminated* attributes of a task may be evaluated both within and outside of the named task. For example, a thread of control may evaluate T'Callable just before it calls the task T. Note, however, that this use of the attribute is problematic, for in the code

```
if T'Callable then
   T.E;
end if;
```

the evaluation of the attribute may yield True, but before the entry call can be executed, *T* may become abnormal, may complete, or may terminate. Thus, checking the *Callable* attribute beforehand is no guarantee that the execution of a later entry call will not raise Tasking_Error.

The task in the problem statement can conclude that it has been made abnormal. Such a situation can be useful to detect, as it may allow the task to reclaim storage, close files, or relinquish other resources before being completed.

[Ada83]   9.9(1 .. 3); 9.10(7)

17.2.3 The Count Attribute

difficulty: designer

Is the following code legal?

```
procedure P is
   task T is
      entry E (Boolean);
   end T;

   task body T is
      function F return Boolean is
      begin
         return E (True)'Count /= 0;
      end F;
   begin
      loop
         accept E (F);
      end loop;
   end T;
begin
   T.E (T.E (True)'Count /= 0);
end P;
```

◇◇◇◇◇

The *Count* attribute may only be used immediately within the task body for which the specified entry is defined. Thus, the uses of the *Count* attribute within the sequence of statements of the function *F* and the procedure *P* are illegal.

The *Count* attribute returns the number of entry calls that are currently queued for the specified entry. The attribute can return any value greater than or equal to zero. All forms of entry calls, including timed and conditional calls, can place an entry call on a queue and thus affect the value of the *Count* attribute. If a timed entry call enqueues a call and the delay expires, the call is simply dequeued. For a conditional entry call, a call may or may not be enqueued. If a call is enqueued and the rendezvous does not occur, the call is dequeued. Lastly, a call is dequeued at the beginning of each rendezvous.

Since entries may be overloaded, an anomaly arises when forming names using this attribute, as in the following code:

```
task type T is
  entry E;
  entry E (Int : in Integer);
end T;
```

It is not possible for tasks of this type to use the *Count* attribute: An expression of the form *E'Count* will always be illegal, even if one of the entries is hidden by a procedure.

[Ada83]   9.6(15); 9.9(5 .. 7)
[ARG]   AI-00034/06, 07-23-86

17.3 ACTIVATION AND EXECUTION

The behavior of a thread of control is composed of four phases: activation, execution, completion, and termination. Activation of a task is the process of elaborating the declarative part of the body of the task. The way in which a task is created determines when activation occurs.

If activation of a task proceeds without raising or propagating an exception to the declarative part of the task, the task begins execution. Execution of a task is simply execution of the sequence of statements in the body of the task. This section presents some of the more intricate semantics of the activation and execution phases.

17.3.1 Exceptions during Activation

difficulty: designer

What will the following program print?

```
with Text_Io;
procedure P_Opus is
  task type T1;
  task type T2;
  type R is
    record
      X : T1;
      Y : T2;
```

```ada
        end record;
     Z : R;

     task body T1 is
        P : Positive := -1;
     begin
        Text_Io.Put_Line ("T1 says hi.");
     end T1;

     task body T2 is
     begin
        Text_Io.Put_Line ("T2 says hi.");
     end T2;

begin
   Inner:
   declare
      T : T2;
      S : String (1 .. 10) := "";
   begin
      null;
   end Inner;
exception
   when Program_Error =>
      Text_Io.Put_Line ("Program_Error.");
   when Tasking_Error =>
      Text_Io.Put_Line ("Tasking_Error.");
   when Constraint_Error =>
      Text_Io.Put_Line ("Constraint_Error.");
end P_Opus;
```

◇◇◇◇◇

The program will print some combination of the following characters and line terminators:

```
T2 says hi.
Tasking_Error.
```

The elaboration of a task object (e.g., Z.X) does not include activation of the task designated by the object. First, the declarative part in which the object declaration appears is elaborated, then the task designated by the object is activated, and then the sequence of statements associated with the declarative region in which the object declaration appears is executed. These three steps proceed sequentially. If multiple objects (e.g., Z.X and Z.Y) are declared within a single declarative part, the activations of the designated tasks proceed in parallel. Activation of a task consists of the elaboration of the declarative part associated with the task's body. The distinction between the two declarative parts, one in which the task object is declared and one in the task body, must be carefully noted.

The difference between the elaboration of a declarative part in which a task object is declared and the activation of the designated task is similar to the difference between the elaboration of a subprogram body and the elaboration of the declarative part within the subprogram body.

The preceding program focuses on the activation of tasks under conditions where exceptions are raised. If an exception is raised or propagated to the declarative part of a task, the task immediately becomes completed and the exception is not propagated further. Instead, Tasking_Error is raised before execution of the first statement (within the sequence of statements) associated with the declarative region in which the task object is declared.

If an exception is raised during the elaboration of a declarative part, any task objects in the declarative part that are not already activated do not become activated; instead, such tasks become terminated. The exception is propagated to the enclosing scope, as usual.

After elaboration of the types, object, and bodies in the declarative part of *P_Opus*, the two tasks designated by the objects *Z.X* and *Z.Y* begin activation. These tasks are activated in parallel. Execution of the sequence of statements of *P_Opus* will not begin until both tasks have completed their activations.

During activation of the task designated by *Z.X*, Constraint_Error is raised (but is not propagated). The raising of the exception during activation prevents further execution of this task (the task becomes completed), but does not affect the activation and further execution of the task designated by *Z.Y*. After both tasks have completed activation, Tasking_Error is raised immediately before the first statement of *P_Opus*. Tasking_Error is raised because the activation of one of the tasks did not finish without exception. This exception is handled and *Tasking_Error* is printed. Note that elaboration and execution of the block statement named *Inner* never takes place.

Execution of the exception handler of *P_Opus* and execution of the call to *Text_Io* within the task designated by *Z.Y* proceed in parallel. Thus, the two lines could be printed in any order, or in fact, could be printed intermixed, e.g., as

```
T2 says Tasking_hi.Err
or.
```

Now suppose the block statement were executed. Then the object *T* would be elaborated, and Constraint_Error would be raised during the elaboration of *S*. The task designated by *T* would never begin activation, but instead would immediately become terminated. Constraint_Error would then be propagated to the outer scope. Note the difference between an exception being raised during activation of a task and an exception being raised after elaboration of a task object declaration, but before the task's activation. The former circumstance causes only the activating task to become completed, while the latter can cause multiple tasks to terminate. The differences between a completed task and a terminated task are presented in Section 17.6.

[Ada83]   9.3(3 .. 4); 11.4.2(1, 5 .. 7)
[ARG]   AI-00809/01, 05-18-90

17.3.2 Activation by Allocation

difficulty: programmer

What will the following program print?

```
with Text_Io;
procedure P is
   task type T;
   type A is access T;
   X : A := new T;

   task body T is
   begin
      null;
   end T;
begin
   Text_Io.Put_Line ("I do not see the big deal here.");
exception
   when Program_Error => Text_Io.Put_Line ("Program_Error!");
   when Tasking_Error  => Text_Io.Put_Line ("Tasking_Error!");
end P;
```


◇◇◇◇◇

The program will not print anything, since Program_Error will be raised in the declarative part of *P*.

There are two methods of activating a task: by declaring a task object or by allocating a task object. In the former case, activation occurs immediately before execution of the sequence of statements of the declarative region in which the object appears. In the latter case, activation occurs as part of the execution of the allocator.

Prior to the activation of a task, an implementation must check to make sure that the corresponding task body has been elaborated. (Note that this semantics is similar to that of calling a subprogram before its body has been elaborated.) In the simple case, where the task type and object declarations appear in the same declarative part, elaboration of the task body is not a problem. This is because activation of such tasks occurs after the complete elaboration of the declarative part. Such is not the case, however, for tasks created by allocators. If a task is created by an allocator and the corresponding task body has not yet been elaborated, Program_Error is raised during execution of the allocator and the task is never allocated.

The activation of a dynamically allocated task is part of the execution of the allocator. If an exception is raised during the activation of a task created by an allocator, Tasking_Error is raised. Note that this exception is raised whenever the activation of a task causes an exception. The important difference between raising Tasking_Error for a task created by an object declaration and one created by an allocator is *where* the exception is raised. In the case of an allocator, Tasking_Error is raised at the point where the allocator is executed.

   In the foregoing program, an attempt is made to activate a task before its body has been elaborated. Thus, Program_Error is raised at the point of the allocator and propagated outside of the procedure *P*.

   A Related Problem: If the following declaration appeared immediately before the declaration of *X* in the preceding program, would the tasks designated by *Y* ever be activated?

         Y : **array** (Character) **of** T;

[Ada83]   3.9(4 .. 8); 9.3(3 .. 4, 6 .. 8)
[ARG]   AI-00149/09, 02-23-87; AI-00198/09, 05-23-88

17.3.3 Spawning Siblings

difficulty: designer

Show how a task of type T may create another task of type T.

◇◇◇◇◇

The following procedure illustrates such a task type:

```
procedure Spawn is
   task type T is
      entry Siblings (Num : in Natural);
   end T;
   subtype S is T;
   type Acc is access T;

   First_Born : T;

   task body T is
      A : Acc;
   begin
      accept Siblings (Num : in Natural) do
         if Num /= 0 then
            A := new S;
            A.Siblings (Num − 1);
         end if;
      end Siblings;
   end T;
```

```
begin
   First_Born.Siblings (4);
end Spawn;
```

The key to solving this problem is the use of the subtype S: Within the body of task T, the identifier T denotes a task object, yet S denotes a subtype. Only through the use of a subtype can the body of a task name its own type. An alternative method of creating tasks within the body of T is to use an array, as in

```
Peers : array (1 .. 4) of S;
```

If such a declaration is placed within the declarative part of the body of T, infinitely recursive activation will occur.

[Ada83]   9.1(4); 9.3(2, 6)

17.3.4 Activation and Execution Order

difficulty: designer

What will the following program print?

```
package Recorder is
   function Note (Int : in Integer) return Integer;
   function The_Record return String;
end Recorder;

package body Recorder is
   type Text is access String;
   So_Far : Text := new String'("");

   function Note (Int : in Integer) return Integer is
   begin
      So_Far := new String'(So_Far.all & Integer'Image (Int));
      return Int;
   end Note;

   function The_Record return String is
   begin
      return So_Far.all;
   end The_Record;
end Recorder;

with Recorder, Text_Io;
procedure Bill_T_Cat is
   task type T1;
```

```
    task type T2;
    A, B : T1;
    Int    : Integer := Recorder.Note (1);
    C, D : T2;

    task body T1 is
        Int : Integer := Recorder.Note (2);
    begin
        Int := Recorder.Note (3);
    end T1;

    task body T2 is
        Int : Integer := Recorder.Note (4);
    begin
        Int := Recorder.Note (5);
    end T2;

    package Pfft is
        Int : Integer := Recorder.Note (6);
        type Acc is access T2;
        Y : Acc := new T2;
    end Pfft;
begin
    Int := Recorder.Note (7);
    Text_Io.Put_Line (Recorder.The_Record);
end Bill_T_Cat;
```

◇◇◇◇◇

The exact output of the program is indeterminate. It could print

```
1  6  4  5  2  3  4  5  4  5  2  3  2  3  7
```

among other things.

This program illustrates the indeterminism inherent in parallel execution. Recall that execution and activation of multiple tasks occur in parallel. An understanding of parallel execution requires the reader to examine the differences between elaboration, activation, and execution. Figure 17.1 depicts the execution of the foregoing program: e_1 denotes the environment task calling *Note* with the value *1*, x_3 denotes task *X* calling *Note* with the value *3*, and so on. Arrows between calls represent ordered (sequential) execution; calls not connected by any path occur in parallel.

The first call to *Note* occurs during the elaboration of the object *Int*. This elaboration occurs sequentially, no other tasks are executing yet. The next call to *Note* occurs during the elaboration of *Pfft.Int*. Again, this elaboration occurs sequentially. The elaboration of object *Y* causes a task to activate. This activation, which includes a call to *Note*, takes place during the evaluation of the allocator: the activation of the task designated by *Y*.**all** takes place before the elaboration of *Bill_T_Cat* proceeds. Thus, the first three

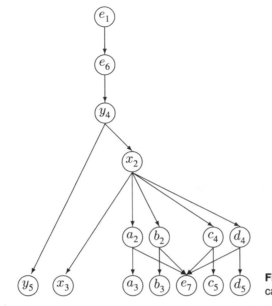

Figure 17.1 Ordered and concurrent calls to *Note*.

calls to *Note* will be associated with the actual parameters *1, 6*, and *4*, in that order. This part of the program's execution is deterministic. Observe that, since the task designated by *Y*.**all** has been activated, it can at any subsequent time call *Note* with the parameter *5*.

Next, the activation of the task designated by *Pfft.X* occurs, and *Note (2)* is called. This task completes its activation before the tasks designated by *A, B, C,* and *D* begin their activations, since *Pfft.X* is declared in an inner scope. The body of the package *Pfft* is implicitly provided at the end of the declarative part of *Bill_T_Cat*. More precisely, the activation of the task designated by *Pfft.X* occurs at the end of the elaboration of the declarative part of the (implicit) body of *Pfft*. (If several package bodies are to be implicitly provided within a single declarative part, the order in which they are elaborated is not defined by the language.) Again, since the task designated by *Pfft.X* is activated, it can execute the call *Note (3)* at any time.

At this point, the elaboration of the declarative part of *Bill_T_Cat* has completed. Now the activation of the tasks designated by *A, B, C,* and *D* will occur in parallel. After these activations, seven individual threads of control could be executing: *A, B, C, D, Pfft.X, Pfft.Y*.**all**, and the task executing *Bill_T_Cat*. The remaining calls to *Note* can occur in any order or, in fact, concurrently.

Some of the more interesting situations that might arise have to do with concurrent updates of the shared variables *Recorder.So_Far* and *Recorder.So_Far*.**all**. Consider the following scenario:

1. The activations of *X* and *Y*.**all** have occurred.
2. The execution of *Y*.**all** evaluates the right-hand expression of the assignment to *Recorder.So_Far*.

3. The activation and execution of all tasks except *Y*.**all** become completed.
4. The call *Note (7)* in procedure *Bill_T_Cat* is executed.
5. The assignment to *So_Far* by the execution of the task *Y*.**all** takes place.
6. The call to *Put_Line* is executed.

In this case, the program would print

```
1 6 4 2 5
```

As the preceding situation illustrates, not all calls to *Note* need be reflected by the output, even though 15 calls to *Note* will take place. In any case, if *7* is printed, it will follow all occurrences of *2* and *4*.

If concurrent updates to *Recorder.So_Far* occur, then the execution of the program is erroneous. The reader should carefully distinguish between erroneous execution and a program that is simply indeterminate. The execution of the preceding program would be indeterminate even if all 15 values were printed. Indeterminism does not imply erroneous execution, but erroneous execution is always indeterminate.

In general, if a task reads a variable and then another task updates the variable before the first task reaches a *synchronization point*, the execution is erroneous. (Synchronization points are presented in detail in Sections 17.7 and 17.8.) Furthermore, if a task updates a variable and then another task reads or updates the variable before the first task reaches a synchronization point, the execution is erroneous. These restrictions are placed on tasks in order to allow for the use of local copies of variables.

In the preceding program, all tasks except that executing the main program do the following:

1. Read the shared variable.
2. Update the shared variable.
3. Read the shared variable again.
4. Update the shared variable again.

If the task designated by *A* updates the shared variable, and then the task designated by *B* reads the variable before *A* is completed, the execution is erroneous. The only synchronization points in tasks of the types *T1* and *T2* are at

- the beginning of activation,
- the end of activation, and
- completion.

The program can be fixed simply by guarding the shared variable. This involves adding a task to the body of *Recorder* so that updates of *So_Far* are serialized:

```
package body Recorder is
    type Text is access String;
```

```
task Guard is
   entry Note          (Int : in        Integer);
   entry The_Record (T   :      out Text);
end Guard;

task body Guard is
   So_Far : Text := new String'("");
begin
   loop
      select
         accept Note (Int : in Integer) do
            So_Far := new String'(So_Far.all & Integer'Image (Int));
         end Note;
      or
         accept The_Record (T : out Text) do
            T := So_Far;
         end The_Record;
      or
         terminate;
      end select;
   end loop;
end Guard;

function Note (Int : in Integer) return Integer is
begin
   Guard.Note (Int);
   return Int;
end Note;

function The_Record return String is
   T : Text;
begin
   Guard.The_Record (T);
   return T.all;
end The_Record;
end Recorder;
```

This modification assures that executions of the program will not be erroneous, although they will still be indeterminate. Specifically, it still need not be the case that all 15 values will be printed.

A Related Problem: What could one infer if execution of the preceding program did print 15 values? What are the implications of the explicit exclusion of composite variables from the discussion of shared variables in [Ada83, §9.11(3 .. 6)]?

[Ada83]   9.3(1 .. 2, 6); 9.11(3 .. 8)

17.4 THE RENDEZVOUS

Two important aspects of using multiple tasks to solve one problem are communication and synchronization. Both of these functions can be performed using many different methods. The rendezvous is a language feature that provides a way for tasks to perform them.

In order for a rendezvous to begin a task must issue an entry call to another task that, in turn, must accept the call. When an entry call is executed, the call is placed in an *entry queue*. To engage in a rendezvous, the called task simply selects and removes the first call in the entry queue.

For a rendezvous used as a communication mechanism, the execution of the rendezvous is defined by a sequence of statements given in the body of the accepting task. This section addresses the semantics of the rendezvous itself; Section 17.5 addresses different methods of determining when a rendezvous is to take place.

17.4.1 Brief Encounters

difficulty: programmer

Given the task specification

```
task T is
   entry A;
   entry B (Int1 : out Integer);
   entry C (Boolean);
   entry D (Character) (Int2 : in Integer);
end T;
```

are the following accept statements legal?

```
accept A;
accept B (Int1 : out Integer);
accept C (True);
accept D ('Z') (Int2 : in Integer) do null; end accept;
```

◇◇◇◇◇

The accept statement for the entry D ('Z') is syntactically illegal. Any execution of the accept statement for B is potentially erroneous.

If a formal part (parameter list) is included in an entry declaration, it must be repeated in any accept statement for the entry. The formal parts specified in an entry declaration and corresponding accept statements must conform with each other under the same rules used for conformity of subprogram formal parts. The syntax for an accept statement is

```
accept entry_simple_name [(entry_index)] [formal_part] [do
   sequence_of_statements
end [entry_simple_name]];
```

An accept statement does not include either a declarative part or exception handlers. Note that regardless of the specification of parameters, an accept statement need not include a sequence of statements. The semantics of the modes associated with parameters in a formal part is equivalent to that of procedures.

The accept statement for *A* is legal and illustrates the simplest form of the statement. Such an accept statement is often used when two tasks must *synchronize* but need not exchange data.

The next accept statement is also legal. As with the previous one, no sequence of statements is supplied. However, because *B* specifies a parameter of mode out, after the execution of the accept statement the value of the actual parameter will be indeterminate. In fact, Constraint_Error could conceivably be raised upon leaving the accept statement if the value associated with the formal parameter is not within range of the type *Integer*. As with procedures, Ada does not require that, for an entry, formal parameters of mode out be assigned values during execution of an accept statement. A program that calls entry *B* is therefore potentially erroneous.

The third accept statement is for the entry *C (True)*. Recall that an entry family defines zero or more distinct entries. In the case of *C*, the names of these entries are *C (False)* and *C (True)*. The entry index used in an accept statement may be a nonstatic expression. Such indices are evaluated when the entry name is evaluated. In the case of a simple accept statement (one that is not an alternative of a selective wait), the entry name is evaluated at the very beginning of execution of the statement. The evaluation of an entry name includes a constraint check to ensure that the entry index belongs to the subtype specified in the entry declaration. As always, if such a check fails, Constraint_Error is raised.

If an accept statement includes a sequence of statements, the optional identifier following the reserved word **end** must be the simple name of the entry, not the reserved word **accept**. Thus, the accept statement for *D* could be made legal by replacing **end accept** with **end** or **end** D.

[Ada83]   6.4.1(5, 7 .. 8); 9.5(1 .. 3, 6 .. 7, 10, 21)

17.4.2 Where to Accept

difficulty: programmer

Is the following code legal?

```
task T is
   entry E;
end T;
```

```
task body T is
  procedure P is
  begin
    accept E;    -- 1.
  end P;
begin
  P;
  accept E do    -- 2.
    accept E;    -- 3.
  end E;
end T;
```

◇◇◇◇◇

The first and third accept statements are semantically illegal.

An accept statement for an entry may appear only within the body of the task for which the entry is defined. Furthermore, the innermost program unit in which the accept statement appears must be the task. Lastly, although accept statements may be nested, accept statements for the same entry or for entries of the same family may not be nested.

The first accept statement is illegal because it appears within a procedure, rather than immediately within the body of the task *T*. The third accept statement is illegal because it is nested within another accept statement for the same entry.

The reason why accept statements for a given task type may not appear within other program units is to prevent a task from accepting an entry other than its own. In order to preserve the rendezvous model, it must be illegal for some task T2 to accept a call to the entry T1.E. Consider the following code:

```
task T1 is
  entry E;
end T1;

task body T1 is
  task T2;

  procedure Back_Door is
  begin
    accept E;    -- Illegal.
  end Back_Door;

  task body T2 is
  begin
    Back_Door;
  end T2;
begin
  Back_Door;
```

end T1;

If this code were legal, the task *T2* could accept the entry *T1.E*. In order to prevent this from happening, we can do any of three things:

1. Disallow the accept statement within the procedure *Back_Door*.
2. Disallow the call to *Back_Door* within the body of *T2*.
3. Raise an exception at run time.

The first of these was selected by the designers of the language to simplify the implementation of static semantic checking.

Checking the second would become complex if separate compilation, call chains, and separation of specifications and bodies had to be taken into account. Separate compilation would require the program library to keep track of which program units accept certain entries. Call chains (e.g., procedure A calls procedure B, which calls *Back_Door*) would require an implementation to make the accept relation transitive. To see how separation of specifications and bodies is problematic, simply consider the semantics if *T2* also defined an entry named *E*.

The third solution was not chosen for a number of reasons. First, accepting an entry of a different task is a logic error that should be detected as soon as possible, e.g., at compilation time. Second, requiring all accept statements to appear immediately within the sequence of statements of a task body centralizes intertask behavior. Finally, though the intent of a procedure such as *Back_Door* is to facilitate modularity, the reality is that it would be more difficult to distinguish between the functional (subprograms) and tasking aspects of a program. Not allowing subprograms to accept entries preserves the simplicity of subprogram behavior while isolating tasking behavior.

Reasons why nested accept statements for the same entry or entry family are not allowed have to do with the scope of an entry declaration and the FIFO (first-in, first-out) semantics of rendezvous. An entry declaration and all corresponding accept statements form a single declarative region that is the scope of entry parameters. If nested accept statements such as

```
accept F (X : in Integer) do
  accept F (X : in Integer) do
    :
  end F;
end F;
```

were allowed, one would have two integer objects *X* declared immediately within the same declarative region, resulting in an illegal homograph. One might think that a reasonable solution to this problem would be to make each accept statement its own declarative region. But in fact, this is not possible, because the entry declaration must be in the same declarative region as the accept statements in order to ensure the conformity of formal parts.

Another aspect of this problem has to do with the FIFO semantics of the rendezvous. Suppose that all entry calls in the program were unconditional and untimed. Suppose further that task A called and was enqueued for entry T.E, and then task B called the same entry. Then the semantics of the language assure that the rendezvous with A is completed before the rendezvous with B begins. Since the call by task A was enqueued first, it would be the first to begin the rendezvous. If nested accept statements for the same entry were allowed, the rendezvous with B would be completed before the rendezvous with A would.

A Related Problem: Why are nested accept statements for the same family not allowed, even if each accept statement names a distinct entry?

[Ada83]   4.1.3 (3, 9 .. 10, 13, 16 .. 18); 9.5(8)

17.4.3 Calling Families

difficulty: programmer

Is the following code legal?

```
with  Text_Io;
procedure Calls is
    task T is
        entry E (Character) (Int : in Integer; F : in Float);
    end T;

    S : constant String := "An Array of Entries";
    :
    :
begin
    for Int in S'Range loop
        T.E (S (Int)) (Int, Float (Int));
    end loop;
end Calls;
```

◇◇◇◇◇

The code is legal.

An entry call statement is comprised of two parts: an entry name and an optional actual parameter part. In the program, *T.E (S (Int))* is the entry name and *(I, Float (Int))* is the actual parameter part.

During execution of an entry call, first the entry name is evaluated. This name denotes both a task and an entry of that task. As shown in the program, the entry name may include a nonstatic expression. In fact, the entry name may be comprised of two nonstatic expressions, as in

```
A : array (1 .. 10) of T;
⋮
A (Int).E (S (Int)) (Int, Float (Int));
```

Once the entry name has been evaluated, the actual parameters, if there are any, are evaluated, in some order. The semantics of evaluating the actual parameter part of an entry call is the same as that for a procedure call.

This program shows that since tasks are a type class and individual tasks are represented by objects, the name of a task object can be an arbitrary expression. It is not uncommon to see entry calls formed by complex expressions, especially when access types and composite types are used in conjunction with task types. One situation that calls for such expressions is that wherein the number of tasks required cannot be determined until execution time and a linked list or tree of tasks is created.

A Related Problem: Can an entry name ever be ambiguous?

[Ada83]   4.1(2, 5); 9.5(2, 10, 18)

17.4.4 Raising Exceptions

difficulty: programmer

What will the following program print?

```
with Text_Io;
procedure Exceptional is
   task T is
      entry E;
   end T;

   Ooops : exception;

   task body T is
   begin
      accept E do
         raise Ooops;
      end E;
   exception
      when Ooops =>
         Text_Io.Put_Line ("T says ooops.");
      when others =>
         Text_Io.Put_Line ("T says foo" & Ascii.Bar);
   end T;
begin
   T.E;
```

```
exception
  when Ooops =>
    Text_Io.Put_Line ("Main says ooops.");
  when others =>
    Text_Io.Put_Line ("Main says foobar.");
end Exceptional;
```

◇◇◇◇◇

The program will print some combination of the following characters and line terminators:

```
T says ooops.
Main says ooops.
```

If an exception is raised and not handled during execution of the sequence of statements forming a rendezvous, the rendezvous is completed; the exception is then propagated within the accepting task, as well as raised in the calling task at the point of the call. The exception is raised in both tasks in order to provide information to both. It is meaningful for the caller to receive an exception that points to the cause of the exceptional condition. An alternative semantics could be always to raise Tasking_Error in the caller. However, under such a semantics, the caller would not be able to distinguish between a rendezvous that cannot take place (for example, because the called task has completed) and a rendezvous that does take place, but encounters some exceptional condition.

The exception is propagated outside the accept statement within the called task, following normal propagation rules. (Conceptually, it is the called task which is actually executing the sequence of statements forming the rendezvous.) In no case is an exception ever propagated beyond the scope of a task body. If a task never handles an exception raised in its body, the task simply is completed. Note that the execution of a rendezvous is the only case where raising an exception can lead to propagation of the same exception to more than one thread of control.

A more common case where an entry call raises an exception involves calling a completed task. If a completed, terminated, or abnormal task is called, Tasking_Error is raised at the point of the call. Note that the entry name and any actual parameters are evaluated before Tasking_Error can be raised. Timed and conditional entry calls *are* entry calls and, therefore, will also cause Tasking_Error to be raised under these circumstances.

A Related Problem: Consider the following accept statement and corresponding entry call:

```
accept E (X : out Integer) do
  X := 0;
end E;
  ⋮
```

```
P  :  Positive;
   ⋮
T.E  (X  =>  P);
```

In which threads of control will an exception be raised? Will Constraint_Error or Tasking_Error be raised?

[Ada83]   9.5(10, 16); 11.5(3 .. 4)

17.4.5 Minimalist Accept Statements

difficulty: designer

Compare and contrast the two accept statements in the following code:

```
Buffer  :  String  (1  ..  1_000);
Last    :  Natural;
   ⋮
accept  Send  (S  :  in  String)  do     accept  Send  (S  :  in  String)  do
   Last  :=  S'Length;                       Text_Io.Put_Line  (S);
   Buffer  (1  ..  Last)  :=  S;          end  Send;
end  Send;
Text_Io.Put_Line  (Buffer  (1  ..  Last));
```


◇◇◇◇◇

The left-hand accept statement attempts to minimize the time in which the calling task is suspended. The right-hand accept statement imposes no limitations on the size of the string to be output.

During execution of a rendezvous, the calling task is suspended. This simply means that the calling task does not execute; it must wait for the rendezvous to be completed before continuing. From the point of view of a single sequence of statements, an entry call is similar to a procedure call. That is, any statements after the call will not be executed until the call has been completed. In order to maximize parallelism, it is desirable to minimize the execution time of a rendezvous.

The left-hand example makes an effort to minimize the time during which the caller is suspended. It does this by copying needed data into local variables, releasing the caller, and then performing the desired operation. The right-hand example suspends the caller for the duration of the execution of the desired operation, the implicit assumption being that the execution of the desired operation takes considerably longer than the assignments to the local variables.

Another aspect of evaluating the two accept statements has to do with confirming that the desired operation has been performed. Suppose the call to *Text_Io.Put_Line* propagates Use_Error. Then, using the left-hand example, the calling task might have to inquire through another entry call whether the data have been output successfully. Otherwise, it would have to ignore this possibility. In contrast, the right-hand example would immediately notify the caller of the inability to complete the operation by raising Use_Error at the point of the call.

[Ada83]   9.5(14); 11.5(1, 3 .. 4)

17.5 THE MULTITALENTED SELECT STATEMENT

In Ada, there exists a compound statement called the select statement. This statement is widely viewed as one of the most complex in programming language history; it is difficult to comprehend even by the experienced Ada programmer. The semantics of this statement allows for most of the actions that can be performed on or by a task.

An important aspect of task synchronization and communication is determining when these events are to take place. The select statement provides a means of allowing a task some leeway in committing itself to a specific rendezvous. There are three forms of the select statement:

- selective wait,
- timed entry call, and
- conditional entry call.

The first form is used by tasks to accept calls while the last two are used by tasks to issue calls. This section presents the semantics of all three forms.

17.5.1 Selecting among More than One Accept

difficulty: designer

Compare and contrast the three following selective waits:

```
  << One >>        << Two >>         << Three >>
  select           select            select
     accept A;        accept A;          accept A;
  or                  accept B;       or
     accept B;     else                  accept B;
  else                null;           end select;
     null;         end select;
  end select;
```

◇◇◇◇◇

The following table illustrates four run time conditions and for each the resulting behaviors of the three statements. The Count attribute is used for notational purposes only, viz., it indicates whether the queues are empty.

	One	Two	Three
A'Count > 0 B'Count > 0	accept A or accept B	accept A then accept B	accept A or accept B
A'Count > 0 B'Count = 0	accept A	accept A then wait for B	accept A
A'Count = 0 B'Count > 0	accept B	execute else part	accept B
A'Count = 0 B'Count = 0	execute else part	execute else part	wait for A or B; accept the first one called

The major differences between the statements have to do with the arbitrary selection of accept alternatives and when each statement must wait for calls. As the fourth condition in the table shows, if the queues are empty when statements *One* or *Two* execute, no waiting occurs since the else part is executed. However, the execution of statement *Three* in this condition must wait for a call to arrive. If the queues for entries *A* and *B* are each nonempty (i.e., the first condition), either accept alternative in statements *One* and *Three* may be selected.

[Ada83] 9.7.1(1 .. 3, 6 .. 7, 9)

17.5.2 Inherent Nature of Indeterminism

difficulty: novice

What will the following program print?

```
with Text_Io;
procedure Nondeterminism is
   task T is
      entry E;
   end T;

   task body T is
   begin
```

```
   loop
     select
        accept E;   Text_Io.Put ('1');
     or
        accept E;   Text_Io.Put ('2');
     or
        accept E;   Text_Io.Put ('3');
     or
        terminate;
     end select;
   end loop;
 end T;
begin
  for Int in 1 .. 6 loop
    T.E;
  end loop;
  Text_Io.New_Line;
end Nondeterminism;
```

◇◇◇◇◇

The program will print six digits, each of which may be a *1*, *2*, or *3*. Thus, any of the following would be legal results:

```
333333
122223
123321
```

During the first six executions of the selective wait, any one of the three accept alternatives may be selected. The last execution will choose the terminate alternative, causing the task to terminate.

From a tasking point of view, the three accept alternatives are equivalent in that they are always open and each name the same entry. Therefore, the decision as to which one to select is totally arbitrary.

This program illustrates one small example of indeterminism in the Ada tasking model. By their very nature, concurrent systems have properties which are indeterminate. In many cases, this is unavoidable and also desirable. The novice tasking programmer should not be overly concerned by these properties. An indeterministic program need not be erroneous or incorrect. Equating the term *indeterministic* with *erroneous* or *incorrect* would be a mistake.

Another simple example of the indeterminism inherent in concurrent systems is given in the following code:

```
with Text_Io;
procedure More_Nondeterminism is
  task T1 is
```

```
      entry  E  (Boolean);
    end  T1;

    task  T2;

    task body  T1 is
    begin
      loop
        select
          accept  E  (True);     Text_Io.Put  ('T');
        or
          accept  E  (False);    Text_Io.Put  ('F');
        or
          terminate;
        end  select;
      end  loop;
    end  T1;

    task body  T2 is
    begin
      for  Int  in  1 .. 10  loop
        T1.E  (True);
      end  loop;
    end  T2;
begin
    for  Int  in  1 .. 10  loop
      T1.E  (False);
    end  loop;

    Text_Io.New_Line;
end  More_Nondeterminism;
```

This program will print 10 *T* characters and 10 *F* characters. The order in which these characters are printed is indeterminate.

[Ada83]   9.7.1(3, 6, 14)
See also   [Cohen88]

17.5.3 Guard Expressions

difficulty: programmer

What will the following program print?

```
with  Text_Io;
procedure  Guard_It is
  task  T is
```

```
      entry  A;
      entry  B;
   end  T;

   task  body  T  is
      Bool : Boolean := True;
   begin
      loop
        select
          when  Bool  =>
            accept  A;
            Text_Io.Put_Line ("Entry  A  selected.");
        or
          when  Bool  =>
            accept  B;
            Text_Io.Put_Line ("Entry  B  selected.");
        end  select;

          Bool := not  Bool;
      end  loop;
   end  T;
begin
   T.A;
   T.B;
exception
   when  Tasking_Error  =>
      Text_Io.Put_Line ("Oooh!  Not  what  I  expected.");
   when  Program_Error  =>
      Text_Io.Put_Line ("Guards  must  have  been  closed.");
   when  others  =>
      Text_Io.Put_Line ("Heck  if  I  know.");
   end  Guard_It;
```

◇◇◇◇◇

The program will print

```
Entry  A  selected.
Oooh! Not what I expected.
```

The selective wait in the program is formed by two accept alternatives. The execution of the statement begins by determining which alternatives are *open*. An alternative is considered open if it has no *when condition*, or if the *when condition* evaluates to True. (The expressions in the when conditions may be of any Boolean type.) Any accept, delay, or terminate alternative may be guarded in this way, but an else part may not. If an alternative is not open, it is said to be *closed* and thus cannot be selected. Note that in determining which alternatives are open, all when conditions are evaluated before any alternative is selected. Also, the entry names for all open accept alternatives are evaluated at this time. The order in which the when conditions and entry names are evaluated is not defined by the language, but they are evaluated sequentially.

Now consider the semantics of the selective wait in the absence of any delay alternatives, a terminate alternative, and an else part. If only one accept alternative is open, it is selected regardless of whether a call is queued. When two or more accept alternatives are open and only one of these alternatives has a waiting call, that call is accepted. If two or more open alternatives have waiting calls, one of them is selected arbitrarily. If none of the open accept alternatives have waiting calls, the select statement waits until one of the selected entries is called; then the rendezvous for that accept statement, and consequently the execution of that accept alternative, takes place. Note that while a task is waiting for a call, when conditions and entry names are not reevaluated. Such evaluations take place only once per execution of the selective wait.

During the first execution of the preceding selective wait, both alternatives are open. For this execution, entry A is accepted. In the next iteration, both alternatives are closed. Whenever all alternatives are closed and there is no else part, the exception Program_Error is raised at the point of the selective wait. Since it is not handled, this exception will cause the task designated by T to complete. Note that Program_Error is not propagated beyond the body of T.

Since the task designated by T is completed before the call to B can be accepted, Tasking_Error is raised at the point of the call. Whenever an entry call is enqueued and the called task is completed or terminates before the call can be accepted, Tasking_Error is raised at the point of call. Similarly, if a call is issued to a task that is already completed or terminated, Tasking_Error is raised.

[Ada83]   9.5(16); 9.7.1(2 .. 6, 11); 11.4.1(4, 8); 11.5(2)
[ARG]   AI-00029/01, 03-13-84; AI-00030/07, 07-23-86

17.5.4 Count, Families, and Priorities

difficulty: designer

For the code

```
type Priority is (Low, Medium, High);
task T is
  entry E (Priority);
end T;
```

can the following selective wait be used to rank the acceptance of entry calls?

```
select
  accept E (High) do ...
or
```

```
     when  E  (High)'Count  =  0  and
             E  (Medium)'Count  +  E  (Low)'Count  /=  0  =>
          accept  E  (Priority'Val  (
                   Boolean'Pos  (E  (Medium)'Count  /=  0)))  do  ...
     end  select;
```

◇◇◇◇◇

The selective wait provides a ranking, but with a number of limitations.

In the program fragment, the accept alternative for *E (High)* is always open. The intention is that the other accept alternative will be open only when no calls are pending for *E (High)* and at least one call is pending for the other two entries. That is, when there is a call waiting for *E (High)*, it is always accepted. When there is a call waiting for *E (Medium)* and there is no call waiting for *E (High)*, the call to *E (Medium)* is always accepted. Finally, a waiting call to *E (Low)* is accepted only when no calls are waiting for the other two entries.

Now suppose that the selective wait is executed and no entry calls are currently queued. Then only the first alternative will be open, causing the task to wait indefinitely for a call to *E (High)*. While the task is waiting in this manner, subsequent calls to the other two entries cannot be accepted until a rendezvous at *E (High)* has taken place. One might attempt to alleviate such semantics by also placing a when condition on the accept alternative for *E (High)*, thus:

```
    select
       when  E  (High)'Count  /=  0  =>
          accept  E  (High)  do  ...
    or
       ┊   -- Same  as  in  the  problem  statement.
    end  select;
```

Unfortunately, this will not work in the presence of timed and conditional entry calls. For suppose that during the evaluation of the first when condition, there is one call queued at *E (High)* and one queued at *E (Low)*. Then the first condition will evaluate to True. One might then suppose that the second when condition must evaluate to False, leaving only the first alternative open. But suppose that before the second when condition is evaluated, the call to *E (High)* expires. In that case, the second when condition will also evaluate to True, leaving both alternatives open. Now suppose further that before the task is ready to accept a call, a new call to *E (High)* is enqueued. Then a situation is created wherein either accept statement may be immediately selected. So *E (Low)* can be accepted instead of *E (High)*.

A different approach to ranking entry calls is by means of a loop statement, as in the following code:

```
    for  P  in  reverse  Priority  loop
       select
```

```
            accept E (P) do
               ⋮

            end E;
            exit;
        else
            null;
        end select;
    end loop;
```

This approach does not suffer from some of the reliability problems just discussed. Another advantage is that the approach can easily handle any size of entry family. Nevertheless, efficiency may be compromised because entries are required to be polled until a call is found. A situation in which many entries are polled for which no calls are pending is sometimes called a *busy wait*. Another disadvantage of this approach is that polling does not allow for the use of a terminate alternative.

Note that the use of static task priorities by means of the pragma Priority will not, in general, solve the problem of ranking entry calls. In deciding which accept alternative to select, a task need not examine its entry queues to determine which of the waiting tasks has the highest priority. This does not prevent an implementation, however, from using such a heuristic.

A Related Problem: Using the polling method in the preceding loop statement, would it be possible to accept a low-priority call when a higher priority call is queued?

[Ada83]   9.5(4 .. 6); 9.9(5 .. 7)
[ARG]   AI-00034/06, 07-23-86; AI-00233/12, 06-16-89; AI-00594/08, 03-01-90
See also   [Burns87] and [Elrad87]

17.5.5 The Delay Alternative

difficulty: programmer

What will the following program print?

```
with Text_Io;
procedure Its_All_Relative is
    task T is
        entry E;
    end T;

    task body T is
    begin
        select
            accept E;
```

```
      or
        delay  86_400.0;
        Text_Io.Put_Line ("Another  day,  another  compiler  bug.");
      or
        delay  1.0;
        Text_Io.Put_Line ("Just  wait  a  second.");
      end  select;
    end  T;
  begin
    null;
  end  Its_All_Relative;
```

◇◇◇◇◇

The program will print *Just wait a second.*

A selective wait may include one or more delay alternatives. Note that delay alternatives, a terminate alternative, and an else part are mutually exclusive.

A delay alternative limits the amount of time that the execution of a selective wait will wait before accepting a call. If a call cannot be accepted within the amount of time specified in the shortest open delay alternative, then the shortest delay alternative is selected. If more than one delay alternative specifies the shortest delay, and no entry is accepted within this time, then one of these delay alternatives is selected arbitrarily. (The unit of time specified in a delay alternative is seconds.)

In the foregoing program, since no call to entry E is ever issued, one of the delay alternatives will be selected. Because the second alternative clearly specifies the shortest delay, it will be selected.

A Related Problem: If all accept alternatives are closed, is a delay alternative selected immediately?

[Ada83]   9.7.1(3, 7 .. 8, 14)

17.5.6 The Meaning of "Immediately"

difficulty: designer

Will the following program ever finish execution?

```
procedure Passing_Ships is
  task T is
    entry E;
  end T;
  task body T is
  begin
    loop
```

```
            select
               accept E;    exit;
            else
               null;
            end select;
        end loop;
     end T;
  begin
    loop
       select
          T.E;    exit;
       else
          null;
       end select;
    end loop;
  end Passing_Ships;
```

◇◇◇◇◇

The answer to this question is implementation dependent. There is no requirement that the rendezvous ever take place.

The selective wait statement provides a task with additional freedom in accepting entry calls. There are many forms of this statement; it may be comprised of one or more *accept alternatives* and at most one of the following:

- any number of *delay alternatives*
- an *else part*
- a *terminate alternative*.

The selective wait in the body of *T* executes as follows:

- A check is made to see whether a call to entry *E* is queued.
- If such a call is waiting, the accept alternative is selected.
- If no call is queued, the else part is executed.

Selecting an accept alternative means that the rendezvous associated with the accept statement is executed, followed by the sequence of statements after the accept statement. An accept alternative is thus formed by an accept statement and an optional sequence of statements. The execution of an else part simply involves the execution of the sequence of statements of the else part.

For any given execution of a selective wait, at most one alternative is selected and executed. The model of executing a selective wait is very similar to that of executing conditional statements.

The statement inside the loop of procedure *Passing_Ships* is a conditional entry call statement. A conditional entry call statement is comprised of two parts: an entry call followed by an optional sequence of statements, and an else part. Like the selective wait, this else part is simply a sequence of statements. The semantics of the conditional entry call statement in *Passing_Ships* is as follows:

- If the entry call can be accepted *immediately*, it is executed. The sequence of statements following the entry call is executed upon return from the rendezvous.
- If the entry call cannot be accepted *immediately*, the sequence of statements comprising the else part is executed.

Conceptually, execution of the conditional entry call statement in the preceding program will enqueue a call to *T.E.* If *T* does not accept this call *immediately*, then the call is removed from the queue and the else part is executed.

The focus of this program is to examine the semantics of *immediately*. If the caller is always in the process of enqueuing the call while the acceptor is in the process of determining whether a call is ready, then the program will never finish. These "windows of opportunity," where the call is enqueued and the acceptor is ready to rendezvous, can be arbitrarily small. If the windows never overlap, the program will loop infinitely.

The reader should note that an implementation need not actually enqueue a call when executing a conditional entry call. There are many ways to implement an Ada run-time system. However, it is easiest to understand the semantics of the conditional entry call statement if one thinks of a call as always being enqueued.

A Related Problem: Can a conditional entry call ever raise Tasking_Error?

[Ada83]   9.7.1(1 .. 3, 6 .. 7, 9); 9.7.2(1 .. 4)
[ARG]   AI-00443/02, 10-13-86; AI-00444/05, 08-06-87

17.5.7 Timed versus Conditional Calls

difficulty: designer

Explain the semantic differences between the following two statements:

```
select                      select
   T.E;                         T.E;
or                          else
                               ⋮
  delay Duration'Small;        ⋮
                            end select;
   ⋮
end select;
```

◇◇◇◇◇

The timed entry call in the left-hand statement will rendezvous if it can be accepted within *Duration'Small* seconds. The conditional entry call on the right will rendezvous if it can be accepted *immediately*. One of the issues in this section is to examine the meaning of *immediately* within this context.

First, consider the conditional entry call. The entry call and following sequence of statements, if any, will be executed if the call can be accepted immediately. In this context, immediately means the following:

1. There are no calls already queued for the called entry.
2. The called task is ready to accept the called entry.

These can be called the preconditions to beginning the rendezvous. The point is that *immediately* does not imply an infinitely small, bounded, or even static amount of time. The length of *immediately* is simply the amount of time required to evaluate the preceding conditions. A conditional entry call must always evaluate these conditions, regardless of how long such evaluation may take.

A timed entry call, on the other hand, has slightly different semantics, depending on the value of the delay specified. Consider the following four cases:

```
(1) delay  value   <=   0.0
(2) 0.0            <    delay  value   <   immediately
(3) delay  value   =    immediately
(4) delay  value   >    immediately
```

In case (1), in which the delay value is less than or equal to zero, a timed entry call is semantically equivalent to a corresponding conditional entry call. That is, a timed entry call with a nonpositive delay must evaluate the preceding preconditions and act accordingly.

The remaining three cases have a semantics that may be characterized as follows: Place the entry call in the corresponding entry queue, and start the *timer*; if the timer expires before the call is accepted, remove the call from the queue and execute the sequence of statements in the delay alternative; if the entry call is accepted before the timer expires, cancel the timer and begin the rendezvous.

It is worthwhile examining the last three cases in further detail. A timed entry call whose delay is positive but less than *immediately* implies that the preconditions cannot be evaluated in the amount of time provided. In this case, the rendezvous cannot take place and the sequence of statements in the delay alternative will be executed. In fact, the preconditions required for the call to be accepted need never be evaluated, because doing so would be unobservable since the delay alternative is going to be selected anyway. The reader should note the counterintuitive semantic differences between the first and second cases. Even though the first case specifies a delay value that is strictly less than that of the second case, the language requires that the rendezvous preconditions be evaluated in the first case, but not in the second.

In the third case, it is indeterminate how the tie will be decided. The language does not specify the winner of a tie. The rendezvous could take place if the preconditions evaluate to True. Alternatively, the sequence of statements in the delay alternative could be executed.

In the last case, there is sufficient time to determine whether the rendezvous can take place. It is this case for which the timed entry call was designed. Note that here no semantics for polling or busy waiting is required. Thus, the calling task need not continually evaluate the preconditions. Since the call has been placed in the corresponding entry queue, the calling task simply waits for one of two things to occur: the call to be accepted or the timer to expire.

A Related Problem: When does the timer on a timed entry call start? On what logical process is the timer executed?

[Ada83]   9.7.2(1, 3 .. 5); 9.7.3(1, 3 .. 4)
[ARG]   AI-00276/07, 02-23-87

17.5.8 The Impatient Callee Task

difficulty: designer

Explain the semantic differences between the following two syntactic forms of the selective wait:

```
select              select
   accept E;           accept E;
else                or
   null;               delay 0.0;
end select;         end select;
```

◇◇◇◇◇

The two statements are semantically equivalent.

The left-hand statement uses the else part to specify that no action is to be performed if a call to entry E cannot be accepted immediately. The right-hand statement achieves the same effect by specifying a delay alternative with a nonpositive value. If an open delay alternative specifies a length of time less than or equal to zero, it has the same semantics as an else part.

The focus of the two statements is to show that the delay statement in a delay alternative does not have the same semantics as a delay statement appearing in a sequence of statements. Recall that regular delay statements specify the minimum amount of time to delay. Thus, even the simple statement

```
delay 0.0;
```

can result in a lengthy delay.

A Related Problem: Suppose the first statement of the else part was "**delay** 0.0;". Would this change the preceding explanation?

[Ada83]   9.7.1(7 .. 9)
See also   [VMNM85]

17.5.9 The Terminate Alternative

difficulty: programmer

Explain how the terminate alternative can be used to prevent deadness errors. A deadness error is when a task is waiting for something that will never happen.

◇◇◇◇◇

An open terminate alternative allows the run-time system to determine whether an accept alternative could ever be selected, e.g., to determine whether a task can ever again be called. If it cannot be called, the terminate alternative provides a means of terminating the task. For example, the following fragment provides for task termination when no more requests to the secretary are forthcoming:

```
task body Secretary is
begin
  loop
    select
      accept Phone_Call ...
    or
      accept Dictation ...
    or
      accept Write_Letter ...
    or
      accept Run_Errand ...
    or
      terminate;
    end select;
  end loop;
end Secretary;
```

To understand the semantics of task termination in general, one must first examine the concept of the (direct) *master* of a task. The (direct) master of a task is one of the following:

- another task
- a block statement
- a subprogram

- a library package.

A task is dependent on its master. There are two ways that tasks can be created: by an allocator and by a task object declaration. Determining the master of a task depends on the means of creation. If a task is created by allocation, the master of the task is the (innermost) task, block, subprogram, or package in which the corresponding access type definition is elaborated. If the task is created by means of an object declaration, the master is the scope immediately enclosing the object declaration.

Furthermore, a task is indirectly dependent on masters other than its direct master. If a master is a block statement or a subprogram, then this master is dependent on the task executing the block statement or subprogram. The task can be thought of as a master of the block or subprogram. Thus, a task is indirectly dependent on the master of its master, in a transitive manner.

When the execution of a task reaches an open terminate alternative, the task will terminate if:

- Some master on which the task is dependent is completed, and
- All other tasks dependent on this same master are terminated or have reached an open terminate alternative.

The master-dependency relation can be thought of as defining a tree structure. On the path to the leaves of any node of the tree are the tasks that are dependent on that node. On the path to the root of any node are the masters on which the node is dependent. The root of the tree is the environment task, which calls the main program. Immediately following the root are nodes representing the main program and library packages. Given this tree structure model, termination can be thought of as occurring bottom up: A given task cannot terminate until all tasks underneath it have terminated or are ready to do so.

Now consider a specific selective wait that contains a terminate alternative:

```
select
    accept E;
or
    terminate;
end select;
```

If there are no calls pending at E, one of two actions can be performed: (1) Wait for a call to E, accept this call, and continue execution, or (2) terminate when the preceding conditions have been met. Regardless of which action is performed, the task might first have to wait for some time. The point is that the preceding conditions governing the terminate alternative may need to be evaluated repeatedly for a given execution of a selective wait.

The terminate alternative can be used to reduce the risk of *deadness* errors. An example of a deadness error is a state where a task is waiting for calls, but no calls will ever be issued. For example, consider a task that acts as a buffer. Such a task is said to be a *server*; that is, it never calls or creates other tasks. The terminate alternative relieves server tasks from deciding when to terminate. In accordance with the nature of server tasks, the terminate alternative allows a task to terminate only when its services are no longer needed. By its very definition, the terminate alternative cannot be selected if there is a possibility of future demands upon the task. Note, however, that if the only open alternative is a terminate alternative, the task must select it. In this case, the terminate alternative may lead to deadlock. One such situation is when calls to the task are issued after the terminate alternative has been selected.

A Related Problem: Is there any justification for closing a terminate alternative?

[Ada83]   9.4; 9.7.1(7, 10)

17.6 COMPLETION AND TERMINATION

Completion and termination are the final two phases of a task's execution. Informally, a task is completed when it has finished the execution of its body. A completed task cannot perform any actions. Termination is the final state of all tasks. This section presents the ways in which tasks can be completed and the semantics of becoming terminated after completion has occurred.

17.6.1 Impatient Masters

difficulty: designer

What will the following program print?

```
with Text_Io;
procedure Be_Careful_Out_There is
   task type T;
   task body T is
   begin
      Text_Io.Put_Line ("Not quite dead yet.");
   end T;
begin
   declare
      type Acc is access T;
      X : Acc := new T;
      P : Positive := -4444;
   begin
      Text_Io.Put_Line ("Cannot be!");
   exception
      when Tasking_Error =>
```

```
            Text_Io.Put_Line ("Tasking_Error in block.");
        when others =>
            Text_Io.Put_Line ("Block says others.");
    end;
exception
    when Constraint_Error | Numeric_Error =>
        Text_Io.Put_Line ("Constraint_Error.");
    when Program_Error => Text_Io.Put_Line ("Program_Error.");
    when Tasking_Error => Text_Io.Put_Line ("Tasking_Error.");
end Be_Careful_Out_There;
```

◇◇◇◇◇

The program will print

```
Not quite dead yet.
Constraint_Error.
```

A scope cannot be exited until all tasks dependent on it have terminated. If dependent tasks have not yet terminated and the thread of control has completed the execution of its scope, the thread of control simply waits. The following are the ways in which a thread of control can complete a scope:

- Finish the execution of all statements.
- Execute a return, exit, or goto statement.
- Raise an exception in the sequence of statements that is not handled within the scope.
- Propagate an exception raised in the declarative part of the scope.

These four cases define ways that a master can be *completed*. Completion refers to the situation where a thread of control executing a scope is *ready* to leave the scope, but has not yet done so. For example, reaching a return statement in a procedure is an example of completion. (A master can also be completed as the result of being made abnormal. This is addressed in Section 17.7.)

The program illustrates the fourth means of completion. The task designated by *X*.**all** is dependent on its master, the block statement. Since this task is created by means of an allocator, its activation occurs during execution of the allocator. After activation, the elaboration of *P* raises Constraint_Error or Numeric_Error in the declarative part. The exception cannot be propagated until the task *X*.**all** has terminated.

Because of the dependency between tasks and scope, care must be taken when subprograms create tasks. Thus, in the subprogram template

```
procedure P is
    task T;
    task body T is
```

```
        begin
            :
        end  T;
    begin
        :
    end  P;
```

any invocation of procedure *P* cannot return until *T* has terminated.

[Ada83]   9.4(5 .. 6)
[ARG]   AI-00173/05, 12-01-86

17.6.2 Death by Exception

difficulty: programmer

What does the following program print?

```ada
with  Text_Io;
procedure  Main  is
   X : Integer;

   task  T  is
      entry  E  (X : out  Positive);
   end  T;

   task  body  T  is
   begin
      loop
         accept  E  (X : out  Positive)  do
            X := -1;
         end  E;
      end  loop;
   end  T;
begin
   begin
      T.E  (X);
   exception
      when  Constraint_Error  =>
         Text_Io.Put_Line  ("1: Constraint_Error.");
      when  Tasking_Error  =>
         Text_Io.Put_Line  ("1: Tasking_Error.");
   end;

   T.E  (X);
```

```
exception
  when Constraint_Error =>
    Text_Io.Put_Line ("2: Constraint_Error.");
  when Tasking_Error =>
    Text_Io.Put_Line ("2: Tasking_Error.");
end Main;
```

◇◇◇◇◇

The program will print

1: Constraint_Error.
2: Tasking_Error.

When an exception is raised but not handled within a task, the task is completed. This is the same semantics as for an exception being raised in any scope—that is, the scope is completed.

In the foregoing program, an exception is raised during a rendezvous. The exception is not handled, thus forcing the rendezvous to be completed. Constraint_Error is raised within two threads of control: the task designated by T and the task executing the main program. Because the main program provides a handler for the exception, but T does not, the task designated by T will complete execution.

After handling Constraint_Error, the main program again calls $T.E$. A rendezvous cannot take place, since T will be completed before any more calls can be accepted. Hence, Tasking_Error will be raised at the point of this second call. The main program also handles this exception.

[Ada83]   9.4(5); 9.5(16); 11.5(1 .. 5)

17.6.3 Naming Terminated Tasks

difficulty: designer

Can a task ever be named outside the scope of its master?

◇◇◇◇◇

A task can be named outside the scope of its master when a subprogram or entry call returns a value of a task type. The following program is a pathological example of referencing a task outside of its master:

```
with Text_Io;
procedure Dead_Tasks_Dont_Talk is
  task type T;
  task body T is
```

```
      begin
        null;
      end T;

      function F return T is
        X : T;
      begin
        return X;
      end F;
begin
    Text_Io.Put_Line (Boolean'Image (F'Callable xor F'Terminated));
exception
    when Tasking_Error => Text_Io.Put_Line ("Tasking_Error.");
end Dead_Tasks_Dont_Talk;
```

Here, the function F creates a task object X that is returned to the caller. As discussed in Section 17.6.2, execution of the return statement must first wait for the dependent task designated by X to terminate. Therefore, any execution of the function F will return a terminated task. (Note that F is called twice in this program, returning a different task each time.)

Originally, the Ada Rapporteur Group ruled that, since F returned a terminated task, the program would print *TRUE*. This interpretation is straightforward and intuitive. However, experience with the language has shown that the effect on implementations is drastic. To conform to the interpretation, many implementations had to change their algorithms for deallocating memory used by tasks. The algorithms conforming to the original interpretation were much less efficient. The Ada Rapporteur Group deemed the inefficiency too severe to justify supporting pathologies such as the foregoing. Therefore, the new interpretation is simply that any naming of a task after the completion of its master is erroneous. Accordingly, any execution of the preceding program is erroneous.

A Related Problem: Is there any way to rewrite the program such that function F returns a task that has not yet terminated?

[Ada83]   9.4(5 .. 6)
[ARG]   AI-00167/05, 12-13-90; AI-00867/03, 12-13-90

17.6.4 Library Tasks

difficulty: designer

Consider the following program:

```
      package P is
        task type T is
          entry E;
```

```
      end T;
    X : T;
  end P;

  package body P is
    task body T is
    begin
      loop
        select
            accept E;
        or
            terminate;
        end select;
      end loop;
    end T;
  end P;

  with P;
  procedure Main is
    Y     : P.T;
    Excep : exception;
  begin
    P.X.E;
    Y.E;
    raise Excep;
  end Main;
```

When will the tasks terminate?

◇◇◇◇◇

The task designated by Y will terminate after execution of the main program has been completed. That is, it will terminate after the two statements in the main program have been executed. The task designated by X can, but need not, terminate.

The only instance in which a task of the type T terminates is if its terminate alternative is selected. In order for this alternative to be selected, the master of the task must be completed. The master of the task designated by X is the library package P. But completion does not apply to packages. For this reason, the language does not define when, if ever, the task designated by X terminates. However, the task cannot terminate while it can still be called. This means that it will not terminate before the main program finishes executing.

The Ada Rapporteur Group has elaborated the conditions under which library tasks (those tasks whose immediate master is a library package) terminate. A library task that is suspended on an open terminate alternative, and whose dependents (if any) are terminated or likewise suspended, must terminate when the main program terminates normally. This stipulation follows the intuitive meaning of the terminate alternative.

However, a different interpretation exists when the main program terminates as a result of an unhandled exception. The Ada Rapporteur Group maintains that in that case the termination of library tasks is still implementation dependent. For this reason, task X need not ever terminate.

The termination of the task designated by Y is much different. Its master is a procedure, so the task will terminate when the procedure has been completed.

A Related Problem: If the body of the library package P contained a sequence of statements that raised, but did not handle, an exception, would the task designated by X then terminate? Would the task designated by Y ever activate?

[Ada83]   9.4(1, 5 .. 10, 12 .. 13)
[ARG]   AI-00399/14, 06-16-89

17.7 THE TASK STATE MODEL

At this point, the reader should be aware that there are a number of phases (or states) of a task's execution. The main purpose of this section is to explain further and reenforce the transitions between these states. Figure 17.2 is a state diagram that illustrates the various states of a task and the transitions between states.

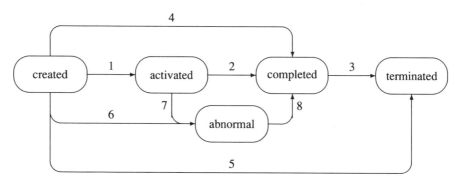

Figure 17.2   Task state diagram.

Arcs 1, 2, and 3 are associated with "normal" execution, regardless of how the task is created. The following is a brief explanation of the transitions represented by the arcs:

1. A task is activated if its activation can begin and does occur without raising an exception.
2. After a task has been activated, it may become completed. Note that a task can never become terminated without first becoming completed if it has the chance to create dependents.

3. Once a task has been completed, it can terminate when all its dependents have terminated.

4. If, during the activation of a task, an exception is raised within the task, the task becomes completed.

5. Before a task has a chance to begin activation, an exception may be raised within the elaboration of the task's direct master. In such a case, the task becomes terminated. Note that this transition can never be undertaken by a task created by an allocator.

6. A task may be aborted any time after it is created. Once a task is aborted, it becomes abnormal.

7. A task may also be aborted while it is active.

8. After becoming abnormal, a task may be completed.

17.7.1 Deadness Errors

difficulty: programmer

What will the following program print?

```
with Text_Io;
procedure Dead_Head is
   task T1 is entry E; end T1;
   task T2 is entry E; end T2;
   task T3 is entry E; end T3;

   task body T1 is
   begin
      accept E;
   exception
      when Tasking_Error =>
         Text_Io.Put_Line ("Tasking_Error in T1.");
   end T1;

   task body T2 is
   begin
      T3.E;
   exception
      when Tasking_Error =>
         Text_Io.Put_Line ("Tasking_Error in T2.");
   end T2;

   task body T3 is
   begin
      T2.E;
   exception
      when Tasking_Error =>
```

```
            Text_Io.Put_Line ("Tasking_Error in T3.");
      end T3;
begin
   null;
exception
   when Tasking_Error =>
      Text_Io.Put_Line ("Tasking_Error in Dead_Head.");
end Dead_Head;
```

◇◇◇◇◇

The program will not print anything.

 Two tasking states not explicitly addressed by the language are circular deadlock and global blocking. Both of these states are examples of what is generally referred to as deadness errors. Circular deadlock occurs when two or more tasks must synchronize with each other before they can continue execution, but the synchronization must occur in an order that cannot take place. Global blocking, a state of the program as a whole, is the state in which all active tasks are blocked and cannot continue execution. The preceding program experiences both circular deadlock and global blocking.

 The task designated by *T1* reaches a state in which it is blocked, waiting for a call. The tasks designated by *T2* and *T3* reach a circular deadlock state in which they are attempting to call each other. This results in global blocking: all tasks are blocked, including the one executing the main program, and none can terminate. (The task executing *Dead_Head* is blocked because it cannot exit the scope of *Dead_Head* until the dependent tasks have terminated.) No exception is raised when a program reaches these states. The semantics of the preceding program are such that all four tasks remain blocked forever.

A Related Problem: Does a task always deadlock when it calls one of its own entries?

[Ada83] 9.5(11 .. 13)

17.7.2 Synchronization Points

difficulty: designer

What will the following program print?

```
with Text_Io;
procedure Sync is
   task Caller;
   task Callee is
      entry E;
   end Callee;
```

```
task body Caller is
begin
  loop
    Callee.E;
  end loop;
exception
  when Tasking_Error => Text_Io.Put_Line ("Callee died");
end Caller;

task body Callee is
begin
  loop
    accept E;
  end loop;
end Callee;
begin
  abort Caller, Callee;
end Sync;
```

◇◇◇◇◇

The program can, but need not, print *Callee died*.

The abort statement names one or more task objects. A consequence of this semantics is that one cannot abort all tasks of a given type by providing the type mark. Execution of an abort statement causes the named tasks to become *abnormal* in some order. Furthermore, any tasks dependent on an abnormal task themselves become abnormal. In this way abnormality is a transitive property. Like completion and termination, abnormality is a state of a task. Note that the named tasks become abnormal immediately, but, as will be discussed, this need not have an immediate or direct effect on the tasks themselves. The abortion of a task that is already abnormal, completed, or terminated has no effect.

If a task becomes abnormal during execution, the actions that can be performed by the task are restricted. An abnormal task becomes completed no later than when it reaches one of the following *synchronization points* during its execution:

- the end of its activation
- the activation of another task
- an entry call
- the beginning or end of an accept statement
- a select statement (selective wait, timed call, and conditional call)
- a delay statement
- an exception handler
- an abort statement.

Similarly, a task becomes completed if it is suspended or blocked as a result of executing either a delay statement, a select statement, an accept statement, or an entry call, and then becomes abnormal. In the last case, the entry call is also removed from the entry queue. Finally, a task becomes completed if it becomes abnormal before it begins its activation.

Note the conceptual differences in the ways in which a task can become completed. The ways presented in Section 17.6 arose through actions of the task itself. By contrast, the abort statement can cause a task to become completed as a direct result of actions performed by other tasks.

Calling an abnormal task will result in Tasking_Error being raised. Similarly, when a task becomes abnormal, any calls in its entry queues will result in Tasking_Error being raised at the point of each call.

A special case is the abortion of tasks engaged in a rendezvous. If the calling task becomes abnormal while in a rendezvous, it does not become completed until the end of the rendezvous. Note that such a case has no observable effect on the called task: it is important that the rendezvous be allowed to complete to ensure the integrity of the data passed.

Quite a different situation exists if the called task becomes abnormal during a rendezvous. The called task need not become completed until it reaches a synchronization point. The called task will become completed no later than the end of the rendezvous. Regardless of the actual effect on the called task, Tasking_Error will be raised in the calling task at the point of the call. The exception will be raised after the called task becomes abnormal, but no later than the completion of the called task.

The semantic ramifications surrounding the latency of raising Tasking_Error in the caller are drastic. The semantics allows for the case where the called task is still executing the rendezvous, perhaps changing the values of parameters, while the calling task is no longer blocked. In handling Tasking_Error in such circumstances, the calling task cannot suppose that the rendezvous has been completed normally. This means that, even during localization of the declaration of objects, concurrent updates cannot always be prevented. (Consider the situation where entry parameters are passed by reference.)

The program presented in this subsection is neither erroneous nor incorrect; it is simply indeterminate. There are many cases where execution of the program will cause nothing to be printed. The interesting cases are those in which a call to *Put_Line* is executed. In order for *Callee died* to be printed, the task designated by *Callee* must become abnormal before that designated by *Caller*. Furthermore, the calling task must not become abnormal until after Tasking_Error has been handled.

Given these restrictions, there are three states that the calling task can be in when the called task becomes abnormal:

1. enqueued
2. in a rendezvous
3. executing the loop.

In all three cases, Tasking_Error is raised. In the last case, it is raised when the entry call is reached.

The program can be made deterministic by replacing the single abort statement with two consecutive abort statements. If *Caller* is aborted first, then nothing will be printed.

One should be aware that there exist cases wherein an abnormal task need never become completed. Consider, for example, the following task body:

```
task body T is
begin
  loop
    Text_Io.Put_Line ("Kill me if you can!");
  end loop;
end T;
```

If another task aborts *T* after *T* has been activated, execution of *T* need not be affected. *T* can become completed anytime after becoming abnormal, but it need not ever become completed. A ramification of this situation is that completion can occur during execution at places other than synchronization points. If completion occurs while a variable is being updated, the value of the variable is undefined.

A Related Problem: When a task is made abnormal, why is there no need to purge its entry queues?

[Ada83]   9.5(14); 9.10; 11.5(3, 5)
[ARG]   AI-00360/05, 04-12-88; AI-00446/05, 09-25-87; AI-00837/03, 12-13-90

17.7.3 Self-abortion

difficulty: designer

Consider a task type *T* and the following template of its body:

```
task body T is
  ⋮
begin
  loop
    select
      accept A ...
    or
      accept B ...
    or
      accept Die ...
    end select;
```

end loop;
end T;

Suppose that whenever a rendezvous takes place at *Die*, the called task should become completed as soon as possible. How may the accept statement for *Die* be filled in?

◇◇◇◇◇

Here are three of many possible solutions:

Solution 1	*Solution 2*	*Solution 3*
accept Die; **raise** Complete;	**accept** Die; **abort** T; **delay** 0.0;	**accept** Die; **exit**;

The first solution simply raises an exception that is never handled. Since exceptions raised in tasks (outside of rendezvous) are not propagated beyond the task, this solution does not directly affect any other tasks. The third solution is somewhat similar. In both the first and the third solutions, completion takes places because the sequence of statements has finished executing.

The second solution works because the task designated by *T* becomes abnormal during the execution of the abort statement, and the delay statement itself is a synchronization point. Thus, the task also becomes completed no later than the execution of the delay statement. An effect of using the abort statement is that all dependent tasks of the named task also become abnormal, in a transitive manner. Thus, this solution would have radically different semantics than the other two solutions if the task in question created any dependent tasks.

A Related Problem: Is the fact that abnormality is transitive an advantage or a disadvantage of the second solution?

[Ada83]   9.4(5); 9.10(1 .. 6)
[ARG]   AI-00224/03, 03-14-90

17.8 SHARED VARIABLES

If one were to read the *Reference Manual for the Ada Programming Language* as a linguist, divorced from the many assumptions about and allusions to the history of computer science, [Ada83, §9] would likely be misunderstood. If a linguist were to read [Ada83, §9] and attempt to derive an operational semantics (a low-level, target-dependent behavior) from it, the resulting semantics would most likely differ a great deal from that which the designers intended. The novice Ada programmer, like the linguist, cannot hope to understand Ada tasking solely by reading [Ada83]: tasking is one of the few aspects of Ada that relies heavily on knowledge and experience of previous programming languages. In employing such phrases as "proceed in parallel," "logical processor," and "proceed independently except at points where they synchronize," the introduction to [Ada83, §9] alludes to this knowledge. Neither "parallel" nor "synchronize" is well defined by [Ada83] itself.

Reliance on a previous understanding of these concepts becomes critical when attempting to understand the semantics of shared variables. After all, task activation is conceptually similar to package elaboration, and entry calls are analogous to procedure calls. A usable operational semantics for Ada that disregards shared variables can be obtained by ignoring the terms "parallel" and "logical processor." Most certainly, on uniprocessor machines, the operational semantics of Ada is devoid of any reference to these terms. Also, the concept of a "logical processor" need not be limited to Ada's tasking constructs—e.g., in an expression such as $a + b + c + d$, the evaluation of the subexpressions $a + b$ and $c + d$ can often "proceed in parallel."

Only when trying to understand [Ada83, §9.11], on shared variables, does ignorance of the meaning of "parallel" fail the reader. If one derived an operational semantics for shared variables ignoring the term, erroneous executions would result. In this passive manner, by defining some executions as erroneous, Ada requires the programmer to understand the aforementioned concepts.

This section clarifies and defines explicitly the concepts of independent execution and synchronization. A number of programs that use shared variables and the conditions which these programs result in erroneous executions are examined.

17.8.1 Synchronizing Variables

difficulty: designer

What will the following program print?

```
with  Text_Io;
procedure  X is
   V : Positive range 1 .. 5 := 1;

   task  Y is
      entry  E;
```

```
      end Y;
      task body Y is
         package P is end;
         package body P is
         begin
            V := V + 1;
         end P;
      begin
         accept E do
            V := V + 1;
         end E;
         V := V + 1;
      end Y;
   begin
      V := V + 1;
      Y.E;
      begin
         delay 0.0;
         V := V + 1;
      exception
         when others => null;
      end;
      Text_Io.Put_Line ("Survey says..." & Integer'Image (V));
   end X;
```

◇◇◇◇◇

What the program will print is implementation dependent. Some executions of the program will be erroneous.

A shared variable is simply a scalar or access variable that is accessible by multiple tasks. Note that "accessible" and "visible" have different meanings. A variable may be shared by two tasks, even though it is visible to neither—for example, when the variable is hidden in a package body and the two tasks call operations exported by the package, thus accessing the variable.

In the preceding program two tasks—the environment task invoking X and the task designated by Y—share the variable V. (The environment task is often informally referred to simply as X.) To determine whether the use of a shared variable results in an erroneous execution, one must examine the intervals between consecutive synchronization points of a task accessing the variable. If, within such an interval of a task, the task reads from the variable and another task writes to the variable, the execution is erroneous. Further, if, within such an interval of a task, the task *and* another task both write to the variable, then the execution is erroneous. Note that any number of tasks may read a shared variable within an interval between two synchronization points without causing execution to become erroneous. This model of accessing shared variables is sometimes referred to as the CREW model: Concurrent Read, Exclusive Write.

The foregoing rules determine whether an execution is erroneous and thus unpredictable. To determine the value of a shared variable at a given point in an execution, further synchronizations (beyond those given in Section 17.7.2) between pairs of tasks must be considered. Two tasks are synchronized with each other at the following points of execution:

- at the start and end of a rendezvous with each other
- at the start and end of activation if one task causes activation of the other
- at the completion of either task.

These five points are also considered synchronization points. The order of execution of operations on shared variables is determined, then, only by these five means of synchronization. If two tasks each operate on a shared variable between synchronizations, neither may assume that the other's operations have taken effect.

The distinction between synchronizations that determine erroneous executions and synchronizations that determine values of variables is crucial. Intervals between synchronization points within a task are used to determine whether an execution is erroneous; synchronizations between pairs of tasks are used to determine the value of a shared variable.

Figure 17.3 illustrates one possible execution of the program at issue. The diagonal vectors represent synchronizations between the two tasks and are labeled with the corresponding value of V at that point in the execution. The execution starts with X initializing the variable and then causing activation of Y. Since this activation forms a synchronization between X and Y, Y takes on the value of the variable given it by X during initialization. During the activation of Y, the variable is both read and updated (as package P is elaborated). Then Y completes its activation, which is also a synchronization between the tasks. Thus, X observes the new value of the variable computed by Y.

The execution proceeds through a rendezvous, synchronizing the two tasks twice more. Up to this point, the execution is determinate and nonerroneous, and the value of V is 4. After the rendezvous, both tasks read from and write to the shared variable. If the execution proceeds as depicted in Figure 17.3, then Y assigns 5 to V and becomes completed. The completion of Y synchronizes the two tasks, so X observes that V now has the value 5. The final assignment by X then raises an exception that is handled. (The handling of the exception is a synchronization point.) This execution is not erroneous.

Now consider another execution in which X reads the value of the variable before Y is completed. The delay statement and the handling of the exception form an interval in which X reads the variable. Between these points, Y updates the shared variable. That is, relative to some global observer, the delay of X executes before Y updates the variable, and Y updates the variable before X handles the exception. Thus, this execution is erroneous.

A Related Problem: If, between two synchronization points of the preceding program, one task evaluates V'Size and the other writes to V, then would the execution be erroneous?

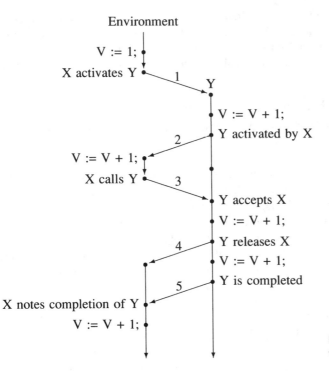

Figure 17.3 Order of access of shared variables.

[Ada83]   9.10(6); 9.11(2 .. 8)
See also   [Bryan89] and [Dewar90]

17.8.2 Finders Keepers

difficulty: designer

What will the following program print?

```
with  Text_Io;
procedure  Finders_Keepers  is
   task  type  T;
   N  :  Natural  :=  0;
   task  body  T  is
   begin
      delay  0.0;
      N  :=  N  +  1;
      delay  0.0;
   end  T;
begin
   declare
```

```
        X, Y : T;
    begin
       null;
    end;
    Text_Io.Put_Line  (Integer'Image  (N));
 end  Finders_Keepers;
```

◇◇◇◇◇

Again, what the program will print is implementation dependent. Some executions are erroneous; nonerroneous executions could print 1 or 2.

For both of tasks X and Y, assignment to N occurs between the synchronization points corresponding to the delay statements. Thus both tasks delay, read from and write to N, delay, and become completed.

It is the interleaving of these operations that can result in erroneous executions. For example, the following sequence is erroneous since both tasks update the variable between pairs of synchronization points of X. For that matter, the sequence is also erroneous since both tasks update the variable between synchronization points of Y.

$$
\textit{interval of } X \left\{ \begin{array}{l} X \;\; \text{delays} \\ Y \;\; \text{delays} \\ X \;\; \text{reads, writes} \\ Y \;\; \text{reads, writes} \\ X \;\; \text{delays} \\ Y \;\; \text{delays} \end{array} \right\} \textit{interval of } Y
$$

A nonerroneous but indeterminate execution is illustrated by

$$
\textit{interval of } X \left\{ \begin{array}{l} X \;\; \text{delays} \\ X \;\; \text{reads, writes} \\ Y \;\; \text{delays} \\ X \;\; \text{delays} \\ Y \;\; \text{reads, writes} \\ Y \;\; \text{delays} \end{array} \right\} \textit{interval of } Y
$$

This execution is indeterminate because tasks X and Y never synchronize other than at completion. Thus, when Y reads the variable, it need not observe the result of the assignment by X. Consequently, both tasks may execute

```
N := 0 + 1;
```

The main program will nevertheless observe the result of both assignments, since it synchronizes with the tasks upon their completion. A nonerroneous execution will print either 1 or 2.

An interleaving in which X and Y synchronize, and one that prints the value 2 is the following:

1. *X* delays
2. *X* assigns
3. *X* delays
4. *X* completes
5. *Y* delays
6. *Y* assigns
7. *Y* delays
8. *Y* completes

Here, *Y* will observe the new value assigned to *N* by *X*, since *X* and *Y* synchronize at the completion of *X*.

[Ada83]   9.10(6); 9.11(1 .. 8)

17.8.3 Transitivity of Synchronization

difficulty: designer

If task X synchronizes with task Y, and then task Y synchronizes with task Z, are X and Z synchronized?

◇◇◇◇◇

X and Z are in fact synchronized because pairwise synchronizations of tasks are transitive. A common method of avoiding erroneous executions is to form critical regions using the following semaphore task type:

```
task Semaphore is
   entry Seize;
   entry Release;
end Semaphore;

task type T;
X, Y : T;
N    : Natural := 0;

task body Semaphore is
begin
   loop
     select
       accept Seize;
       accept Release;
     or
       terminate;
     end select;
```

```
  end loop;
end Semaphore;

task body T is
begin
  Semaphore.Seize;
  N := N + 1;
  Semaphore.Release;
end T;
```

Use of the semaphore prevents the interleaving of assignments, which cause erroneous executions. Now, between any two consecutive synchronization points, at most one assignment may occur. Suppose that X seizes the semaphore first. Then X updates the shared variable and synchronizes with the semaphore at *Release*. Y is now able to seize the semaphore and thus indirectly synchronize with X. In other words, whichever task obtains the semaphore second will observe the assignment previously performed by the other task.

An alternative architecture to the semaphore is to eliminate the shared variable altogether, as in the following task:

```
task Keeper is
  entry Increment;
  entry Observe (Val : out Natural);
end Keeper;

task body Keeper is
  N : Natural := 0;
begin
  loop
    select
      accept Increment;
      N := N + 1;
    or
      accept Observe (Val : out Natural) do
        Val := N;
      end Observe;
    or
      terminate;
    end select;
  end loop;
end Keeper;
```

Within this architecture, the tasks X and Y can simply call the entries of *Keeper*.
Now consider a different architecture for X and Y:

```
task X is
  entry E;
```

```
end X;

task Y;

task body X is
begin
   N := N + 1;
   accept E;
end X;

task body Y is
begin
   X.E;
   N := N + 1;
end Y;
```

This architecture produces nonerroneous executions and a determinate ordering of accesses to the shared variable. However, it totally constrains the order in which X and Y access the variable, and such a constraint may be viewed as overly restrictive.

[Ada83]   9.6(10); 9.11(1 .. 8)

17.8.4 Shared Variables as Parameters

difficulty: designer

Are executions of the following program erroneous? If not, what will they print?

```
with Text_Io;
procedure U_Pass is
   S : String (1 .. 2) := "ab";

   procedure Mess (Str : in out String;
                   N   : in      Positive) is
   begin
      Str (N) := 'c';
   end Mess;
begin
   declare
      task T;
      task body T is
      begin
         Mess (S, 1);
      end T;
   begin
      Mess (S, 2);
```

```
     end;
       Text_Io.Put_Line (S);
   end U_Pass;
```

◇◇◇◇◇

Some executions of this program are erroneous.

The semantics of [Ada83, §9.11] only constrains the use of shared scalar and access variables. One might then wonder about the semantics of shared variables of composite types. Observe that all variables are either scalar, access, task, or composites of variables of these type classes. Though [Ada83, §9.11] does not directly apply to the variable S, it does directly apply to the variables S *(1)* and S *(2)*.

An execution of this program cannot be deemed erroneous solely on the basis of the rules governing shared variables. The assignment within the subprogram *Mess* will execute twice, upon different variables. However, the two assignments may not be the only updates performed on the shared variables. Consider the situation in which the actual parameter S is passed by copy. Then upon returning from *Mess*, both tasks will update the shared variables S *(1)* and S *(2)*. In this case, the output is indeterminate since the order of the updates is not prescribed by synchronizations between the environment task and the task denoted by T.

If, for both calls, S is passed by reference, then the program will print *cc*. Since, in some executions, the effect of the program is dependent on the parameter-passing mechanism employed, the program is erroneous according to [Ada83, §6.2(7)].

Gonzalez [Gonzalez90] points out that this dependency on the passing mechanism can be eliminated through the use of access types. For example, consider the following rewrite of the program:

```
with Text_Io;
procedure U_Pass is
   type Text is access String;
   S : Text := new String'("ab");

   procedure Mess (Str : in Text;
                    N   : in Positive) is
   begin
      Str (N) := 'c';
   end Mess;
begin
   declare
      task T;
      task body T is
      begin
         Mess (S, 1);
      end T;
   begin
      Mess (S, 2);
```

        end;

      Text_Io.Put_Line (S.**all**);
    end U_Pass;

In this version, no additional updates are performed through parameter passing. Thus, all executions of the program are determinate.

A Related Problem: Can the passing of a shared variable of a task type as a subprogram actual parameter of mode in out lead to erroneous executions?

[Ada83]   6.2(7); 9.10(6); 9.11(1 .. 8)
See also   [Gonzalez90] and [Dewar90]

chapter 18

Exceptions

*Actually, that's in the spirit of 11.6. It
almost solves a whole bunch of problems.*
Professor Robert Dewar, January 13, 1987, at a SIGAda
meeting, Hollywood, Florida (answering a question concerning
the optimization of vector operations and pipelining)

Exceptions can be thought of as software signals. They are included in the language to
increase the reliability of programs by any of the following means:

- predefining the effect of many abnormal run-time conditions
- allowing the user to define abnormal run-time conditions
- allowing user-defined handling of, or reaction to, abnormal run-time conditions.

Ada uses the same mechanisms for both predefined and user-defined conditions.

Throughout the history of programming languages, there have been mechanisms
similar to Ada exceptions. Generally, these mechanisms can be grouped into one of the
following three categories:

1. Execute a handler, and then return to the operation that encountered the abnormal
   condition.
2. Execute a handler, and allow the handler to decide whether to continue with the
   operation that encountered the abnormal condition.
3. Execute a handler, and abandon execution of the operation that encountered the
   abnormal condition.

Ada exceptions fall into the last category.

Unlike hardware interrupts or exceptions in other languages, an Ada exception has an effect that is dependent on the scope in which it is raised. A program can have many handlers for the same exception. The handler to be executed is determined by the thread of control and the scope in which the abnormal condition is encountered.

This chapter focuses on user-defined exceptions and the handling of all exceptions. The conditions under which predefined exceptions are raised are covered throughout the text, in appropriate chapters. Sections 18.1 and 18.2 address issues that every Ada programmer should be aware of. Section 18.3 addresses very intricate semantical issues involving advanced code generation strategies. The issues presented in Section 18.3 are not fundamental to an understanding of the use of exceptions.

18.1 DECLARATION OF EXCEPTIONS

Like most entities in Ada, exceptions must be explicitly declared before they can be used. This section presents the syntax and semantics of exception declarations.

18.1.1 Exceptions as Objects

difficulty: novice

Is the following code legal?

```
procedure Exceptional_Objects is
   X, Y, Z : exception;
   A       : exception;
   B       : array (1 .. 5) of exception;

   procedure Q is
   begin
      null;
   end Q;

   C : exception;
begin
   null;
end Exceptional_Objects;
```

◇◇◇◇◇

The declarations of *B* and *C* are syntactically illegal.

Exceptions are not types or objects; rather, they are a unique class of entities within the language. Thus, exceptions cannot be components of a composite type. Also, an exception declaration is a basic declarative item. The declarations of *X, Y, Z*, and *A* are legal.

[Ada83]   3.1(3); 3.9(2); 11.1(1 .. 3)

18.1.2 Hiding Exceptions

difficulty: programmer

What will the following program print?

```
with  Text_Io;
procedure  A_Johnson  is
   Constraint_Error  :  exception;
   P  :  Positive;
begin
   P  :=  −42;
exception
   when  Constraint_Error  =>
      Text_Io.Put_Line  ("Handling  Constraint_Error.");
   when  others  =>
      Text_Io.Put_Line  ("Very  interesting,  but  stupid.");
end  A_Johnson;
```

◇◇◇◇◇

The program will print *Very interesting, but stupid.*

In general, exception declarations follow the same scope and visibility rules as all other declarations. Thus, local declarations can hide outer declarations.

The declaration of the exception in this program hides the predefined exception *Constraint_Error* declared in package Standard. The assignment statement, however, causes the predefined exception to be raised. Since the first exception handler names only the user-defined *Constraint_Error*, this handler is not executed. Instead, the second handler, which handles all other exceptions, is executed. If the intent was to handle the predefined exception explicitly, the expanded name Standard.Constraint_Error should have been used.

[Ada83]   11.1(5); 11.2(5)

18.1.3 Generic Exceptions

difficulty: novice

What will the following program print?

```
generic
package P is
  E : exception;
end P;

with Text_Io, P;
procedure Exception_Space is
  package P1 is new P;
  package P2 is new P;
begin
  raise P1.E;
exception
  when P2.E   => Text_Io.Put_Line ("Alias city.");
  when others => Text_Io.Put_Line ("Too much name space.");
end Exception_Space;
```

◇◇◇◇◇

The program will print *Too much name space.*

If an exception is declared within a generic unit, then each instance of the unit defines a unique exception. Although all exceptions in all instances have the same simple name, they are declared within distinct program units and thus are distinct exceptions.

The program instantiates the generic unit *P* twice, resulting in two distinct exceptions. Since the exception *P1.E* is raised, the handler naming *P2.E* will not be executed.

A Related Problem: Explain the rationale for the predefined library unit Io_Exceptions.

[Ada83]   11.1(3); 11.2(5)

18.1.4 Recursive Exceptions

difficulty: programmer

What will the following program print?

```
with Text_Io;
procedure Diffy_Qs is
  procedure Q (N : in Natural) is
    X : exception;
  begin
    if N /= 0 then
      Q (N − 1);
    else
      raise X;
    end if;
```

```
    exception
       when X => Text_Io.Put ("Handling X. "); raise;
       when others => Text_Io.Put ("Not X. ");
    end Q;
begin
    Q (N => 2);
exception
    when others => Text_Io.Put_Line ("Ooops.");
end Diffy_Qs;
```

◇◇◇◇◇

The program will print *Handling X. Handling X. Handling X. Ooops.*

The name of an exception declared within a subprogram denotes the same exception in all invocations of the subprogram. Note this difference between an exception declaration and an object declaration. In the case of an object declared in a subprogram, a new object is created each time the subprogram is invoked. This is not the case for exceptions. The difference is important when considering recursive subprograms. An exception declared in a recursive subprogram can be handled by name in an outer recursive invocation. Because of this rule, all exceptions of a program can be identified at compilation time. Thus, exceptions cannot be "created" during execution. One consequence of this rule is that, for any exception, the handler to be executed can be determined at compilation time.

Note that regardless of the innermost scope of an exception declaration, only one exception is declared. That is, if a subprogram contains a local declare block or a package which in turn contains an exception declaration, the preceding rule still applies. For example, consider the following code:

```
generic
package Gp is
    E : exception;
end Gp;

with Gp;
procedure Recursive is
    package Np is new Gp;
    ⋮
end Recursive;
```

Regardless of the number of invocations of the procedure *Recursive*, only one instantiation of *Gp* exists. Like exceptions, instantiations are determined at compilation time. This is not to say that the elaboration of the instance denoted by *Np* occurs only once: elaboration and instantiation are two different concepts. The elaboration of *Np* indeed occurs once per invocation of *Recursive*. Nevertheless, no elaboration of *Np* creates a new exception. Therefore, only one exception named *Np.E* exists within all invocations of *Recursive*.

[Ada83]   11.1(3)
[ARG]   AI-00334/01, 02-12-87

18.2 RAISING, PROPAGATING, AND HANDLING EXCEPTIONS

Throughout previous chapters, programs have made simple uses of exceptions. This section provides a more complete presentation of the use of exceptions.

In order to understand the effect of raising an exception, one must understand the concepts of propagating and handling an exception. An exception is either handled within the frame where it is raised, or propagated from frame to frame until it is handled. A *frame* is simply a region of code in which an exception can be raised. A frame is formed by a block statement, or a subprogram, package, task, or generic unit body. Any frame can include exception handlers.

18.2.1 Static Semantic Issues

difficulty: programmer

Given direct visibility to the package and exceptions given by

```
package  P  is
   X, Y, Z : exception;
end  P;
```

are the following exception handlers legal?

```
exception                        exception
  when  X | Y | Z =>  ...          when  X  =>  ...
  when  others  =>  ...            when  P.X  =>  ...
  when  Z  =>  ...                 when  others  | Z  =>  ...
end;                             end;
```

◇◇◇◇◇

Both *groups of exception handlers* are semantically illegal.

A group of exception handlers may appear after the sequence of statements in any frame. A group of handlers is simply a sequence of one or more *exception handlers*. The syntax of an exception handler is

```
exception_choice   ::=  exception_name  |  others
exception_handler  ::=  when  exception_choice {|  exception_choice}  =>
                        sequence_of_statements
```

An exception may be named only once within a group of handlers. If the exception choice **others** appears within a group of handlers, it must appear alone and in the last handler. More than one exception name can appear in the same handler when separated by the vertical bar (|). The semantics of the vertical bar, within this context, is similar to that when it appears in a case statement alternative or aggregate.

Any statement that can appear within the sequence of statements of a frame can also appear within the sequence of statements of a handler for the frame. For example, a return statement can appear within a handler.

[Ada83]   11.2(2 .. 5, 8)

18.2.2 Propagation Logs

difficulty: programmer

What will the following program print?

```
with  Text_Io;
procedure  Lumberjack  is
    Int  :  Integer;

    procedure  Log  (Name  :  in  String)  is
    begin
        Text_Io.Put_Line  ("Logging  "  &  Name);
        raise;
    end  Log;
begin
    Int  :=  Integer'Last  +  2;
exception
    when  Storage_Error  =>  Log  ("Storage_Error");
    when  others          =>  Log  ("Unknown  Exception");
end  Lumberjack;
```

◇◇◇◇◇

The program will not print anything because it is semantically illegal. Both handlers are legal, but the use of the raise statement in *Log* is illegal. A raise statement that does not name an exception may only appear within a sequence of statements of an exception handler.

Exceptions can be raised either implicitly or explicitly, or they can be reraised. Predefined exceptions can be raised implicitly by the implementation's run time system. For example, the attempted invocation of a subprogram before the elaboration of its body causes Program_Error to be raised. Only predefined exceptions are raised implicitly.

A raise statement that names an exception explicitly raises the named exception when executed. Both user-defined and predefined exceptions may be named in a raise statement .

A raise statement that does not name an exception reraises the exception being handled. This form of the raise statement can only appear within a sequence of statements of an exception handler, and not within a program unit declared within such a sequence of statements.

When many handlers appear within a group of handlers, it is often the case that the code associated with the handlers is similar. Such code can be modularized. The only restriction is that the reraising of the exception must be performed within each handler. The preceding program could be made legal by removing the raise statement from within *Log* and placing it after each call to *Log*.

Consider the case where a certain number of exceptions are always handled in a similar manner. Suppose that, when handling these exceptions, only a small fraction of the code executed is specific to each exception. Then the common code need be written only once if it is placed in subprograms. Alternatively, the handlers can be constructed as follows:

```
exception
   when Stack_Overflow   => ...
   when Stack_Underflow  => ...
   when others =>
      ...    -- Common code.
    begin
      raise;
    exception
      when Constraint_Error => ...    -- Exception specific code.
      when Tasking_Error    => ...    -- Exception specific code.
      when others => ...
    end;
      ...    -- Common code.
end;
```

In this example, the stack-related exceptions are specific to the group of handlers shown and are treated as such. The predefined exceptions *Constraint_Error* and *Tasking_Error* are always handled in the same way in all groups of handlers. The block statement forms a construct analogous to a case statement governed by the exception being handled.

[Ada83]   11.1(4 .. 9); 11.3; 11.4.1(21)

18.2.3 Raising Another Exception

difficulty: programmer

What will the following program print?

```
with Text_Io;
procedure Change_It is
begin
  begin
    begin
      raise Program_Error;
    exception
      when Program_Error => raise Storage_Error;
    end;
  exception
    when Program_Error =>
      Text_Io.Put ("Handling Program_Error.");
    when Storage_Error =>
      Text_Io.Put ("Handling Storage_Error.");
    when others =>
      Text_Io.Put ("Handling others.");
  end;
  Text_Io.Put_Line (" Fine.");
end Change_It;
```

◇◇◇◇◇

The program will print *Handling Storage_Error. Fine.*

The purpose of this program is to illustrate that when an exception is handled, the sequence of statements of the handler can cause a different exception to be propagated. Note that *Program_Error* is handled before execution of the second raise statement begins; it is never the case that two exceptions can be simultaneously propagating within the same thread of control.

The program also illustrates that once an exception is handled, flow of control continues normally: after execution of the exception handler naming *Storage_Error*, flow of control simply continues with the statement following the outer block statement.

[Ada83]   11.4.1(3, 10)

18.2.4 Call Stack Tracing

difficulty: programmer

What will the following program print?

```
with Text_Io;
procedure Wilbur is
  procedure P (C : in Character) is
  begin
    Text_Io.Put (C);
    if C = 'f' then
```

```
            raise Constraint_Error;
        else
            P (Character'Succ(C));
        end if;
    exception
        when others => Text_Io.Put (C);   raise;
    end P;
begin
    P ('a');   Text_Io.Put_Line (" okay.");
exception
    when others => Text_Io.Put_Line (" done.");
end Wilbur;
```

◇◇◇◇◇

The program will print *abcdeffedcba done.*

When an exception is raised, the normal flow of control is abandoned. Control is immediately passed to a handler for the exception, if one exists. A handler can handle a raised exception if the handler either names the exception or specifies the **others** choice. If, within the same group of handlers, both of these situations exist, the handler that names the exception is executed.

When an exception is raised within a sequence of statements, the group of handlers associated with this sequence is considered first. If no handler for the raised exception exists within this group, the exception is *propagated.* If an exception is raised within a declarative part, the exception is immediately propagated.

There are three cases of propagation to consider:

1. propagation from a block statement
2. propagation from a subprogram
3. propagation from the elaboration of a package.

(Note that all three refer to both the declarative part and the sequence of statements of the construct.) Conceptually, when an exception is propagated from a block statement, it is reraised at the point of the statement, in the (innermost) enclosing scope. When an exception is propagated from a subprogram, it is reraised at the point of the subprogram call. When propagated during the elaboration of a package, the exception is reraised at the point of the program that caused the elaboration to take place. The following program fragments are illustrative:

```
begin
    begin
        raise E;
    end;
    -- E is reraised at this point.
```

```
        ⋮
    end;


    declare
      package P is end P;
      package body P is
        P : Positive := -3;
      end P;
      -- Constraint_Error is reraised at this point.
        ⋮
    begin
        ⋮
    end;
```

In the second fragment, since the exception is propagated to a declarative part, it is again propagated to the scope enclosing the block statement. Propagation continues until a handler for the exception is found, or until the exception is propagated within the outermost scope of a thread of control. Propagation ceases as soon as the execution of an exception handler begins.

The original program is an example of propagating an exception from a subprogram. Observe that *P* is called recursively five times. At the innermost recursive level, *Constraint_Error* is raised. This exception is handled at this level and then is reraised using the raise statement. This causes the exception to be propagated to the previous recursive level, where it is again handled and reraised. Propagation of the previous level and reraising continues until *Constraint_Error* is propagated to the main program, where it is handled, and execution of the program is completed normally.

[Ada83]   11.4; 11.4.1; 11.4.2

18.2.5 Preventing Propagation

difficulty: programmer

What will the following program print? (Suppose no optimization is performed.)

```
    with Text_Io;
    procedure Proposition_13 is
      procedure Q is
        S : String (1 .. 2) := "Hello There";
      begin
        null;
      exception
        when Constraint_Error =>
```

```
        Text_Io.Put_Line ("Constraint_Error in Q.");
   end Q;

   procedure R is
      S : String (1 .. 2);
   begin
      S := "Nice Try";
   exception
      when Constraint_Error =>
         Text_Io.Put_Line ("Constraint_Error in R.");
   end R;
begin
   begin
      Q;
   exception
      when others =>
         Text_Io.Put_Line ("Q missed it.");
   end;

   R;
exception
   when others =>
      Text_Io.Put_Line ("R missed it.");
end Proposition_13;
```

◇◇◇◇◇

The program will print

```
Q missed it.
Constraint_Error in R.
```

This program illustrates that when an exception is raised within the declarative part
of a subprogram, the exception cannot be handled by that execution of the subprogram.
Instead, it is propagated to the point of the call. In the program, *Constraint_Error*
is raised in the declarative part of *Q* and is propagated to the block statement within
the main program; the exception is handled within the block statement. The execution
of *R* also raises *Constraint_Error*. However, since it is raised within the sequence of
statements, it can be handled locally.

The same propagation rule applies to all declarative parts. For example, if an
exception is raised during the elaboration of the declarative part of a block statement, it
cannot be handled by handlers appearing at the end of the block statement.

[Ada83]   11.4.1(3); 11.4.2(1 .. 2, 8)

18.2.6 Propagation from Packages

difficulty: programmer

If an exception is raised during the elaboration of a package, where can it be handled?

◇◇◇◇◇

The following two cases exist:

1. If an exception is raised within a declarative part (a visible part, private part, or body) of a package, it can only be handled by an enclosing scope.
2. If an exception is raised within the sequence of statements at the end of a package body, it can be handled by a handler following the sequence of statements. If not handled, the exception is propagated to the enclosing scope.

A special case to consider is the elaboration of a library package. For such packages, there is no observable enclosing scope. If an exception is propagated from the elaboration of a library package, execution of the program is abandoned. Abandoning the program means that no other library packages are elaborated and execution of the main subprogram never begins.

[Ada83]   11.4.1(4, 7, 9, 20); 11.4.2(1, 4, 6 .. 8)

18.2.7 Handling an Exception outside of Its Scope

difficulty: programmer

What will be printed when the procedure *Main* is executed?

```
package P is
   procedure P1;
   procedure P2;
end P;

procedure Q;

with Text_Io, Q;
package body P is
  X : exception;
  procedure P1 is
  begin
     Q;
  exception
     when X => Text_Io.Put ("P1:X "); raise;
```

```
      when others => Text_Io.Put ("P1:others "); raise;
    end P1;

    procedure P2 is
    begin
      raise X;
    exception
      when X => Text_Io.Put ("P2:X "); raise;
    end P2;
end P;

with Text_Io, P;
procedure Q is
  X : exception;
begin
  P.P2;
exception
  when X => Text_Io.Put ("Q:X "); raise;
  when others => Text_Io.Put ("Q:others "); raise;
end Q;

with Text_Io, P;
procedure Main is
begin
  P.P1;
  Text_Io.Put_Line (" okay.");
exception
  when others => Text_Io.Put_Line (" done.");
end Main;
```

◇◇◇◇◇

The program will print *P2:X Q:others P1:X done.*

In this program, an exception is twice propagated beyond its scope and then propagated back within its scope. Exceptions are one of the few entities in Ada that can have an effect outside their scope. The program illustrates why an exception must "exist" outside its scope.

The exceptions *P.X* and *Q.X* are distinct exceptions. *P.X* is visible only within the body of *P*, and *Q.X* is visible only within the body of *Q*. In particular, *P.X* is not visible within *Q*, even though *P.X* may be propagated to *Q*.

The program begins with a call to *P.P1*; *P1* then calls *Q*, which in turn calls *P.P2*. Within *P.P2*, the exception *P.X* is raised. This exception is handled within *P.P2* and then propagated to *Q*. Within *Q*, the exception is not visible. Although not visible, the exception is handled by the **others** handler and propagated back to *P.P1*. In *P.P1*, the exception is handled by name and propagated to the main program. Once again, within the main subprogram, the exception is not visible but is handled by the **others** handler.

[Ada83]   11.1(1 .. 3); 11.2(5 .. 6); 11.4.1(4 .. 5, 9)

18.2.8 Propagation Styles

difficulty: designer

Suppose the exceptional condition *underflow* is used to denote a situation in which an attempt is made to "pop" an empty stack. Compare and contrast the following three implementations of reporting an overflow:

```
package Stack_1 is          package Stack_2 is
   :                            :
   Underflow : exception;      procedure Pop (
   procedure Pop (                E           :   out Element;
      E:    out Element;          S           : in out Stack;
      S: in out Stack);          Underflowed :   out Boolean);
   :                            :
end Stack_1;                 end Stack_2;


package Stack_3 is
   :
   Underflow : exception;
   procedure Pop (
      E           :   out Element;
      S           : in out Stack;
      Underflowed :   out Boolean;
      Propagate   : in     Boolean := True);
   :
end Stack_3;
```

◇◇◇◇◇

The first implementation propagates the exception *Underflow* whenever the condition is encountered. By propagating an exception, this implementation forces the caller to address the condition or complete execution of the thread of control.

The second implementation does not use an exception. Instead, a Boolean value is returned indicating whether the condition occurred. A problem with this implementation is that the caller is free to ignore the returned Boolean value.

The third implementation attempts to combine the capabilities of the first two. The caller may choose how the condition is reported. If *Propagate* is True, the exception is propagated when the condition occurs; if *Propagate* is False, the value of *Underflowed* indicates whether the condition occurred.

Stack_1 should be considered the most reliable implementation. It requires an immediate reaction to the exceptional condition: the exceptional condition cannot be ignored without causing the completion of a thread of control. *Stack_2* does not require an immediate reaction: the caller may continue the computation with invalid assumptions about the value of the stack. This can lead to a computational error much later during execution. The error would then be far removed from its cause.

The decision of how to report an exceptional condition should be based on the severity of the condition. Note that, given any one of the preceding implementations, the others can easily be derived. For example, given *Stack_1*, *Stack_2.Pop* can be implemented as follows:

```
procedure Pop (E            :    out Element;
               S            : in out Stack;
               Underflowed :    out Boolean) is
begin
   Stack_1.Pop (E, S);
   Underflowed := False;
exception
   when Stack_1.Underflow => Underflowed := True;
end Pop;
```

In another debatable use of exceptions, suppose that the type *Stack* is defined as follows:

```
type List is array (1 .. 100) of Element;
type Stack is
   record
      Data : List;
      Top  : Natural := 0;
   end record;
```

Consider the following two implementations of *Pop*:

```
begin                          begin
   if S.Top = 0 then              E := S.Data (S.Top);
      raise Underflow;            S.Top := S.Top - 1;
   else                        exception
      E := S.Data (S.Top);        when Constraint_Error =>
      S.Top := S.Top - 1;            raise Underflow;
   end if;                     end Pop;
end Pop;
```

The left-hand example explicitly checks for the underflow condition. A check is made for each call to *Pop*. The right-hand example allows the condition to be reported implicitly by the run-time system. A problem with this solution is that it assumes that the only way *Constraint_Error* can be raised is when *S.Top* is zero. But this need not be the case. When the type *Element* is an unconstrained record type, *Constraint_Error* could be raised by the constraint check performed by the assignment, and not the constraint check performed by the array indexing. In that case, *Underflow* would be propagated for the wrong reason.

The problems with the right-hand example illuminate some of the common criticisms of exceptions in Ada. Among these criticisms is that exceptions may report an error too late after its actual cause or report an error inaccurately. Discussions of some of these criticisms, and responses to them, can be found in the following references:

[Ada83]   11.1(4 .. 5); 11.4; 11.4.1(4 .. 5)
See also   [ACGE85] and [Hoare81]

18.3 OPTIMIZATION AND REORDERING

Throughout [Ada83], an order of execution is specified for language features. For some constructs, the language explicitly states that several orders of execution are allowed. This section focuses on why an implementation is allowed to alter the order of execution of a single thread of control, even when the order of execution is uniquely specified by the language. We focus on Section 11.6 of [Ada83], fewer than two pages of text.

[Ada83, §11.6] has some rather astonishing semantic ramifications. More than four years after the language was standardized, many of these ramifications are still not well understood. In fact, some of those that are understood are not well liked. Professors Robert Dewar and Paul Hilfinger, members of the Ada Rapporteur Group, summed up the situation nicely when they wrote:

> Section 11.6 of the Ada Standard was intended to give implementors some limited license to perform standard code transformations to enhance performance. It has proven less than satisfactory for this purpose. It disallows any number of familiar optimizations, some of them potentially important. It introduces obvious portability problems. It makes some programs difficult if not impossible to write. Finally, the set of allowed transformations is ill-defined.[1]

This is an area of the language that continues to be researched. The ramifications of Section 11.6, and indeed, the text of the section itself, are extremely likely to change. The problems presented here are presented with a "current" and rather conservative reading of the text.

---

[1]From Ada Rapporteur Group Notes, AI-00315/13, August 15, 1990, pages 27–28.

18.3.1 Eliminating Operations

difficulty: language lawyer

What are the possible outputs of the following program?

```
with Text_Io;
procedure Eliminated is
   type N is range 1 .. 10;
   X : N := 6;
begin
   if X > 999 then
      Text_Io.Put_Line ("Very interesting application of 11.6");
   else
      Text_Io.Put_Line ("What an easy problem");
   end if;
exception
   when others =>
      Text_Io.Put_Line ("How could this be canonical");
end Eliminated;
```

◇◇◇◇◇

The program can print either *How could this be canonical* or *What an easy problem.*
    The evaluation of the Boolean expression would seem to raise Numeric_Error or Constraint_Error if *999* is not within the base type of *N*. However, this need not be the case: an implementation is allowed to evaluate the expression using a base type larger than the base type of *N*. For example, an implementation is free to use the ">" operation of a 64-bit integer type and thus always satisfy the constraint check associated with the implicit conversion of the numeric literal *999*. In this case, the expression would yield False.
    If the Boolean expression is not optimized and *999* is not a member of the base type of *N*, the implicit conversion will raise either Numeric_Error or Constraint_Error. This is the "normal" semantics of integer operations and is what one would expect.
    The point of the preceding program is to begin to show the surprisingly wide latitude allowed an implementation when performing predefined numerical operations. One must thus take great care when assuming that an operation will raise an exception.
    As an example, if the expression in the declaration

```
X : Integer := Integer'Last + 1 - 32;
```

were evaluated from left to right, an exception might be raised. But the language allows an implementation to change the association of the expression in order to remove the possibility of raising an exception, thus:

```
Integer'Last + (1 - 32)
```

Conversely, an association can be changed such that an exception is introduced where one did not exist in left-to-right evaluation. The programmer can enforce a specific association by the use of parentheses and short-circuit control forms.

A Related Problem: The elaboration of the following declarative part will propagate Program_Error. Can the predefined addition operation thus be eliminated?

```
declare
    function F return Integer;
    X : Integer := F + 1;
    function F return Integer is ...
begin ...
```

Suppose the declaration of *X* were changed to the following:

```
    X : Integer := F;
```

Could the elaboration or initialization of *X* be eliminated?

[Ada83]   4.5(4); 4.5.7(3 .. 7); 11.6(5 .. 6, 8 .. 9)
[ARG]   AI-00387/05, 02-23-87

18.3.2 Reordering Operations

difficulty: designer

List all possible outputs of the following program:

```
with Text_Io;
procedure Cba is
    A, B, C : Integer := 1;
begin
    A := 2;
    B := 3;
    C := Integer'Last + 1;
exception
    when Numeric_Error | Constraint_Error =>
        Text_Io.Put_Line (Integer'Image (A) & Integer'Image (B) &
                          Integer'Image (C) );
    when others => Text_Io.Put_Line ("Lost me again");
end Cba;
```

◇◇◇◇◇

The program can print any of the following lines:

    2 3 1
    1 1 1
    2 1 1

An implementation is free to reorder the evaluation of right-hand expressions. The actual assignment operations, however, cannot be reordered. Reordering is allowed in order to take full advantage of architectures such as vector processors, data flow machines, and pipeline architectures.

The order of execution expected by most programmers is called the *canonical order*. The canonical order of execution is the order specified by the language and is the order that [Ada83, §11.6] allows an implementation to alter. (Note that the order of execution specified by the language is a partial order, not a total order. For example, the language does not prescribe the order of evaluation of subprogram actual parameters.)

If the preceding program is executed in canonical order, *2 3 1* will be printed. However, the expression *Integer'Last + 1* may be evaluated at any point after the elaboration of the declarative part. This means that the expression can be evaluated, and an exception raised, before either of the assignments to *A* and *B* is executed. In that case, *1 1 1* is printed. Alternatively, the expression could be evaluated after the assignment to *A*, but before the assignment to *B*, resulting in *2 1 1* being printed.

To complicate the matter further, the evaluation of *Integer'Last + 1* need not raise an exception. (Section 18.3.1 discusses the reasons for this.) It may instead be the assignment operation to *C* that raises the exception (*Constraint_Error*). In any case, an exception will be raised within the execution of the assignment statement for *C*.

Note that the program cannot print *1 3 1*, as that would imply a reordering of the assignment operations to *A* and *B*. The distinction between an *assignment operation* and an *assignment statement* is critical. An assignment statement is comprised of many operations, including at the very least, the following:

- evaluation of the right-hand expression
- evaluation of the left-hand name
- performance of a constraint check on the value of the right-hand expression
- assignment of the value.

Only the last two comprise the actual assignment operation. The point is that the evaluation of the expression *Integer'Last + 1* is not part of the assignment operation to *C*.

A Related Problem: The foregoing program shows that the evaluation of right-hand expressions of assignment statements can be reordered. Can an implementation reorder the evaluation of the left-hand names as well?

[Ada83]   3.3(5); 11.6(2 .. 4)
[ARG]   AI-00315/13, 08-15-90

18.3.3 Delayed Reactions

difficulty: language lawyer

List all possible outputs of the following program:

```ada
with  Text_Io;
procedure  Time_Bomb  is
   X, Y : Integer := 2;
begin
   begin
      X := 1 / 0;
      Y := 3;
   end;
   Text_Io.Put_Line ("okay" & Integer'Image (X) &
                        Integer'Image (Y));
exception
   when Numeric_Error | Constraint_Error =>
      Text_Io.Put_Line ("boom" & Integer'Image (X) &
                           Integer'Image (Y));
   when others => Text_Io.Put_Line ("surprise");
end Time_Bomb;
```

◇◇◇◇◇

The program can print any of the following lines:

```
boom  2  2
okay  2  3
boom  2  3
```

A reading of [Ada83] would indicate that *Numeric_Error* must be raised upon execution of the first assignment statement. In fact, either *Numeric_Error* or *Constraint_Error* may be raised. In many cases, it is confusing as to which of these exceptions will be raised by an operation. In order to reduce second-guessing and portability problems, the Ada Rapporteur Group has decided that whenever the language specifies that *Numeric_Error* is raised, an implementation is free to raise *Constraint_Error* instead. Thus, whenever one handles *Numeric_Error* by name, the same group of handlers should include a handler for *Constraint_Error*. Note that *Constraint_Error* can be raised wherever *Numeric_Error* may be raised, but not vice versa.

When executed in canonical order, the program will print *boom 2 2*. This is the behavior most would expect.

If *okay 2 3* is printed, one can infer that the first assignment statement has been eliminated. An implementation is free to eliminate any predefined operation (including assignment) whose sole effect is to *propagate* a predefined exception. (Note that the exceptions declared in the predefined package Io_Exceptions are not considered predefined exceptions; only those declared immediately within package Standard are predefined.) Clearly, the only effect of the division operation is to propagate either *Constraint_Error* or *Numeric_Error* outside the block. Thus, this operation can be removed. Anc once the division operation is removed, the assignment operation to *X* can be removed, since it cannot have any effect.

Note how the semantics of this program change if the block statement is removed but both assignment statements remain. In that case, an exception is not propagated and, thus, no operations can be removed.

In order for *boom 2 3* to be printed, the division operation must be performed after the assignment operation to *Y*. These two operations may be reordered since no assignment operations are being reordered. Note that there is no assignment operation to *X*. This is because an exception would be raised by the evaluation of the division operation, in which case the assignment operation to *X* would not take place. Once the assignment operation to *X* is eliminated, the remaining operations within the block can be reordered as follows:

- Y := 3
- 1 / 0

The focus of this program is that the raising of *Numeric_Error* and *Constraint_Error* within a frame can occur practically anyplace within the frame. The programmer can restrict the location where these exceptions are raised simply by reducing the size of frames using block statements. Operations can never be reordered between frames.

A Related Problem: If the block is removed, but both assignment statements remain, can *Y* be assigned the value *3*? Would the set of allowed outputs change if *X* and *Y* were declared to be of the predefined type Float and the integer literals were changed to real literals?

[Ada83]   3.3(5); 4.5.5(12); 11.6(3 .. 4, 7)
[ARG]   AI-00159/05, 10-19-90; AI-00315/13, 08-15-90; AI-00387/05, 02-23-87

18.3.4 Erroneous Reorderings

difficulty: language lawyer

If a program is not erroneous when executed in canonical order, can an allowed optimization make it erroneous?

◇◇◇◇◇

An allowed optimization can make such a program erroneous. In fact [Ada83, §11.6(10)] includes such an example. The following fragment is another:

```
declare
   P : Positive := -1;
begin
   Text_Io.Put_Line (Integer'Image (P));
end;
```

Since the only effect of the assignment operation is to propagate *Constraint_Error*, the assignment can be eliminated. But if the assignment is eliminated, the value of *P* will be undefined.

As a final remark in this section, consider what it means for an operation to propagate a predefined exception. The following two statements do not include operations, although they may propagate predefined exceptions:

> **raise**;   **raise** Constraint_Error;

The optimization rules only apply to predefined and basic operations. Thus, although the two statements

> P := Positive'(-1);   **raise** Constraint_Error;

have the same effect when each is executed in canonical order, only the left-hand statement is comprised of predefined and basic operations. For this reason, only the left-hand statement can be eliminated if it propagates a predefined exception.

[Ada83]   1.6(6 .. 7); 3.2.1(17); 3.3(5); 3.3.3(2 .. 7); 11.6(7, 10 .. 11)
[ARG]   AI-00315/13, 08-15-90

chapter 19

Generic Units

*It was another world, the world of the
eagle, the world of fierce abstraction.*
D. H. Lawrence

Generic software has absolutely no value.
Bill Joy, February 15, 1989, at the Stanford
Computer Forum, Stanford, California

Generic units are a relatively new feature of procedural programming languages. Parameterization of code has evolved from assembly language macros to subprogram parameters. Now, in Ada, generic units provide the next step in this evolution.

In order to understand the design of generic units, one must remember that Ada is a strongly typed language. Generic units provide the capability of reusing units while preserving strong typing and circumventing the need for the programmer to duplicate a unit every time it is used. For example, one who requires a linked list of integers and a linked list of strings need only write the linked list operations once. Generic units are a language feature that directly supports software abstraction and reuse.

19.1 DECLARATION OF GENERIC UNITS

The three forms of a generic unit are a generic package, a generic procedure, and a generic function. The specifications of these units are very similar to their nongeneric counterparts, the only difference being that a generic unit includes a *generic formal part*. This formal part defines how the generic unit is parameterized. The parameters of a generic unit are called, simply, generic formal parameters. Generic units are not overloadable, although instances of generic subprograms are.

There are three types of generic formal parameters:

- generic formal objects
- generic formal types
- generic formal subprograms.

It is the last two types of parameters that extend parameterization capabilities beyond those of subprograms.

The body of a generic unit is syntactically identical to its nongeneric counterpart. The main difference between writing a generic body versus a nongeneric one has to do with the assumptions that can be made about visible types and operations. For example, within different instances of the same generic unit, the properties of a type can differ.

This section focuses on the construction of generic unit specifications and, specifically, on generic formal parts. Generic unit bodies are not covered, due to their high degree of similarity to other program unit bodies.

19.1.1 They Are Declarations

difficulty: novice

Is the following unit legal?

```
generic
   type T is private;
   E : exception;
procedure Swap (X, Y : in out T) is
   Temp : constant T := X;
begin
   X := Y;
   Y := Temp;
exception
   when Constraint_Error => raise E;
end Swap;
```

◇◇◇◇◇

The unit is syntactically illegal. A generic unit, like other program units, is comprised of a specification and a body. For generic units, the specification and body must be lexically distinct. Also, an exception declaration may not appear within a generic formal part.

Syntactically, a generic formal part appears at the beginning of a generic specification. The generic formal part begins with the reserved word **generic** and is followed by zero or more *generic parameter declarations*. A subprogram or package declaration follows the generic formal part. Together with this declaration, the formal part forms the declaration of a generic unit.

The declarations allowed within a generic formal part are limited to objects, types, and subprograms. The syntax of these declarations is similar, but not identical, to that of the declaration of these entities when they appear in other declarative regions.

A Related Problem: In what situations would an empty generic formal part be useful?

[Ada83]   12.1(1 .. 2)
See also   [Bryan88]

19.1.2 Unconstrained Formal Objects

difficulty: programmer

Is the following unit legal?

```
generic
    X :  in  String  :=  "Looks  good";
    Y :  in  out  String;
    Z :  Integer  :=  X'First  +  Y'Last  (1);
package  Gp  is  ...  end  Gp;
```

◇◇◇◇◇

The unit is legal. Within an instance of this unit, the constraints of *X* and *Y* are those of the corresponding actual parameters. Note that this semantics is the same as that for formal parameters of subprograms and task entries.

The mode of a generic formal object may be either **in** or **in out**. If no mode is specified in a generic formal object declaration, mode in is used. Object declarations of mode in may include a default expression. Such a default is evaluated during instantiation only if the formal object is not associated with an actual parameter. Object declarations of mode in out may not include a default expression. Again, this semantics is similar to that of subprogram and entry parameters.

A difference between a generic formal part and a subprogram formal part is that the order of evaluation of generic formal parameters is defined, while that of subprogram formal parameters is not. (The order is lexical for generic formal parameters.) Thus, declarations in the generic formal part are visible to subsequent declarations appearing in the same formal part. For example, the following unit is legal:

```
generic
    X :  Integer;
    with  function  F  (Par :  in  Integer  :=  X  +  1)  return  Integer;
    Y :  Positive  :=  F  +  F  (X  −  1);
procedure  Kids_Dont_Try_This_At_Home;
```

A Related Problem: If a generic actual parameter is an unconstrained record object, can instances of the generic unit change the object's subtype?

[Ada83]   12.1(2, 11); 12.1.1(2 .. 5); 12.3(17)

19.1.3 Parameter Modes

difficulty: designer

Why is mode out not allowed for generic formal objects?

◇◇◇◇◇

Consider two possible semantics for such a mode if it were allowed:

1. the semantics of mode in out, except that the generic unit could never read the value of the object
2. assignment of the object only in the sequence of statements at the end of a generic package body.

Generally, there are two ways of viewing a generic formal object: primarily as an object and primarily as a parameter. Only when it is viewed in the latter fashion does there appear to be a form of parameter missing from the language.

One philosophy regarding a generic formal part is that it be used solely to provide information to instances. In this respect, an object of mode out would not be meaningful. Even uses of objects of mode in out are dubious from this viewpoint. If one views a generic formal object primarily as an object and secondarily as a parameter, then disallowing write-only objects keeps all kinds of objects in the language consistent—namely, the language provides only two kinds of objects: constants (i.e., mode in) and variables (i.e., mode in out).

A different philosophy of generic units, one that the language design team did not choose, is that the generic formal part is used to exchange information between the unit containing the instantiation and the instance itself. In this respect, a generic formal object is viewed primarily as a parameter, and the second semantics presented above might then be useful.

The semantics of generic formal objects of mode in and of mode in out are not strictly identical to their subprogram and entry parameter counterparts. The language design team chose to define a generic formal object of mode in as a distinct object whose value is a copy of that provided by the actual parameter; a generic formal object of mode in out is simply a renaming of the actual object.

A Related Problem: Are object parameters of mode in of any use with generic subprograms? What about those of mode in out?

[Ada83]   12.1(2); 12.1.1(1 .. 4)

19.1.4 Limited Formal Objects

difficulty: programmer

Is the following unit legal?

```
with Text_Io;
generic
    File : in Text_Io.File_Type;
package Gu is ... end Gu;
```

◇◇◇◇◇

The unit is semantically illegal. Generic formal objects of mode in cannot be of a limited type. During instantiation, an association of an actual parameter with a generic formal object of mode in is treated as an assignment, meaning that actual parameters are always passed by copy, and never by reference. By always treating these associations as assignments, the potential side-effect problems associated with subprogram formal parameters are eliminated. A generic formal object of mode in out, however, may be of a limited type.

[Ada83]   12.1.1(3)

19.1.5 Generic Formal Type Classes

difficulty: programmer

Ada defines a number of type "templates" that can be used to import types of a given class. These templates do not include definitions for record or scalar types. Show how a generic unit can import record and scalar types.

◇◇◇◇◇

Any nonlimited type can be imported using the private template; any type can be imported using the limited, private template. The following table summarizes the available templates:

Template	*May Be Matched by*
limited private	any type
private	any nonlimited type
(<>)	any discrete type
range <>	any integer type
digits <>	any floating point type
delta <>	any fixed point type

Generic formal types may also be formed by means other than these templates. Generic formal access and array types are formed in the same way that they are formed in regular type declarations. Also, generic formal private type declarations may include a discriminant part. (The semantics of such declarations is discussed elsewhere.) Figure 19.1 summarizes the available forms for generic formal types. For each template in the tree, the set of legal actual parameters is a subset of the legal actual parameters for templates closer to the root of the tree.

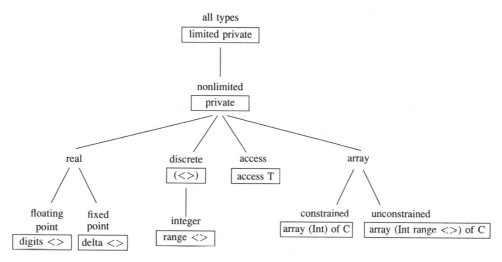

Figure 19.1   Generic formal type classes.

Within a generic unit, the operations implicitly defined for a formal parameter type are those common to all legal corresponding actual parameters. For example, equality is always defined for nonlimited generic formal private types. Conversely, addition is never implicitly defined for such a type, regardless of the actual parameter. As with any type definition, implicit operations are declared immediately after a generic formal type declaration. These "least common denominator" semantics are used so that the legality of a generic unit can be checked independently of instantiations of the unit.

The granularity of the foregoing type templates may not be fine enough for every application. For example, Ada does not provide a primitive for importing a floating point type whose values must include zero. However, such constraints can always be checked explicitly by the instances of a generic unit, as is the case for the following generic unit:

```
generic
    type Constrained is private;
    type Zero_Inclusive is digits <>;
package Self_Checker is ...  end Self_Checker;

package body Self_Checker is
    :
    :
```

```
  begin
    if not Constrained'Constrained or
        0.0 not in Zero_Inclusive then
        ⋮
    end if;
  end Self_Checker;
```

A Related Problem: Write a generic formal part that allows any numeric type to be imported. Does your solution handle complex numbers?

[Ada83]   12.1.2(4 .. 12)

19.1.6 Subtype Indications in Generic Formal Parts

difficulty: programmer

Is the following unit legal?

```
  generic
    X : in Integer range 1 .. 10;
    type Arr1 is array (Positive range 1 .. X)
       of Positive range 1 .. X;
  package Gu is
    type Arr2 is array (Positive range 1 .. X)
       of Positive range 1 .. X;
  end Gu;
```

◇◇◇◇◇

The unit is syntactically illegal. The only form of subtype indication allowed within a generic formal part is a type mark. Range, accuracy, index, and discriminant constraints are not allowed within a generic formal part. (Note that there are similar rules for subprogram formal parts, entry formal parts, and discriminant parts.) Although such constraints cannot appear in formal type declarations, one may still achieve their effects simply by moving the constraint out of the generic formal part.

It is not uncommon that type declarations are needed before a formal part can be written. Such types can be declared with explicit constraints in a different scope, as in the following code:

```
  with System;
  package Nester is
```

```
    subtype Lowercase is Character range 'a' .. 'z';
    type Instrumentation is range 0 .. System.Max_Int;

  generic
      type D is (<>);
      type A is array (D range <>) of Lowercase;
      Int : in out Instrumentation;
    package Gu is ... end Gu;
  end Nester;
```

[Ada83]   12.1(2, 4); 12.1.2(2)

19.1.7 Formal Types with Discriminants

difficulty: designer

Is the following unit legal?

```
  generic
      type Disc is (<>);
      Init : in Disc;
      type R (D : Disc := Init) is private;
    package Gu is ... end Gu;
```


◇◇◇◇◇

The unit is illegal. A default expression is not allowed in the declaration of a discriminant that appears in a generic formal part.

A purpose of this program is to show that the declaration of a generic formal type may include the name of other generic formal types. If the default expression in the type *R* were removed, the unit would be legal. Although no default expression can appear in a discriminant part of a generic formal private type, the actual type may include such default expressions. One consequence of this semantics is that a generic formal private type with discriminants can never be used within the generic unit to declare unconstrained record objects. Such objects must be constrained by their declarations. However, within the generic part itself, one can declare an object parameter of mode in out. Within some instances, this object may be unconstrained. The following program is illustrative:

```
  generic
      type Enum is (<>);
      type T (E : Enum) is private;
      Obj : in out T;
    package Gen_Pac is
    end Gen_Pac;
```

```
with Text_Io;
package body Gen_Pac is
begin
    Text_Io.Put_Line (Boolean'Image (T'Constrained) & ' ' &
                      Boolean'Image (Obj'Constrained));
end Gen_Pac;

with Gen_Pac;
procedure Main is
    type R1 (D : Integer) is record null; end record;
    type R2 (D : Integer := 1) is record null; end record;

    Obj1            : R1 (3);
    Obj2            : R2 (3);
    Obj3            : R2;

    package P1 is new Gen_Pac (Integer, R1, Obj1);
    package P2 is new Gen_Pac (Integer, R2, Obj2);
    package P3 is new Gen_Pac (Integer, R2, Obj3);
begin
    null;
end Main;
```

This program will print

```
FALSE TRUE
FALSE TRUE
FALSE FALSE
```

One may question why the language does not allow default expressions for discriminants of generic formal types. The major reason has to do with the complexity of the matching rules that would result. If one wishes to import a record type whose objects can change subtypes, a private type without discriminants can be used.

[Ada83]   12.1.2(3)

19.1.8 Importing Operations

difficulty: designer

Is the following unit legal?

```
generic
    type P is private;
    with function "=" (L, R : in P) return Boolean is <>;
```

```
    type Lp is limited private;
    with procedure Proc (X : out Lp);
    with function Eq (L, R : in Lp) return Boolean is "=";
package Gu is
    procedure Q (X : out Lp);
    end Gu;
```

◇◇◇◇◇

The unit contains three semantic errors.

The generic formal function "=" is illegal simply because predefined equality may never be explicitly hidden, except by a renaming declaration. (Recall that "=" for the type P is implicitly declared immediately after the declaration of P.) The declaration of the generic formal parameter Eq is also illegal. In this declaration, a default subprogram is specified. If an explicit default subprogram is given, the named subprogram must be visible where it is named. Since Lp is a limited type, equality is not predefined for this type and thus is not visible within the generic formal part.

The declaration of Q is also semantically illegal. Mode out cannot be used for explicit subprogram formal parameters of a limited type, except within the package defining the corresponding limited, private type. Although the type Lp is declared within the generic unit Gu, it is not defined within the visible part of Gu; also, technically, Gu is not a package, but rather, a generic unit.

The reader should be aware of the similarities in the rules governing the use of the "two kinds" of private types. Private types may be declared either immediately within the visible part of a package or within a generic formal part. In the former case, the package exports the type while other units import it. In the latter case, the generic unit imports the type while the unit performing the instantiation exports it. In both cases, it is the exporting unit that may have visibility to the complete definition of the type and the importing unit that has visibility to the restricted set of operations defined for private types.

There are two methods of specifying default subprograms within the declaration of a generic formal subprogram: implicitly or explicitly. The implicit method uses the box, $<>$, while the explicit method uses the name of a subprogram. An implicit default subprogram is matched during instantiation if

1. The generic formal subprogram is not associated with an actual parameter.
2. Directly visible at the point of instantiation, there exists a subprogram with the same designator and parameter and result type profile as the generic formal subprogram has.

If, at the point of instantiation, the first rule holds but the second does not, the instantiation is semantically illegal. If both rules hold, the directly visible subprogram is used as the actual parameter.

An explicit default for a generic formal subprogram must have the same parameter and result type profile as does the generic formal parameter. A conformance check

for this condition is made during compilation of the generic unit. An explicit default
subprogram is matched if the instantiation does not associate an actual parameter with
the generic formal subprogram. The following is an example of default subprogram
matching:

```
with Text_Io;
generic
   with procedure Write (X : String) is Text_Io.Put;
   with procedure Read (Int : out Integer; W : in Natural) is <>;
procedure Gp;

with Gp, Text_Io;
package User is
   package Int_Io is new
      Text_Io.Integer_Io (Num => Integer);
   procedure Read (Q : out Integer; W : Integer)
      renames Int_Io.Get;
   procedure P is new Gp;
end User;
```

In the instance *P*, the default *Text_Io.Put* is associated with *Write* and *Int_Io.Get* is
associated with *Read*.

[Ada83]   6.7(4); 7.4.4(4); 8.3(15, 17); 12.1.2 (4 .. 5, 13 .. 14); 12.1.3(1)

19.1.9 Binding Time

difficulty: designer

Compare and contrast the design of the following two generic units:

```
generic
   type Component is private;
   type Index is (<>);
   type Items is array (Index range <>) of Component;
   with function "<" (L, R : in Component)
            return Boolean is <>;
package Sort_1 is
   procedure Sort (This_Stuff : in out Items);
end Sort_1;


generic
   type Component is private;
   type Index is (<>);
   with function "<" (L, R : in Component)
```

```
          return Boolean is <>;
   package Sort_2 is
      type Items is array (Index range <>) of Component;
      procedure Sort (This_Stuff : in out Items);
   end Sort_2;
```

◇◇◇◇◇

In the first unit, the array type is imported from the context of the instantiation, and in the second unit it is exported by the instance. The array type does not add any new information; it is composed of other generic formal types. Use of the first package requires the user to declare an array type, even if the type is not otherwise needed until after the point of instantiation. Use of the second package requires that the user declare all objects to be sorted after the instantiation or resort to explicit type conversion.

The decision as to which unit to implement has to do with the expected context of instantiations. If it is thought that users will most often already have an array type declared before instantiation, then the first unit is most applicable. In a case like sorting, this will most likely be true. Generally, applications that perform sorting also perform many other operations on arrays.

The second unit can still be used, even if the user already has an array type declared. In this case, an explicit type conversion would have to be performed when calling the exported *Sort* subprogram. Another consideration is that each instance defines an abstraction. Some hold that sorting in ascending order versus sorting in descending order are different abstractions. On such a view, one may want to enforce strong typing by exporting a different array type for each instance. The second unit implements these considerations, while the first unit allows arrays of the same type to be shared among more than one instance.

The second unit *binds* the array type to the instance, rather than to the context in which the instantiations occur. In general, to increase the reusability of a generic unit, bindings should be delayed until the context of the instantiation. Delayed bindings allow the instance to be more easily incorporated into different contexts. Rather than define a new context with new types, a generic unit should be easily usable within a wide variety of contexts.

[Ada83]   12.1.2(4, 6)
See also   [Mendal86]

19.1.10 Empty Parts

difficulty: designer

Write code to illustrate two good uses for empty generic formal parts.

◇◇◇◇◇

The following code illustrates the use of an empty generic formal part to control the order of elaboration:

```
generic                          with A;
package A is                     package B is
   function F return Integer;        package C is new A;
end A;                              X : Integer := C.F;
                                 end B;
```

The following code illustrates the use of an empty generic formal part to produce multiple copies of a package's state:

```
generic                          with Text_Io;
package Simple_Io is             package body Simple_Io is
   procedure Open (                 The_File : Text_Io.File_Type;

   File : in String);               ⋮
   procedure Put (               end Simple_Io;
   S : in String);
   procedure Get (
   S : out String;
   L : out Natural);

   ⋮

end Simple_Io;
```

At first thought, it might seem that there would be no use for generic units with empty formal parts, since the most obvious advantages of a generic package over a package are to separate data from algorithms and to parameterize an algorithm itself. However, generic units can also be used to circumvent common problems relating to order of elaboration. In the first example above, suppose that package A was not generic. Then, if package B were elaborated before the body of A, the exception Program_Error would be raised during the assignment to B.X. By specifying A as a generic unit, the language guarantees that the body of the function F is elaborated at the point of instantiation. Thus, the assignment cannot raise Program_Error. The point here is that both the specification and the body of an instance are elaborated as part of instantiation.

Empty generic formal parts are also useful for obtaining multiple copies of a package's state. The unit *Simple_Io* above is an example of hiding a piece of the program state. If this package were not generic, then each program could use the package with only one file at a time. If multiple parts of a system were to use a nongeneric version of this package, all would be sharing the same file. Such global coupling is undesirable. Generic units allow one to obtain distinct versions of the state of a package. Each instantiation of *Simple_Io* creates a new object named *The_File*.

The reader should note that, instead, private types can be used to solve the state problem illustrated by the second example. Abstract data structure packages, for example, usually export a private type rather than implement a single structure in the package body.

However, there are cases where the state of a package cannot easily be encapsulated by a private type. For example, consider a package body that includes an instantiation of a generic package; the state of the first package body then includes the state of the instance. The state of the instance cannot easily be encapsulated into a type definition. The state of the instance can, however, be encapsulated into the full definition of a private type by using the following scheme:

1. Place the instantiation in the body of a task type.
2. Export a private type that includes a component of this task type.

This solution is obviously laborious and somewhat convoluted. Its major advantage is that any number of copies of the state can be created during execution. This is not so in the case of using generic units. However, generic units with empty formal parts provide the easiest mechanism for addressing this state problem.

A Related Problem: Are there any uses for an empty generic formal part associated with a generic subprogram?

[Ada83]   12.1(2); 12.3(5)

19.2 INSTANTIATION

This section presents the syntax and semantics of generic unit instantiation. Conceptually, instantiation is the process of creating an instance from a generic unit. An important part of this process is the association of actual parameters with formal parameters. This association is called *matching*.

An instantiation can appear as both a basic and a later declarative item. Also, an instantiation may be a library unit.

19.2.1 Self-instantiation

difficulty: programmer

Can a generic unit directly or indirectly instantiate itself? If so, give an example.

◇◇◇◇◇

Within a generic unit, the name of the unit denotes an instance, not a generic unit. Thus, a generic unit cannot directly instantiate itself. This feature allows generic subprograms to be recursive and is similar to the rule that within the body of a task type, the name of the type denotes a task.

The compilation unit dependencies of Ada may seem to indicate that "mutual instantiation" is possible. But the following code is illegal:

```
generic                               generic
procedure P;                          procedure Q;

with Q;                               with P;
procedure P is                        procedure Q is
   procedure X is new Q;                 procedure X is new P;
begin                                 begin
   X;                                    X;
end P;                                end Q;
```

Such circular instantiations are expressly forbidden by the language. The conflict is that instantiation occurs at compilation time, whereas a possible reading of the preceding code is that "infinite recursion" takes place at run time. But the latter is not the case: the recursion is detected during compilation.

Although generic units cannot instantiate themselves in the foregoing manner, instances of a generic unit can instantiate nested generic units. A common example of this is the following:

```
generic
   type Item is private;
   ⋮
package B_Trees is
   type Tree is limited private;
   ⋮
   function Number_Of_Nodes (In_Tree : in Tree) return Natural;

   generic
      with procedure Visit (Node : in Item);
   procedure Traverse (The_Tree : in Tree);
private
   type Node is
      record
         The_Item                 : Item;
         Left_Branch, Right_Branch : Tree;
      end record;
   type Tree is access Node;
end B_Trees;

package body B_Trees is
   ⋮
   function Number_Of_Nodes (In_Tree : in Tree) return Natural is
      Count : Natural := 0;
      procedure Increment (Int : in Item) is
      begin
         Count := Count + 1;
```

```
      end Increment;
      procedure Walk is new Traverse (Increment);
   begin
      Walk (In_Tree);
      return Count;
   end Number_Of_Nodes;
   .
   .
   .
   procedure Traverse (The_Tree : in Tree) is
   begin
      if The_Tree /= null then
         Visit (The_Tree.The_Item);
         Traverse (The_Tree.Left_Branch);
         Traverse (The_Tree.Right_Branch);
      end if;
   end Traverse;
end B_Trees;
```

Note that the body of *Number_Of_Nodes* instantiates the generic unit *Traverse*. This is legal, since within instances of *B_Trees*, *Traverse* denotes a generic unit. Finally, note that *Traverse* is recursive.

A Related Problem: Can an instantiation have the same simple name as the corresponding generic unit?

[Ada83]   12.1(10); 12.3(18)

19.2.2 Discriminants

difficulty: programmer

Are the following units legal?

```
generic
   type Ft1 is private;
   type Ft2 (Int : Integer) is private;
package Gu is
   X : Ft1;
   Y : Ft2 (2);
end Gu;

with Gu;
package P is
   type At1 (X : Integer) is record null; end record;
   type At2 (X : Positive := 666) is record null; end record;
   subtype At3 is At2 (2);
```

```
    package U1 is new Gu (At1, At2);
    package U2 is new Gu (At2, At1);
    package U3 is new Gu (At3, At3);
end P;
```

◇◇◇◇◇

The instantiations *U1* and *U3* are semantically illegal.

A generic formal private type without discriminants can be matched by any non-limited type, including an unconstrained composite type. However, if the generic unit includes object declarations for the private type, then the instantiation is illegal if the private type is matched by

- an unconstrained array type, or
- an unconstrained record type without defaults.

For this reason, the matching of *At1* to *Ft1* in the instantiation *U1* is semantically illegal. The reason for the restriction is that within the instance, the formal type is treated in the same manner as the actual type. The first instantiation is illegal for the same reason that the declaration

```
    R : At1;   -- Illegal.
```

is illegal. That is, the declaration of *X* within the instance denoted by *U1* is similar to the preceding declaration.

Note that in the first instantiation, the matching of *At2* to *Ft2* is legal: even though the subtypes of the two discriminants differ, their base types are the same. However, during instantiation, a check is made to determine whether the constraints of the formal discriminants are those of the actual discriminants. If this check fails, Constraint_Error is raised. Thus, if *At2* is matched to *Ft2*, Constraint_Error will be raised at the point of instantiation.

When a generic formal private type includes a discriminant part, it must be matched by an unconstrained record type (i.e., a type with discriminants). The conformance rules for this matching are more relaxed than those governing an incomplete type declaration with discriminants and its corresponding full declaration. First, a generic formal private type with discriminants cannot specify defaults; nevertheless, the matching type may have defaults. Second, the syntactic form of the matching type's discriminant part need not conform to that of the formal type. Finally, the identifiers of the discriminants need not be the same.

The discriminant parts of the actual and the formal type must satisfy the following rules:

- The number of discriminants must be the same.

- The base type of each discriminant in the actual type must be the that of the corresponding discriminant in the formal type.
- The actual subtype must be unconstrained.

The instantiation *U2* is legal. The matching of *At2* to *Ft1* is legal because *At2* includes defaults. Note that this instantiation will not raise Constraint_Error during elaboration.

At3 can only be used as an actual type for a formal type that does not include discriminants, since *At3* is constrained. For this reason, the instantiation *U3* is illegal.

A Related Problem: Can an access type whose designated type is an incomplete type be used as a generic actual parameter?

[Ada83]   12.1.2(3); 12.3.2(1, 3 .. 5)
[ARG]   AI-00037/12, 12-01-86

19.2.3 Type Matching

difficulty: designer

For each generic formal type on the left-hand side, state which of the actual types on the right-hand side can be used to match it.

```
type F1 is (<>);              type A1 is new Integer;
type F2 is range <>;          subtype A2 is Character
                                 range 'a' .. 'z';
type F3 is digits <>;         subtype A3 is Character;
type F4 is delta <>;          task type A4;
type F5 is private;           subtype A5 is Float
                                 range 0.0 .. −1.0;
type F6 is limited private;   subtype A6 is Calendar.Time;
type F7 is array (1 .. 10)    type A7 is access A3;
   of F5;
type F8 is array (            subtype A8 is String (1 .. 10);
   F1 range <>) of F5;
type F9 is access F5;         type A9 is new String;

                              type A10 is access A2;
```

◇◇◇◇◇

	F1	F2	F3	F4	F5	F6	F7	F8	F9
A1	yes	yes	no	no	yes	yes	no	no	no
A2	yes	no	no	no	yes	yes	no	no	no
A3	yes	no	no	no	yes	yes	no	no	no
A4	no	no	no	no	no	yes	no	no	no
A5	no	no	yes	no	yes	yes	no	no	no
A6	no	no	no	no	yes	yes	no	no	no
A7	no	no	no	no	yes	yes	no	no	maybe
A8	no	no	no	no	yes	yes	maybe	no	no
A9	no	no	no	no	maybe	maybe	no	maybe	no
A10	no	no	no	no	yes	yes	no	no	maybe

The matching of the first six formal types is straightforward:

- *F1* can be matched by any discrete type.
- *F2* can be matched by any integer type.
- *F3* can be matched by any floating point type.
- *F4* can be matched by any fixed point type.
- *F5* can be matched by any nonlimited type.
- *F6* can be matched by any type.

Note that the matching of private and limited, private formal types is also dependent on the use of the type within the generic unit. If the actual type is an unconstrained composite type, then matching may or may not be legal. For example, *A9* may not match *F5* or *F6* if the generic unit includes the declaration of an object of the formal type.

Matching of the last three formal parameters depends on what the actual parameters for *F1* and *F5* are. *A8* may match *F7* only if the actual parameter for *F5* is a subtype of *Character*. Note, however, that if the constraints on the actual type for *F5* differ from those of *Character*, Constraint_Error will be raised during instantiation.

When a generic unit includes formal array types, the following checks are made during instantiation:

- The constraints on the index types of the formal array type are the same as those of the actual array type.
- The constraints on the component type of the formal array type are the same as that of the actual array type.

If either check fails, Constraint_Error is raised. The following code is an example of violating the former check:

```
generic
   type Index is (<>);
   type Arr is array (Index range <>) of Character;
procedure Gp;

with Gp;
procedure Proc is new Gp (Natural, String);
```

If *A2* were matched to *F5* and *A8* were matched to *F7*, then Constraint_Error would be raised. Similar matching rules and constraint checks apply when associating *A9* with *F8*.

A7 and *A10* may match *F9* only if *F5* is matched by a subtype of *Character*. Similarly to constraint checks for array index subtypes, array component subtypes, and discriminant subtypes, the constraints of the designated subtype of a generic formal access type must be the same as that of its actual type. For example, if *F9* were matched by *A7* and *F5* were matched by *A2*, the instantiation would be legal, but Constraint_Error would be raised during elaboration of the instantiation.

A Related Problem: Can a generic actual type be specified as a subtype indication with a constraint?

[Ada83]   12.3.4; 12.3.5

19.2.4 Generic Actual Subprograms

difficulty: programmer

Are the following units legal?

```
generic
   with function F return Boolean;
   with function Increment (Int : in Integer) return Integer;
   with procedure P;
package Gu is ...  end Gu;

with Gu;
package P is
   task T is
      entry E;
   end T;
```

```
    package U is new Gu (
        F => False, Increment => Integer'Succ, P => T.E);
    end P;
```

◇◇◇◇◇

The units are legal. This code illustrates that generic formal subprograms can be matched by enumeration literals, certain attributes, and task entries. In this context, enumeration literals are treated as parameterless functions and entries are treated as procedures. As with all generic formal subprogram matchings, the actual parameter must have the same parameter and result type profile as the formal parameter. Additionally, the modes of any subprogram parameters must be the same.

Certain attributes are classified as functions. The following table provides an example of each of these attributes and a corresponding generic formal subprogram to which it can be matched:

Actual	*Formal*
Integer'Image	**with function** F (Int : **in** Integer) **return** String;
Boolean'Value	**with function** F (S : **in** String) **return** Boolean;
Character'Pos	**with function** F (C : **in** Character)
	return *any_integer_type*;
Boolean'Val	**with function** F (Int : **in** *any_integer_type*)
	return Boolean;
Character'Pred	**with function** F (C : **in** Character)
	return Character;
Integer'Succ	**with function** F (Int : **in** Integer) **return** Integer;

A Related Problem: If, in the problem statement, *T* were defined as a task type, would the instantiation *U* still be legal?

[Ada83]   12.1.3(3); 12.3.6(1, 5 .. 6)
[ARG]   AI-00847/03, 04-15-90

19.2.5 Default Actual Subprograms

difficulty: programmer

What will the following program print?

```
    generic
        type Int is range <>;
        X, Y : in Int;
        with function "+" (L, R : in Int) return Int is <>;
    package Gu is end Gu;
```

```
with  Text_Io;
package body  Gu  is
begin
   Text_Io.Put  (Int'Image  (X  +  Y)  &  ' ');
end  Gu;

with  Gu,  Text_Io;
procedure  Test  is
   function  "+"  (L,  R  :  in  Integer)  return  Integer  is
   begin
      return  L;
   end  "+";

   package  U1  is  new  Gu  (Integer,  3,  4);
   package  U2  is  new  Gu  (Integer,  3,  4,  "+");
   package  U3  is  new  Gu  (Integer,  3,  4,  Standard."−");
begin
   Text_Io.New_Line;
end  Test;
```

◇◇◇◇◇

The program will print *3 3 −1*. The (implicit) generic actual subprogram used in the first instantiation is the user-defined addition, *Test*."+". Because the declaration of the generic formal subprogram does not name a specific default (rather, it uses the box compound delimiter), the actual subprogram is determined by the scope in which the instantiation is defined. Note that if the generic formal subprogram had named the default as in

```
with function  "+"  (L,  R  :  in  Int)  return  Int  is  "+";
```

then predefined addition would have been associated in the first instantiation.

  Test."+" is also the actual parameter used in the second instantiation. If the actual parameter were specified as Standard."+" rather than simply "+", then the predefined addition for *Integer* would have been used.

  The third instantiation illustrates that the generic actual subprogram need not be an operator with the same designator as the formal parameter. In fact, the actual subprogram need not even be an operator.

  A Related Problem: Can a default generic formal subprogram ever be an attribute, a task entry, or an enumeration literal? Can an implicit generic actual subprogram ever be an attribute, a task entry, or an enumeration literal?

[Ada83] 12.1.3(2); 12.3(3, 17); 12.3.6(2 .. 3)

19.2.6 Overload Resolution

difficulty: designer

Are the following units legal?

```
generic
   with procedure Put (S : in String);
   with procedure Put (C : in Character);
   type T is private;
   with procedure Y (A : in out T);
package Gp is ... end Gp;

with Gp, Text_Io;
package P is
   procedure A (X : out Boolean);
   procedure A (X : in out Integer);

   package P1 is new Gp (
      Text_Io.Put,
      Put => Text_Io.Put,
      T   => Integer, Y => A);
   package P2 is new Gp (
      Text_Io.Put,
      Text_Io.Put,
      Y => A,
      T => Boolean);
end P;
```

◇◇◇◇◇

Both instantiations are semantically illegal.

In order to match an actual subprogram to a generic formal subprogram, the following must hold:

- Both subprograms must have the same parameter and result type profile.
- The mode of all subprogram parameters must be the same.

The following may differ between the actual and the formal subprogram:

- the designator
- subprogram parameter names
- the use of default expressions
- implicit or explicit specification of the mode of mode in parameters
- subprogram parameter and result subtypes.

The instantiation *P1* is illegal simply because named association cannot be used for a generic formal subprogram when the designator of the formal parameter is over-loaded within the generic formal part. If the named association for *Put* were changed to positional association, the instantiation would be legal.

The second instantiation is illegal because, at the point of instantiation, there is no visible subprogram named *A* that has the same parameter profile and subprogram parameter modes as the generic formal *Y*. The determination of the actual parameter for *Y* is dependent on the actual parameter used for *T*. Since *Boolean* is matched to *T* and the designator *A* is associated with *Y*, the actual parameter for *Y* must be a subprogram of the form

```
procedure A (Identifier : in out Boolean);
```

But there is no such subprogram visible at the point of the second instantiation.

This subsection illustrates that the disambiguation of a generic actual subprogram can be fairly complex. However, like overload resolution for subprogram calls, this complexity falls largely on the implementation, and not the programmer. The instantiations in the following code are common manifestations of these issues:

```
generic
   type T is private;
   with function "<" (L, R : in T) return Boolean;
package Gu is ... end Gu;

package U1 is new Gu (Integer, "<");
package U2 is new Gu ("<" => ">", T => Boolean);
```

A Related Problem: Is it ever the case that an identifier appearing in a generic formal part must be matched by the same identifier?

[Ada83]   6.6(1 .. 2, 6); 8.5(7); 12.3(3); 12.3.6(1, 5)

19.2.7 Program_Error

difficulty: designer

What will the following program print?

```
with Text_Io;
procedure Main is
begin
   declare
      procedure P;

      generic
         with procedure P is <>;
```

```
package Q is end Q;

package Instance is new Q;

package body Q is
begin
    P;
end Q;

    procedure P is begin null; end P;
begin
    Text_Io.Put_Line ("So what?");
end;
exception
    when Program_Error =>
        Text_Io.Put_Line ("Elaboration problems.");
    when others =>
        Text_Io.Put_Line ("Lost in space.");
end Main;
```

◇◇◇◇◇

The program will print *Elaboration problems.*

If a generic unit is instantiated before its body has been elaborated, Program_Error is raised at the point of instantiation. This situation is similar to that of calling a function before its body has been elaborated: Program_Error is raised at the point of call. The preceding instantiation raises Program_Error because Q is instantiated before its body has been elaborated.

Even if the instantiation were moved to a point immediately after the body of Q, Program_Error would still be raised during instantiation. In this case, the elaboration of the instance would call the procedure P. But the call would occur prior to the elaboration of the body of P, and thus Program_Error would still be raised. This problem illustrates the difference between the elaboration of the body of a generic unit and the elaboration of the body of an instance. If the instantiation were moved to a point after the body of P, the instantiation would proceed without exceptions and the program would print *So what?*

[Ada83]   3.9(4 .. 5, 7 .. 8); 11.1(7)

19.3 INSTANCES

This section presents the semantics of instances of generic units. Instantiation forms an instance with the simple name used in an instantiation denoting the created instance. For example, in the instantiation,

```
package Int_Io is new Text_Io.Integer_Io (Integer);
```

Int_Io is not the instance, but rather denotes the instance. It is this instance which is a package.

19.3.1 Predefined Exported Operations

difficulty: designer

Are the following units legal?

```
generic
   type T1 is private;
   type T2 is limited private;
package Gu is
   type A1 is array (1 .. 10) of T1;
   type A2 is array (1 .. 10) of T2;
end Gu;

with Gu;
package P is
   package U is new Gu (
      T1 => Character, T2 => Integer);
   function "<=" (L, R : in U.A2) return Boolean
      renames U."<=";
   X : U.A1 := "0123456789";
   Y : U.A2 := (others => 33);
   B : constant Boolean := Y <= Y;
end P;
```

◇◇◇◇◇

The units are legal.

These units focus on the operations defined for the types *A1* and *A2*. There are two sets of operations to consider:

1. those defined within the generic unit
2. those defined within instances.

These two sets may differ; however, the first is always a subset of the second. Within a generic unit, the operations defined for a formal type include those that are predefined for the class of the type. Similarly, the operations defined for an array type whose component type is a generic formal type depend on the class of the generic formal type. For example, within the generic unit *Gu*, catenation is defined for *A1*, but not *A2*.

Conceptually, within instances of a generic unit, the operations defined for a formal type are those of the actual type. For example, addition is defined for the type *T2* within the instance denoted by *U*. Similarly, within instances, operations defined for an array type whose component type is a generic formal type depend on the class of the corresponding generic actual type.

The type *U.A1* is simply a one-dimensional array of characters. Similarly, *U.A2* is an array of integers. Thus, string literals are defined for *U.A1*, and the relational operations are defined for *U.A2*.

A Related Problem: What predefined operations of the type *A2* would exist in an instance for which *T2* was matched by a task type?

[Ada83]   12.1.2(4 .. 14); 12.3(5, 9, 15)
[ARG]   AI-00398/08, 06-18-87

19.3.2 Types Are Types

difficulty: designer

Are the following units legal?

```
generic
   type T1 is range <>;
   type T2 is range <>;
package Gp is
   subtype S1 is T1;
   subtype S2 is T2;
   X1 : S1 := 1;
   X2 : S2 := 2;
end Gp;


with Gp;
procedure A_Type_By_Any_Other_Name is
   package P is new Gp (Positive, Positive);
   Y1 : P.S1;
   Y2 : P.S2 := 22;
begin
   P.X1 := P.X2;
   Y1    := Y2;
end A_Type_By_Any_Other_Name;
```

◇◇◇◇◇

The units are legal. This program is similar to the one in Section 19.3.1. Within the generic unit *Gp*, the types *T1* and *T2* are treated as having different base types. That is, *X2* could not be directly assigned to *X1*. However, within the instance denoted by *P*, *T1* and *T2* are both subtypes of the predefined type Integer. Thus, the two assignment statements are legal.

Note that the names of the generic formal parameters are not visible within instances. Conceptually, an instance is constructed from a generic unit by

1. removing the generic formal part,
2. replacing all uses of formal parameters with uses of the corresponding actual parameters, and
3. replacing the name of the generic unit with the name of the instantiation.

[Ada83]   12.1.2(1); 12.3(5 .. 16)

19.3.3 Constraints Are Constraints

difficulty: designer

What will the following program print?

```
generic
   with function F return Positive;
package Gu is
   X : Integer := F;
end Gu;

with Gu, Text_Io;
procedure P is
   function G return Integer is
   begin
      return Integer'First;
   end G;
begin
   declare
      package U is new Gu (G);
   begin
      Text_Io.Put_Line ("Equilibrium achieved.");
   end;
exception
   when Constraint_Error | Numeric_Error =>
      Text_Io.Put_Line ("Out of whack.");
end P;
```

◇◇◇◇◇

The program will print *Equilibrium achieved.* As with generic formal objects of mode in out, the constraints on the parameters and result of generic formal subprograms are those given in the declaration of the actual subprogram. Even though the formal subprogram *F* is declared to return a value of the subtype *Positive*, the constraints of the result subtype within the instance are those of the actual subprogram *G*, namely, *Integer*. For example, if the declaration of *X* specified *Positive* rather than *Integer*, the elaboration of the instantiation would raise Constraint_Error.

In any case, the type marks given in the declaration of generic formal objects of mode in out and generic formal subprograms can lead to confusion. [Ada83] suggests that base types (or first named subtypes) always be used in these declarations. Such a rule of style, however, does not eliminate the confusion. For consider the following generic formal and actual subprograms:

```
with procedure Formal (Int : in Integer);
procedure Actual (P : in Positive);
```

The programmer might suppose that, within the body of the generic unit, negative values may be passed to the procedure. But this might be an invalid assumption since, within the instance alluded to here, Constraint_Error would be raised during such a call.

A Related Problem: Consider a generic subprogram *G* with a generic formal subprogram parameter *P*. Write the code to illustrate mutual recursion between an instance of *G* and the corresponding actual parameter for *P*.

[Ada83]   12.1.3(3, 5); 12.3(5, 11)

19.3.4 Constraints on Formal Objects

difficulty: designer

What will the following program print?

```
generic
   X : in out Positive;
   Y : in out Integer;
package Gu is end Gu;

with Text_Io;
package body Gu is
begin
   begin
      X := -3;   Text_Io.Put ("X okay; ");
   exception
      when Constraint_Error => Text_Io.Put ("X bombed; ");
   end;

   Y := -3;   Text_Io.Put ("Y okay. ");
exception
```

```
        when Constraint_Error => Text_Io.Put ("Y bombed. ");
    end Gu;

    with Gu, Text_Io;
    procedure P is
        A : Positive;
        B : Integer;
        package U1 is new Gu (A, B);
        package U2 is new Gu (B, A);
    begin
        Text_Io.New_Line;
    end P;
```

◇◇◇◇◇

The program will print *X bombed; Y okay. X okay; Y bombed.*

The actual object matching a generic formal object of mode in out must be a renamable variable supporting both read and write operations. Such an object thus cannot be a mode in or a mode out subprogram formal parameter. (Whether an object is renamable is covered in detail in Chapter 22.)

The matching of an actual object to a generic formal object of mode in out is equivalent to a renaming declaration. Thus, the constraints of the formal object are those of the actual object, regardless of the type mark given in the declaration of the former.

In the instance denoted by *U1*, the subtype of *X* is *Positive* and the subtype of *Y* is *Integer*. In the second instance, the subtype of *X* is *Integer* and the subtype of *Y* is *Positive*. This program illustrates that within different instances of the same generic unit, the constraints on actual parameters may differ.

Since matching of generic formal objects of mode in out is equivalent to renaming, aliases are created. In this program, the object *X* within the first instance and the object *Y* within the second instance are both aliases of *P.A*. Similarly, *U1.Y* and *U2.X* are aliases of *P.B*. Thus, although there are six object names in the program, there are actually only two objects.

The program

```
    generic
        C : in out Character;
    procedure P;
    procedure P is
    begin
        C := Character'Succ (C);
    end P;

    with P, Text_Io;
    procedure Main is
        S : String (1 .. 5) := "abcde";
        procedure Q is new P (C => S(4));
```

```
begin
   Q;   Q;   Text_Io.Put_Line (S);
end Main;
```

will print *abcfe*.

[Ada83]   8.5(4 .. 5); 12.1.1(4 .. 5); 12.3(8); 12.3.1(2)

19.3.5 Homographs in Instances

difficulty: programmer

Are the following units legal?

```
generic
   type F1 is digits <>;
   type F2 is digits <>;
package Math_Stuff is
   function X (Left, Right : in F1) return F1;
   function X (Left, Right : in F2) return F2;
end Math_Stuff;

with Math_Stuff;
procedure P is
   package Math is new Math_Stuff (Float, Float);
   A : Float;
begin
   A := Math.X (10.10, 20.20);
end P;
```

◇◇◇◇◇

The call to *Math.X* is illegal. Within the instance of *Math_Stuff*, both functions named *X* have the same parameter and result type profile. This does not, of course, make the instantiation illegal; it does, however, make it impossible to call either function exported by the instance.

This program illustrates a rather precarious aspect of generic units: Ada cannot prevent one from writing useless code. An alternative semantics would be to make the preceding instantiation illegal, because it creates what would otherwise be considered illegal homographs. Such a semantics, however, would involve more complex checking of instantiations.

[Ada83]   6.6(3); 8.3(17); 12.3(22)
[ARG]   AI-00012/06, 05-23-88

19.3.6 Importing Static Properties

difficulty: language lawyer

Are the following units legal?

```
generic
   type Int is range <>;
   X : in Integer;
package Gu is
   subtype S is Int;
   Y : constant Integer := X;
end Gu;

with Gu, Calendar;
package P is
   package U1 is new Gu (Integer, Calendar.Day (Calendar.Clock));
   subtype J is Integer range 1 .. Calendar.Month (Calendar.Clock);
   package U2 is new Gu (J, 6);

   type K is range U1.S'First .. U2.Y;
   type L is range U2.S'Last .. U1.Y;
end P;
```

◇◇◇◇◇

The declaration of the type *L* is semantically illegal.

The focus of these units is determining whether subtypes and objects declared within an instance are static. A reading of [Ada83] would clearly indicate that generic formal types and objects cannot be static. The Ada Rapporteur Group has decided that such a restriction is overly intrusive upon the use of generic units. The current interpretation allows generic formal types and objects to be static if their corresponding actual parameters are static. This interpretation more closely fits in with the rest of the *instance model*. That is, if one recalls that formal parameters do not exist within instances (they are replaced by their actual parameters), then the reinterpretation provided by the Ada Rapporteur Group fits this model far better than do the previous restrictions.

Given the new interpretation, *U1.S* and *U2.Y* are both static, but *U1.Y* and *U2.S* are not. For this reason, the declaration of the type *K* is legal, but the declaration of *L* is not.

Note that generic formal parameters are always nonstatic within a generic unit. For example, within the body of *Gu*, neither *Int* nor *X* could be used in a context where a static expression is required.

[Ada83]   4.9(11); 12.3(5, 17)
[ARG]   AI-00409/05, 09-12-87; AI-00483/04, 08-06-87; AI-00505/03, 06-16-88;
           AI-00878/00, 04-16-90

19.3.7 Breaking the Contract Model

difficulty: designer

Which of the following units are illegal?

```
generic
   type T is private;
   Val : in T;
package Gu is end Gu;

package body Gu is
   X : constant T := Val;
   Y : T;
end Gu;

with Gu;
package Ru is new Gu (String, "Looky here, Looky here...");
```

◇◇◇◇◇

The instantiation *Ru* is illegal. These units illustrate a situation in which a unit (*Ru*) is illegal with respect to a unit on which it is not dependent (the body of *Gu*). If the instantiation were legal, then the body of the instance could not be elaborated, because the array object *Y* would not be of a constrained subtype.

This is a well-understood and often-cited example of a deficiency in the specification and body model. The designers of the language thought it best that implementations address the problem of when to report an illegality, rather than including complex language rules to handle this special case. (In some implementations, the compilation of *Ru* will succeed, but any attempt to link or elaborate a program that includes *Ru* will be illegal.) Such dependencies are examined in detail in Chapter 20.

[Ada83]   10.3(6, 8 .. 9); 10.4(2); 12.3.2(4)
[ARG]   AI-00256/23, 06-16-88

19.3.8 Exceptions in Instances

difficulty: programmer

Consider the following unit:

```
generic
   type F is digits <>;
package Gp is
   Bad_Instance : exception;
```

```
            ⋮
    end Gp;

    package body Gp is
            ⋮
    begin
        if 0.0 not in F then
            raise Bad_Instance;
        end if;
    end Gp;

    with Gp;
    procedure Mk_Instance is
            ⋮
        type Real_Useless is digits 15 range 1.0 .. 0.0;
        package Nu is new Gp (Real_Useless);
            ⋮
    end Mk_Instance;
```

The instance will propagate an exception. Can the exception be handled?

◇◇◇◇◇

The exception can be handled, but not by name. Each instance of *Gp* declares a new exception. Due to the propagation and visibility rules, *Nu.Bad_Instance* cannot be handled by name if it is propagated during instantiation.

It is considered bad style to propagate an exception beyond its scope. In this example, *Bad_Instance* is raised when the generic actual parameter does not meet the requirements of the generic unit. There are a number of ways to raise the exception without propagating it beyond its scope. One method is to nest the generic unit within a scope containing the exception declaration, thus:

```
    package P is
        Bad_Instance : exception;

        generic
            type F is digits <>;
        package Gp is ... end Gp;
    end P;
```

A second method would be to raise the exception at the first use of the instance. For example, within the body of *Gp*, the following procedure could be added:

```
procedure Check_Instance is
begin
   if 0.0 not in F then
      raise Bad_Instance;
   end if;
end Check_Instance;
```

Then, the first statement of each exported subprogram could be a call to this procedure. This solution, however, assumes that the "use" of an instance is defined by a call to an exported subprogram, which need not be the case—for example, consider an instance that exports only objects or types.

[Ada83]   11.1(3); 12.3(5, 13, 17)

chapter 20

The Program Library

It takes them six days to do an Ada build.
And on the seventh day they rested.
Mark Gerhardt and Professor Mark Linton,
April 18, 1989, Stanford University
(remarks on a question posed about the time it takes to
compile the multi-million line AFATDS software system)

In previous chapters, most of the problems presented centered around asking the reader to examine some code and, based on that code alone, determine its semantics. Usually, the surrounding context in which the code appeared was transparent. One aspect of this surrounding context is the contents of the program library. The program library is an abstract data base that stores necessary details and relationships amongst various units of an Ada program. This data base is used to enforce strong typing and the semantics of the language across compilation boundaries.

20.1 PACKAGE STANDARD

The predefined package Standard defines a declarative region that encompasses all other Ada units. This package and the predefined library units together form the predefined programming environment. This section presents a basis for understanding the program library and, specifically, the use of package Standard within the library.

20.1.1 Homographs

difficulty: programmer

Are the following library units legal?

```
package Integer is ... end Integer;
procedure True;
function False return Integer;
function True  return Boolean;
procedure Program_Error;

procedure Text_Io is
  procedure Storage_Error is separate;
begin
  null;
end Text_Io;
```

◇◇◇◇◇

The procedure *True*, the function *False*, and the procedure *Text_Io* are legal.

A library unit is a compilation unit that is nested immediately within package Standard and that can be compiled separately. That is, library units are declared within package Standard. A library unit can be a generic declaration, package declaration, subprogram, or generic instantiation. A compilation unit is simply a unit that can be compiled separately. A compilation unit is either a library unit or a secondary unit (body).

The rules that apply to homographs in a declarative region also govern package Standard. Since the type Integer is already defined in package Standard, a package specification named *Integer* cannot also appear immediately within that declarative region. The same is true for the predefined exception Program_Error. If an implementation provides other predefined declarations that are not library units, such as Long_Integer, then library units cannot also have the same names as such implementation-specific declarations.

The procedure *True* is legal, since the only predefined entity named *True* declared immediately within package Standard is also overloadable and has a different parameter and result type profile. Similarly, the function *False* is legal, since the literal False in package Standard has a different parameter and result type profile than does this function. However, the function *True* is illegal, since its parameter and result type profile is the same as that of the predefined literal True.

Although the language predefines a library unit named Text_Io, a user is allowed to *redefine* a library unit. For this reason, the procedure *Text_Io* is legal. If this procedure were compiled, then any reference to *Text_Io* in a with-clause of another compilation unit would refer to the procedure *Text_Io* instead of the package *Text_Io*. Note that the body stub for *Storage_Error* is legal, since the body stub is not defined immediately within package Standard, thus not resulting in any homograph.

A Related Problem: Can a library unit be named *Ascii*?

[Ada83]   8.3(15, 17); 6.6(1); 8.6(2); 10.1(4)
[ARG]   AI-00192/05, 05-23-88

20.1.2 Hiding the Predefined Package Standard

difficulty: programmer

What will the following program print?

```
package Standard is
   function "+" (L, R : in Integer) return Integer;
end Standard;

package body Standard is
   function "+" (L, R : in Integer) return Integer is
   begin
      return 42;
   end "+";
end Standard;

with Text_Io, Standard;
procedure Main is
   function "+" (L, R : in Integer) return Integer
      renames Standard."+";
begin
   Text_Io.Put_Line (Integer'Image (1 + 2));
end Main;
```

◇◇◇◇◇

The program will print *42*.

    The predefined package Standard is not a library unit; rather, it is the root of the program library and *encompasses* the remainder of the library. Therefore, a user is allowed to define a library unit named *Standard*. After the renaming declaration, the predefined binary addition for the type Integer is hidden, directly and indirectly. That is, within *Main*, even the expanded name Standard."+" denotes the user-defined operation, so that the following calls are illegal:

```
Standard."+" (Left => 33, Right => 22)    -- Illegal.
"+" (Left => 33, Right => 22)             -- Illegal.
```

    If the foregoing program had not defined a library unit named *Standard*, then the context clause would be semantically illegal. One cannot name the predefined package Standard in a with-clause since that package is not a library unit. Note that if *Standard* were removed from the with-clause before *Main*, then the renaming declaration would still be legal, and *3* would be printed.

    A Related Problem: What differences are allowed among implementations of the predefined package Standard?

[Ada83]   8.6(2); 10.1(3 .. 4, 10); 10.1.1(3)

20.2 PACKAGE CALENDAR

The predefined library package Calendar provides a simple interface for modeling wall
clock time. Many of the problems programmers have with this package are attributable
to not knowing what the intended uses of the package are. The package exports only the
minimal characteristics of time; more elaborate requirements are necessarily implementation dependent and need to be provided by means of user-defined (or vendor-supplied)
library units.

20.2.1 Midnight Caller

difficulty: designer

What will the following program print?

```
with Calendar, Text_Io;
procedure Midnight is
   function "=" (L, R : in Calendar.Time) return Boolean
      renames Calendar."=";
begin
   Text_Io.Put_Line (Boolean'Image (
      Calendar.Time_Of (1961, 5, 24, 86_400.0) =
      Calendar.Time_Of (1961, 5, 25, 0.0)));
exception
   when Calendar.Time_Error =>
      Text_Io.Put_Line ("Illegal time formation.");
end Midnight;
```

◇◇◇◇◇

The program will print *TRUE*.
   Package Calendar defines the following subtypes used in the formation and selection of values of the type Time:

```
subtype Year_Number  is Integer  range 1901 .. 2099;
subtype Month_Number is Integer  range 1 .. 12;
subtype Day_Number   is Integer  range 1 .. 31;
subtype Day_Duration is Duration range 0.0 .. 86_400.0;
```

The function *Time_Of* takes values of these types and produces a value of the
type Time. What is not made clear by the standard is whether Day_Duration'Last (i.e.,
86_400.0) signifies a valid Seconds component of the type Time. There are 86,400
seconds in a single day. The intent of the standard, as interpreted by the Ada Rapporteur
Group, is that midnight is defined to be Day_Duration'First (i.e., 0.0) seconds of any

day. The question is then whether 86_400.0 seconds past midnight forms a part of a "proper date" for the Time_Of function.

The intent of the subtype *Day_Duration* is to allow multiple representations of midnight in the formation of a value of the type Time: military time typically uses two different representations of midnight, 00:00 and 24:00. In order to support such usage, the meaning of 86_400.0 as the Seconds parameter to the function *Time_Of* signifies midnight of the following day. Thus, both of the values returned by *Time_Of* in the preceding program yield midnight for the date May 25, 1961.

[Ada83]   9.6(4 .. 6, 7)
[ARG]   AI-00196/05, 07-23-86

20.2.2 Running Out of Time

difficulty: designer

Which of the following expressions will raise an exception? Assume direct visibility to the operations defined in package Calendar.

1. Time_Of (1967, 2, 29, 0.0)
2. Time_Of (2099, 12, 31, 86_399.0) + 1.0
3. Time_Of (2099, 12, 31, 86_399.0) − Time_Of (1901, 1, 1, 0.0)

◇◇◇◇◇

The exception Calendar.Time_Error will be raised upon evaluation of the first two expressions. This exception might also be raised in the third expression.

The first expression specifies an illegal date: February 29, 1967. Thus, Time_Error will be raised by this invocation of *Time_Of*.

The second expression introduces the use of one of the addition operators in package Calendar. Several operators are provided:

```
function "+" (Left : Time;      Right : Duration) return Time;
function "+" (Left : Duration; Right : Time)      return Time;
function "−" (Left : Time;      Right : Duration) return Time;
function "−" (Left : Time;      Right : Time)      return Duration;

function "<"  (Left, Right : Time) return Boolean;
function "<=" (Left, Right : Time) return Boolean;
function ">"  (Left, Right : Time) return Boolean;
function ">=" (Left, Right : Time) return Boolean;
```

The invocation of the addition function attempts to yield midnight of the date January 1, 2100. But since the year 2100 is not in the range of the subtype Year_Number, the exception Time_Error will be raised instead.

The last expression involves two calls to *Time_Of*, the results of which are subtracted from each other using the operator provided in package Calendar. If the result returned by the subtraction operator does not correspond to a value in the range of the type Duration, Time_Error will be raised.

[Ada83]   9.6(5 .. 6)
[ARG]   AI-00196/05, 07-23-86

20.2.3 Subtype Assumptions

difficulty: designer

Does the language require that the following expression evaluate to True?

        Duration'Last >= 86_400.0 **and** Integer'Last >= 2099

◇◇◇◇◇

The language requires that the predefined type Duration support both the values 86_400.0 and −86_400.0. However, there is no requirement that the type Integer support the value 2099.

The implementation of the numeric types *Duration* and *Integer* can vary among implementations. The language requires that any implementation of *Duration* support the minimal characteristics of time required by the package Calendar. However, there is no corresponding requirement on the type *Integer* that is used in defining three subtypes in package Calendar. If the implementation of *Integer* cannot support the value 2099 (or any other value of the integer subtypes in package Calendar), then, upon elaboration of package Calendar, Constraint_Error or Numeric_Error will be raised. This semantics follows the same conventions as for any user-defined subtype.

The intent of the type *Integer* is certainly that it be able to support the ranges of the subtypes in package Calendar, as well as uses of the subtypes Natural, Positive, System.Priority, Text_Io.Field, and Text_Io.Number_Base. The subtype *Positive* is used in the definition of the type String. Thus, any useful implementation must define the range of *Integer* such that these other language features can be employed without exception. The ACVC is the vehicle used to ensure that unreasonable restrictions, such as the type Integer not supporting the value 2099, are otherwise justified.

[Ada83]   3.5.4(7); 9.6(4); C(6, 19)
[ARG]   AI-00325/05, 07-23-86

20.2.4 Time Warps

difficulty: programmer

Can this program ever print *FALSE*? Explain.

```
with Calendar, Text_Io;
procedure Warp is
   Secs : constant Calendar.Day_Duration :=
      Calendar.Seconds (Calendar.Clock);
begin
   Text_Io.Put_Line (Boolean'Image (
      Secs <= Calendar.Seconds (Calendar.Clock)));
end Warp;
```

◇◇◇◇◇

Under some external conditions, the program may print *FALSE*. Under normal conditions, the program will print *TRUE*.

The function *Clock* returns a value of the type Time corresponding to a wall clock defined by the environment. There is no requirement on the function *Clock* that it return monotonically nondecreasing values. If the environment's wall clock gets reset (for example, to account for daylight savings time), then subsequent calls to *Clock* will reflect this change.

A Related Problem: Is the semantics of a pending delay statement or delay alternative preserved when the environment's wall clock is reset?

[Ada83]   9.6(5)
[ARG]   AI-00195/09, 05-23-88; AI-00754/01, 01-30-89

20.2.5 Unsupported Date

difficulty: designer

If the environment's wall clock corresponds to a date before January 1, 1901, or after December 31, 2099, must the exception Time_Error be raised in the following declaration?

```
Month : constant Calendar.Month_Number :=
   Calendar.Month (Calendar.Clock);
```

◇◇◇◇◇

The exception *Time_Error* can be raised only by calls to Time_Of and the operators in package Calendar. Constraint_Error or Numeric_Error might be raised in the preceding declaration, depending on the implementation of the type Time.

The language states the conditions under which *Time_Error* may be raised. This exception is not raised by a call to the functions *Clock* or *Month*. It is thus possible for an implementation to support values of the type Time whose years are outside the range of the subtype Year_Number. If an implementation supports Time values outside the range of Year_Number, any attempt to acquire the year component of such values will result in Constraint_Error or Numeric_Error being raised.

The foregoing declaration may be elaborated without exception, in which case the proper month number will be returned. Alternatively, the call to *Calendar.Clock* may cause Constraint_Error or Numeric_Error to be raised if the implementation does not support values of the type Time outside the range of the subtype Year_Number.

[Ada83]   9.6(6)
[ARG]   AI-00194/00, 03-13-84; AI-00195/09, 05-23-88

20.2.6 Clock Resolution

difficulty: designer

What will the following program print?

```
with Calendar, Text_Io, System;
procedure Resolve is
   Start : Calendar.Time;
   function "=" (L, R : in Calendar.Time) return Boolean
      renames Calendar."=";
begin
   Start := Calendar.Clock;
   delay Duration'Small;
   Text_Io.Put (Boolean'Image (Calendar.Clock = Start) & ' ');

   Start := Calendar.Clock;
   delay Duration (System.Tick);
   Text_Io.Put_Line (Boolean'Image (Calendar.Clock = Start));
end Resolve;
```

◇◇◇◇◇

The program may print any of the following:

```
FALSE  TRUE
FALSE  FALSE
```

```
TRUE  FALSE
TRUE  TRUE
```

The value *System.Tick* is defined to be the basic clock period for an implementation. That is, the clock is updated at the frequency of *System.Tick*. The value of *Duration'Small* must be no greater than 0.020, i.e., 20 milliseconds. *Duration'Small* represents only the accuracy of the values represented by the type Duration. The language does not require a relationship between *Duration'Small* and *System.Tick*. Further, the delay of a delay statement need not conform to any accuracy requirement of either *System.Tick* or *Duration'Small*.

In the absence of external clock anomalies, such as a clock reset, successive calls to Calendar.Clock will return time values that are at least *System.Tick* apart. Therefore, in normal cases, the program will print *FALSE FALSE*. In cases where the external clock has been reset, either equality test may print *TRUE*.

[Ada83]   9.6(4 .. 5); 13.7.1(1, 7)
[ARG]   AI-00201/07, 05-23-88; AI-00223/00, 03-13-84; AI-00366/07, 05-23-88

20.2.7 Multiple Clocks

difficulty: designer

Can the package Calendar be used to model multiple distributed wall clocks in a single Ada program?

◇◇◇◇◇

The definition of package Calendar does not exclude the possibility of modeling more than one external clock.

A library package in an Ada program is shared by all threads of control in the program. That is, the state of the package is a shared resource. For package Calendar, the question then becomes whether this state can account for multiple external clocks. In a distributed environment, it is not uncommon for each node to have its own external clock. It would therefore be useful if the package Calendar could be used to model different external clocks.

The language does not prohibit an implementation from modeling time by means of multiple clocks. Since the function Calendar.Clock need not return monotonically nondecreasing values, it is possible to implement Calendar.Clock by means of more than one external clock. Consider a distributed system corresponding to the following two tasks (assume visibility to packages Calendar and Text_Io):

```
function "<" (L, R : in Calendar.Time) return Boolean
  renames Calendar."<";
```

```
task Server is
  entry E (
     Your_Time : in      Calendar.Time;
     My_Time   :    out  Calendar.Time);
end Server;


task Client;


task body Client is
  His_Time : Calendar.Time;
begin
  Server.E (Calendar.Clock, His_Time);

  if His_Time < Calendar.Clock then
     Text_Io.Put_Line ("Client: server time < my time");
  else
     Text_Io.Put_Line ("Client: server time >= my time");
  end if;
end Client;


task body Server is
  My_Time,
  His_Time : Calendar.Time;
begin
  accept E (
     Your_Time : in      Calendar.Time;
     My_Time   :    out  Calendar.Time) do
     if Calendar.Clock < Your_Time then
        Text_Io.Put_Line ("Server: my time < client time");
     else
        Text_Io.Put_Line ("Server: my time >= client time");
     end if;

     My_Time := Calendar.Clock;
  end E;
end Server;
```

In a distributed system, one would expect that the calls to the *Clock* function denote different external clocks for each task. Further, there can be no direct correspondence of accuracy between such clocks. That is, the client's clock might tick more slowly than the server's clock. Under normal conditions, one would expect to see either of the following as output of the preceding code:

```
Server: my time < client time
Client: server time < my time
```

or

```
Server:  my  time  >=  client  time
Client:   server  time  >=  my  time
```

However, for reasons particular to the external environment, such as an external clock being reset, either of the following two sets of output are also possible:

```
Server:  my  time  <  client  time
Client:   server  time  >=  my  time
```

or

```
Server:  my  time  >=  client  time
Client:   server  time  <  my  time
```

[Ada83]   9.6(5)
[ARG]   AI-00195/09, 05-23-88; AI-00325/05, 07-23-86; AI-00822/00, 04-14-89

20.3 THE WITH-CLAUSE

With-clauses make other library units visible to compilation units. A unit is dependent on the units named in its with-clauses. The dependency relations define a partial ordering over the set of compilation units in the program library. This section presents some of the more important semantic ramifications of defining visibility to other units.

20.3.1 Imported Unit Names

difficulty: novice

If only the predefined library units are in the program library, are the following compilation units legal?

```
package  P  is
  package  Q  is ...
end  P;

with  Ascii,  Standard.Text_Io,  P.Q;
procedure  X;
```

◇◇◇◇◇

All of the names mentioned in the with-clause are illegal.

Syntactically, with-clauses may appear only immediately before a compilation unit. A name mentioned in a with-clause must be a simple name, that is, a name whose syntax is that of an identifier. For this reason, the names *Standard.Text_Io* and *P.Q* are syntactically illegal in this context. Furthermore, the names mentioned must denote library units. Since the predefined package *Ascii* and the package *P.Q* are not library units, they may not be named in a with-clause.

The package Ascii is not itself a library unit, but is rather a predefined package nested within Standard. Although Text_Io is also nested within Standard, it is, by definition, a library unit. The difference between the visibility of the packages Ascii and Text_Io is that Text_Io must be made visible to other compilation units by means of a with-clause, whereas Ascii is inherently visible to all compilation units. Another difference is that Text_Io can be redefined in the program library, but Ascii can only be hidden.

A Related Problem: Why did the designers of Ada choose not to make *Ascii* a library unit?

[Ada83]   10.1.1(1 .. 3); C(15, 22)

20.3.2 Inheriting Visibility

difficulty: novice

Are the following compilation units legal?

```
with  Text_Io;
procedure  P;

with  Calendar;
procedure  P is
   procedure  Q is separate;
begin
   Text_Io.Put_Line (Integer'Image (Calendar.Day (Calendar.Clock)));
end  P;

with  System;
separate  (P)
procedure  Q is
begin
   Text_Io.Put_Line (
      Integer'Image (Calendar.Month (Calendar.Clock)) & ' ' &
      System.Name'Image (System.System_Name));
end  Q;
```

◇◇◇◇◇

The compilation units are legal. If a unit is named in a with-clause of a compilation unit that is a library unit, the named unit is made visible throughout the associated declarative region. This means that the named unit is made visible to the compilation unit body and any subunits. The with-clause appearing before the declaration of *P* makes *Text_Io* visible to the declaration of *P*, the body of *P*, and the subunit *Q*. Similarly, the with-clause before the body of *P* makes the unit *Calendar* visible to this body and its subunit. Finally, the with-clause before the subunit *Q* makes the unit *System* visible only within the body of *Q*.

Note that the effects of a with-clause are not transitive, as shown by the following code:

```
with  Text_Io;
package  A  is end  A;

with  A;
package  B  is
   F  :  Text_Io.File_Type;    ––  Illegal.
end  B;
```

[Ada83]   10.1.1(4); 10.2(6)
[ARG]   AI-00226/06, 07-23-86

20.3.3 Circular Dependency

difficulty: programmer

Which of the following compilation units are legal?

```
procedure  Oneself;
package  Self  is end;
procedure  A;
procedure  B;

with  Oneself;
procedure  Oneself  is  …

with  Self;
package  Self  is end;

with  A;
procedure  C;

with  C;
procedure  A (Int  :  in  Integer);
```

```
with  B;
procedure  D;

with  D;
procedure  B  is  ...
```

◇◇◇◇◇

The declaration and body of *Oneself*, the first declaration of *Self*, the first declaration of *A*, the declaration and body of *B*, and the declarations of *C* and *D* are legal.

The with-clauses that appear before a compilation unit define dependencies between units. A unit *D* is dependent on another unit *U* if

- *D* is the body of *U*,
- *D* is a subunit of *U*,
- *U* is named in a with-clause before the declaration or body of *D*, or
- *D* is dependent on a unit that is dependent on *U*.

Dependencies must not be *circular*. A circular dependency is a dependency in which a unit is dependent on another unit that is dependent on the first unit. Also, a declaration may not be dependent on itself, since such a dependency would prohibit the replacement of the first declaration by the second. The unit *Self* is an example of such an illegal self-dependency. The first declaration of *Self* is legal and is entered into the program library. The second declaration of *Self* must replace the first and, therefore, cannot be dependent on the first *Self*. Notice that the compilations of *Oneself* are legal. In this case, the with clause before the body of *Oneself* is simply redundant: the body is implicitly dependent on its declaration.

The second declaration of *A* is dependent on the unit *C*, which, in turn, is dependent on the first declaration of *A*. Since the second declaration of *A* must replace the first (compilation units are not overloadable), the circularity is not legal. Note the difference between the A-C dependency and the B-D dependency. The declaration of *D* is dependent on the declaration of *B*, and the body of *B* is dependent on the declaration of *D*. This dependency is noncircular and, therefore, legal. Such a dependency is not uncommon. If *B* calls *D* and vice versa, the subprograms are mutually recursive. Allowing for such dependencies is one of the reasons that program units may be formed by a separate declaration and body.

This problem presents a number of interesting dependency issues. Dependencies among units in the program library define a partial ordering. This partial ordering determines a set of one or more total orderings. Each total ordering defines a legal order in which all units of the program library may be recompiled or elaborated. If such a partial ordering does not exist, then, by definition, the dependencies are illegal. Finally, creating unnecessary dependencies is considered bad Ada style because it increases coupling and restricts the partial ordering, and thus the adaptability, of the program library.

A Related Problem: Are the following compilation units legal?

procedure Myself **is** ...

with Myself;
procedure Myself **is** ...

[Ada83]   10.1(3 .. 6); 10.1.1(1, 6); 10.5(5)
[ARG]   AI-00418/06, 08-06-87

20.3.4 Redundant Visibility

difficulty: language lawyer

Are the following compilation units legal?

```
with Text_Io;
with Text_Io, Text_Io;
procedure P;

with Calendar;
package Q is ... end Q;

with Calendar;
package body Q is
   procedure R is separate;
end Q;

with Q, Calendar;
separate (Q)
procedure R is ...
```

◇◇◇◇◇

All of the compilation units are legal.

Any number of with-clauses may appear at the beginning of a compilation unit. Furthermore, these clauses may name a unit more than once. Naming a unit more than once within the with-clauses of a unit has the same effect as naming it once. Thus, the declaration of *P* is legal.

The with-clause before the declaration of *Q* makes the package *Calendar* visible to the body of *Q*. Thus, the namings of *Calendar* in with-clauses before the body of *Q* and the subunit *R* are redundant and have no effect, but are legal. This is not to imply that these latter clauses are considered bad Ada style: such clauses can provide a quick reference to the units needed by a body.

The naming of *Q* in the with-clause before the subunit *R* presents an interesting case focusing on dependencies and their effect on elaboration. The subunit *R* would be dependent on Q even if no with-clause appeared before the body of R. However, the language requires that units named in the context clause of a subunit be elaborated before the body of the ancestor of the subunit. Since Q is the ancestor of R, it appears that Q must be elaborated before itself. This, of course, is impossible. Either of two possibilities must then hold: (1) the with-clause before the subunit is illegal, or (2) a new interpretation of the language is needed. The second possibility has been chosen by the Ada Rapporteur Group. The binding interpretation of the language is that a compilation unit must be elaborated *no later* than itself.

A Related Problem: Can it ever be the case that a unit named in a with-clause of a declaration is not actually needed by the corresponding body?

[Ada83]   8.6(2); 10.1.1(2 .. 5, 8); 10.2(6); 10.5(2)
[ARG]   AI-00113/12, 05-23-88

20.4 COMPILATION AND THE MAIN PROGRAM

A file submitted to an Ada compiler is called a *compilation*. A compilation can include any number of compilation units. A main program is a compilation unit that may be executed directly. This section examines the notion of a compilation, focusing on on the semantics of including more than one compilation unit per compilation and the differences between a main program and other forms of compilation units.

20.4.1 Compilation versus Compilation Unit

difficulty: designer

Consider the three compilations:

Compilation 1	*Compilation 2*	*Compilation 3*
procedure Q;	**procedure** R;	**with** P, R;
procedure P;	**procedure** R (Int : **in** Integer);	**procedure** X **is**
		begin
		P; R (4);
		end X;

If compilation 1 were submitted, and then compilation 2, would the third compilation be legal?

◇◇◇◇◇

The answer to this question is implementation dependent.

Multiple compilation units may be submitted together, forming a single compilation. For example, the declarations of two different units may appear in the same file, which is then submitted in its entirety to the compiler. The foregoing compilations focus on the result of a compilation when some of the units are illegal or are duplicates.

The declaration of *P* is legal, but appears in the same compilation as the illegal declaration of *Q*. Must an implementation be required to add the declaration of *P* to the program library? The language does not constrain the error recovery strategy of an implementation. Therefore, an implementation can choose to regard the entire compilation as illegal and, thus, not alter the program library. Given a compilation containing a number of legal units and at least one illegal unit, an implementation can selectively and arbitrarily add the legal units to the program library. In general, this is an Ada library implementation issue and not an Ada language issue.

Similarly, in the second compilation, the first declaration of *R* may be added to the library and then replaced by the second declaration, the first declaration may be accepted and the second rejected, or the entire compilation may be rejected. In general, any compilation that contains multiple definitions for a single compilation unit may be accepted (or rejected) in whole or in part. If a later unit is replacing an earlier one, then any units dependent on the earlier unit are made obsolete. The third compilation will be legal only when *P* and the second declaration of *R* are added to the program library.

[Ada83]   10.1(1); 10.3(3, 8); 10.4(1 .. 2)
[ARG]   AI-00255/07, 06-15-88; AI-00507/03, 11-04-88

20.4.2 What Can Be a Compilation Unit?

difficulty: programmer

Suppose that the program library contains only the predefined units and that each of the following units is compiled separately:

```
procedure P;

procedure Q is ...

package body R is ...

function "+" (L, R : in Integer) return Float;

with Text_Io;
package Int_Io is new Text_Io.Integer_Io (Integer);

with Text_Io;
procedure Writeln (S : in String) renames Text_Io.Put_Line;
```

Which of these units are legal?

◇◇◇◇◇

The library units *P*, *Q*, and *Int_Io* are legal.
   A compilation unit can be

- a subprogram, package, or generic unit declaration,
- a subprogram, package, or generic unit body,
- a subunit, or
- a generic instantiation.

   The body of procedure *Q* is legal. Since a declaration for this procedure does not appear in the program library, the body of *Q* forms a library unit. Note that this is the only case in which a syntactic entity that is a secondary unit may form a library unit. The body of package *R* is semantically illegal, because a declaration for the package does not exist in the program library. Unlike a subprogram body, a package body can never form a library unit.
   Operators cannot be used as the designator of a compilation unit. For example, an addition function cannot be used to form a library unit or a subunit. Note that since library units are not overloadable, allowing operators to be library units would be of limited utility in any case.
   The instantiation of *Integer_Io* forms a library unit named *Int_Io*. The renaming of *Put_Line* to *Writeln* does not form a subprogram, but rather provides an alias to an existing subprogram. Note the semantic difference between a generic instantiation and a renaming declaration. The instantiation defines a new entity, while a renaming declaration only provides a new name for an existing entity.

[Ada83]   8.5(7); 10.1(2 .. 3, 6, 10)

20.4.3 Recompiling a Unit

difficulty: novice

If the following three units were submitted for compilation separately and in the order specified, could the procedure *Main* then be executed? If so, what will it print?

```
with  Text_Io;
procedure  P  is
begin
   Text_Io.Put_Line  ("hello");
end  P;

with  P;
```

```
procedure Main is
begin
  P;
end Main;

with Text_Io;
procedure P is
begin
  Text_Io.Hello ("world");   -- Illegal.
end P;
```

◇◇◇◇◇

The procedure *Main* can be executed and will print *hello*.

This program illustrates that an illegal compilation does not affect the program library. The second body of *P* would replace the first if it were legal. Since the second body is illegal, the first remains in the program library and can be called by *Main*.

[Ada83]   10.3(3, 5); 10.4(2)

20.4.4 Library Unit versus Secondary Unit

difficulty: designer

Suppose that the program library initially contains only the predefined units and that each of the following units is compiled separately and in the order specified:

```
procedure P is ...

procedure P (C : in Character) is ...

procedure Q;

procedure Q (C : in Character);

generic
procedure R (Int : in Integer);

with R;
procedure Nr is new R;

procedure Nr (F : in Float) is ...

procedure R (F : in Float) is ...
```

```
with Calendar;
function F (Time : in Calendar.Time) return Integer is ...

function F (Time : in Calendar.Time) return Integer is ...
```

Which of these units are legal?

◇◇◇◇◇

Both bodies of P, both declarations of Q, the declaration of R, both units Nr, and the first body of F are legal.

The body of a subprogram that is a compilation unit forms a library unit if

- it is not a subunit,
- the program library does not contain a subprogram declaration with the same name, and
- the program library does not contain a generic subprogram declaration with the same name.

The compilations of both bodies of P form new library units, since the declaration of a subprogram is optional and, when it is absent, the body or body stub acts as the declaration. Syntactically, a secondary unit is simply a body that is a compilation unit. The second body of P simply replaces the library unit formed by the first. Similarly, the second declaration of Q simply replaces the first, so the compilations of both declarations are legal.

The simple names of all library units must be unique. The declaration of R defines a new library unit. Any subsequent secondary unit with the designator R must conform to this declaration. Thus, the body of R is semantically illegal. Note the subtle error in [Ada83, §10.1(6)]: generic subprogram declarations are not accounted for in this explanation. Compiling a subprogram body does not form a new library unit if there already exists in the library a generic subprogram with the same designator.

The instantiation of R declares both a subprogram (an instance) and a library unit (an instantiation). The library unit (the instantiation named Nr) is not itself a subprogram: generic instantiations and subprograms are disjoint forms of library units. The declaration of Nr creates an instance of R that is a subprogram. The second declaration of Nr is legal: it forms a library unit, since no subprogram declaration with the same name exists in the library, although an instantiation named Nr is present. The instantiation and instance are replaced by the second declaration of Nr.

The first function F forms a library unit. No declaration of F is entered into the program library, although the body of F is entered and its specification acts as its declaration. The second body of F is also treated as a library unit. This second body is then illegal, simply because the name *Calendar.Time* is not visible. Redefinitions of library units do not inherit the context clauses of the units they replace.

Consider another example involving library unit declarations (compiled separately):

```
package P is end P;

procedure P is ...
```

In this case, the procedure *P* (a library unit) replaces the package declaration in the program library.

[Ada83]   6.3(3); 10.1(3 .. 6); 12.2(1)
[ARG]   AI-00199/06, 07-23-86; AI-00225/09, 07-23-86; AI-00507/03, 11-04-88

20.4.5 What Can Be a Main Program?

difficulty: programmer

Which of the following subprograms may be used as *main programs*?

```
generic
procedure Gp;

with Gp;
procedure Main_1 is new Gp;

function Main_2 return Integer;
function Main_3 (N : in Natural) return String;

procedure Main_4;
procedure Main_5 (Int :      out Integer;
                  S   :      out String);
procedure Main_6 (Int : in       Integer;
                  S   : in out String);

package Pack is
   procedure Main_7;
end Pack;
```

◇◇◇◇◇

Procedures *Main_1* and *Main_4* can always be used as main programs. An implementation may allow *Main_2*, *Main_3*, *Main_5*, and *Main_6* to be used as main programs.
    A main program is a subprogram that is a library unit. A careful reading of [Ada83] would seem to indicate that the instantiation *Main_1* is a library unit but is not a subprogram. Rather, it would appear that *Main_1* declares a subprogram that is not itself a library unit. But this is clearly counterintuitive. The Ada Rapporteur Group has interpreted [Ada83] such that *Main_1* is a library unit as well as a subprogram and, thus, may be used as a main program.

An implementation must allow a parameterless procedure to be a main program. Furthermore, an implementation may choose to allow other forms of library subprograms to be main programs. The language does not require an implementation to accept *Main_2*, *Main_3*, *Main_5*, and *Main_6* as main programs, but does not prohibit their use as main programs.

A main program is a subprogram that is called by an *environment task* to initiate the execution of a program. The main program is not itself a task. The means by which the environment task calls the main program is an environment issue, not a language issue.

Main_7 cannot be used as a main program: although it is a subprogram, it is not a library unit.

[Ada83]   10.1(8)
[ARG]   AI-00199/08, 07-23-86; AI-00513/08, 11-04-88

20.4.6 The Return of the Main Program

difficulty: designer

Can a main program return before all *library tasks* have terminated?

◇◇◇◇◇

A library task is a task whose master is a library package. For example, any task that is declared immediately within the declarative part of a library package is a library task. Library tasks are dependent not on the main program, but rather, on the environment task (the task that calls the main program). The main program may return before library tasks have terminated, whereas the environment task must wait for them to terminate. In a conventional environment, the environment task is simply a process created by the operating system.

[Ada83]   9.4(13); 10.1(8)
[ARG]   AI-00222/08, 10-29-87; AI-00399/14, 06-16-89

20.5 BODY STUBS AND SUBUNITS

Not only is Ada a strongly typed language, but it preserves strong typing across compilation units. Separate compilation simplifies the development of large programs by partitioning pieces of an Ada program into separately compilable units. The power of being able to change parts of a program, preserving strong typing, without recompiling all other units can be realized in Ada. This section presents the features of Ada that allow a user to compile units separately, while minimizing the recompilations required when changes are made.

20.5.1 Specifying Subunits

difficulty: programmer

Compile the following units separately. Which units are legal?

```
package P is end P;
package body P is
   procedure Q is separate;
end P;
```

```
separate (Standard.P);
procedure Q;
procedure Q is ...
```

◇◇◇◇◇

The declaration and body of *P* are legal. The attempt to define the subunit *Q* results in a number of syntactic errors.

The body of package *P* contains a body stub for the procedure *Q*. Since a declaration of *Q* does not precede the body stub, the body stub provides an implicit declaration of *Q*. A body stub is a later declarative item and may be used to compile the body of a program unit separately. A subunit is the compilation unit that defines the proper body associated with a body stub.

The syntactic form of a subunit is as follows:

```
subunit      ::=  separate (parent_unit_name) proper_body
proper_body  ::=  subprogram_body | package_body | task_body
```

Note that there is no semicolon following the parenthesized parent unit name. Also, the first identifier of the parent unit name must be a library unit. Since *Standard* is not a library unit, the name *Standard.P* is semantically illegal. A *proper_body* cannot be a declaration. The following is a legal subunit for *Q*:

```
separate (P)
procedure Q is ...
```

The reason why no semicolon follows the parent unit name is subtle. Remember that the semicolon is a delimiter. As such, it is used to delimit adjacent declarations, statements, pragmas, or clauses. Since

```
separate (parent_unit_name)
```

is none of these, a semicolon does not apply. The "separate" token, the parentheses, and the parent unit name are simply parts of the syntactic production *subunit* and do not stand by themselves.

Note that although a task cannot be a library unit, the body of a task can form a compilation unit when appearing as a subunit. For example, the following code defines one library unit and two compilation units:

```
procedure  P  is
   task  T;
   task  body  T  is  separate;
begin
   null;
end  P;

separate  (P)
task  body  T  is  ...
```

Finally, an implementation is allowed arbitrarily and selectively to require that the *complete body* of a generic unit appear in the same compilation as the generic declaration. The complete body of a unit includes any subunits of the body, in a transitive manner.

[Ada83]   3.9(2); 10.1(2); 10.2(1 .. 3, 5); 10.3(9)

20.5.2 The Parent Unit

difficulty: programmer

Are the following compilations legal?

```
procedure  A  is  separate;

separate  (Standard)
procedure  A  is  ...

procedure  P  is
   procedure  Q  is
      procedure  R  is  separate;
   ⋮
end  P;
```

◇◇◇◇◇

All of the compilations are illegal.

A body stub may appear only immediately within a declarative part of a compilation unit body. Note that [Ada83, §10.2(3)] seems to imply that a body stub may also appear immediately within the declarative part of a library package. However, since later declarative items cannot appear within package specifications, and a body stub is a later declarative item, placing a body stub in a package specification is syntactically illegal. The [Ada83] wording is simply incorrect. Nonetheless, although it may be misleading, it is innocent due to the independent syntactic restriction.

A body stub is not a compilation unit. For this reason, the body stub of *A* is illegal. Also, since the predefined package *Standard* is not a library unit, it cannot be named as the parent unit (or ancestor unit) of a subunit. Therefore, the subunit *A* is semantically illegal.

The body stub of procedure *R* is semantically illegal because its parent, *Q*, is not a compilation unit. Body stubs cannot be declared within nested declarative parts.

A Related Problem: When can a body stub appear in a block statement?

[Ada83]   10.2(3, 5)

20.5.3 Conformance

difficulty: designer

Are the following compilation units legal?

```
package P is
   procedure Q (X : in Standard.Integer);
end P;

package body P is
   package Stnd renames Standard;
   procedure Q (X : in Integer) is separate;
end P;

separate (P)
procedure Q (X : in Stnd.Integer) is ... end Q;
```

◇◇◇◇◇

The compilation units are all legal. Three specifications for the subprogram *Q* are given:

   1. in a declaration
   2. in a body stub
   3. in a subunit.

The specifications of a declaration and its corresponding body stub must conform. Likewise, the specifications of a body stub and its corresponding subunit must conform. In the foregoing example, both pairs of specifications do conform. The specification in the declaration and that in the subunit of Q do not conform; however, the language does not require this pair of specifications to conform.

[Ada83]   6.3(3); 6.3.1(3); 10.2(4)
[ARG]   AI-00241/07, 06-16-89

20.5.4 Family Trees

difficulty: designer

Are the following compilation units legal? Suppose they are compiled separately.

```
procedure P is
   procedure A is separate;                        -- A_p
   procedure B is separate;                        -- B_p
   procedure Q (C : in Character) is separate;     -- Q_c
   procedure Q (B : in Boolean) is separate;       -- Q_b
   ⋮
end P;


separate (P)
procedure A is                                     -- A_p
   procedure Q (Int : in Integer) is separate;     -- Q_int
   ⋮
end A;


separate (P)
procedure B is                                     -- B_p
   procedure Q (F : in Float) is separate;         -- Q_f
   ⋮
end B;


separate (P)
procedure Q (C : in Character) is                  -- Q_c
   procedure A is separate;                        -- A_q
   ⋮
end Q;


separate (P)
procedure Q (B : in Boolean) is                    -- Q_b
   procedure B is separate;                        -- B_q
```

$\vdots$

end Q;

◇◇◇◇◇

The procedure *P* is semantically illegal, since it specifies two body stubs with the same name. *P* is an ancestor library unit, that is, a library unit whose secondary unit contains body stubs. The names of all subunits with the same ancestor library unit must be unique. This restriction is similar to the restriction that all library unit names must be unique. These rules simplify the design and implementation of the program library.

If a body stub appears within a secondary unit of a library unit, then the library unit is the ancestor and the parent of the corresponding subunit. The parent unit of a subunit is simply the unit in which the corresponding body stub appears. Furthermore, the ancestor of any subunit is the ancestor of its parent.

The set of compilation units corresponds to the (illegal) compilation tree shown in Figure 20.1.

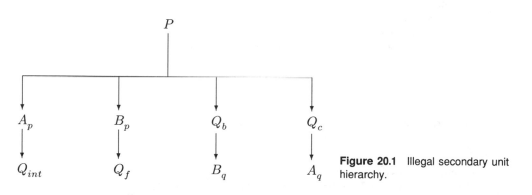

Figure 20.1   Illegal secondary unit hierarchy.

The reader might question the severity of requiring unique names for the subunits of a given ancestor library unit. Overloading is not defined for subunits, since the implementation might then be quite complex. For example, suppose the compilation tree in Figure 20.2 were legal. Then the subunits of both of the units *C* would take the form

separate (P.Q)
procedure C (...) **is** ...

Determining which parent unit *Q* the preceding subunit applied to would require conformance checking on specifications appearing in different scopes. Since the specifications of the units *C* appear in different scopes, they may have the same parameter and result type profile. In such a case, it would not be possible to determine which parent is referred to by the subunit. The language restriction that requires each ancestor to have subunits with distinct simple names eliminates such complexity. Note, however, that

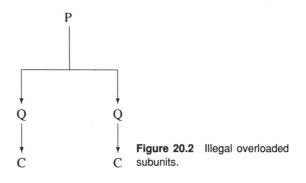

Figure 20.2 Illegal overloaded subunits.

renaming can be used to provide overloaded names for subunits of the same ancestor library unit:

```
procedure Parent is
   procedure Child_1 is separate;
   procedure Child_2 (X : in Integer) is separate;
begin
   declare
      procedure P renames Child_1;
      procedure P (X : in Integer) renames Child_2;
   begin
      P;         -- Call to Child_1.
      P (1);     -- Call to Child_2.
   end;
end Parent;
```

[Ada83]   10.2(5, 8)
[ARG]   AI-00297/06, 06-16-89; AI-00482/04, 11-04-88

20.6 COMPILATION DEPENDENCIES

There are a number of means by which a dependency can be formed between compilation units. These dependencies and the recompilation of units determine when units become *obsolete*, that is, when they must be recompiled. This section explains the circumstances under which units become obsolete.

20.6.1 Forced Recompilations

difficulty: programmer

What are the sets of units that must be recompiled when

- an ancestor library unit
- the secondary unit of an ancestor library unit
- a parent unit
- a subunit

is recompiled?

◇◇◇◇◇

A *complete body* is here considered to be a secondary unit and all subunits that are descendants of the secondary unit. If an ancestor library unit is recompiled, then the complete body of this unit is *potentially affected* and may need to be recompiled. In addition, whenever a library unit is recompiled, any units that name this library unit in a with-clause are potentially affected. *Potentially affected* defines a transitive relation: any units dependent on a potentially affected unit are themselves potentially affected.

If the secondary unit of a library unit is recompiled, only the subunits forming the complete body of the library unit are potentially affected, excluding generic units and instantiations. A parent unit is always a secondary unit. When a parent unit is recompiled, only the subunits forming the complete body of this unit are potentially affected. The same situation exists for subunits, since they are also secondary units.

An implementation is allowed to determine, from the set of potentially affected units, a subset called the *actually affected* units. The language allows an implementation to require recompilation of only the actually affected units. An actually affected unit is one that becomes illegal when another unit is recompiled. Some recompilations might be *upwardly compatible*; that is, the change made to the recompiled unit has no effect on the semantics of dependent units. For example, if the code

```
type Extended_Mode is (Input_File, Output_File, Append_File);

procedure Append (File  : in out File_Type;
                  Mode : in       Extended_Mode;
                  Name : in       String;
                  Form : in       String := "");
```

were added to the specification of Text_Io, then the complete body of Text_Io is potentially and actually affected. However, units that name Text_Io in a with-clause and do not name it in a use-clause are only potentially, and not actually, affected: for such units, an implementation need not force their recompilation. A simple example will illustrate this point:

```
with Text_Io;
procedure P is
begin
   Text_Io.Put_Line ("Hi.");
end P;
```

This procedure is only potentially affected by a change to the specification of Text_Io. The preceding hypothetical changes to Text_Io do not affect the legality of the unit. As an example of an actually affected unit, consider

```
package Q is
   Append : constant := 3;
end Q;

with Q, Text_Io;
use Q, Text_Io;
package R is
   X : constant := Append;
end R;
```

The legality of *R* is affected by the aforementioned changes to Text_Io: when compiled against an unmodified version of Text_Io, *R* is legal; when compiled against the extended version, *R* becomes illegal.

In general, the algorithm for determining the minimal set of actually affected units is nontrivial. For this reason, the language allows an implementation to require the recompilation of all potentially affected units.

Another method that the language allows an implementation to use in order to simplify the aforesaid algorithm involves generic units. An implementation is allowed to require that the declaration, body, and all subunits of a generic unit appear in the same compilation. For such an implementation, the only potentially affected units left to consider are those that name the generic unit in their with-clauses.

[Ada83]   10.3(5 .. 6, 8 .. 9)

20.6.2 Obsolescence

difficulty: novice

Submit the following units separately for compilation in the order specified. Without any further compilations, what will the execution of *Main* print?

```
package P is
   X : Integer := 1;
end P;

package body P is
begin
   X := 22;
end P;
```

```
package P is
   X, Y : Integer := 2;
end P;

with P, Text_Io;
procedure Main is
begin
   Text_Io.Put_Line ("Some like" & Integer'Image (P.X + P.Y));
end Main;
```

◇◇◇◇◇

Execution of the procedure *Main* will print *Some like 4*.

The successful compilation of a library unit replaces an existing library unit with the same name. Also, the complete body of the library unit that has been replaced becomes *obsolete*. An obsolete unit is identical to a potentially affected unit.

The foregoing illustrates a special case in which an obsolete unit is "automatically" replaced. The first two units add the library unit and the secondary unit of *P* to the program library. The compilation of the second declaration of *P* replaces the existing library unit. The secondary unit of *P* is then obsolete, but since it is not needed by the new declaration, it is treated as actually affected. (It is not needed because the new package declaration does not contain subprogram or task declarations, or incomplete type declarations whose full declarations are not provided.) Further, an implicit, empty package body replaces the obsolete secondary unit in the program library.

A Related Problem: Can recompilation of the body of a nongeneric unit make other library units obsolete?

[Ada83]   10.3(5, 16)
[ARG]   AI-00400/06, 03-11-87

20.6.3 Contract Violation

difficulty: designer

Consider the following compilation units:

```
generic
   type T is private;
package Gp is
   procedure P;
end Gp;

package body Gp is
   X : T;
```

```
    procedure P is begin null; end P;
  end Gp;

  with Gp;
  package Np is new Gp (T => String);
```

In both of the following cases, begin with the program library containing only the predefined units. Then compile the preceding units in the order specified. For both cases, which units are legal?

  1. declaration of *Gp*, instantiation *Np*, body of *Gp*
  2. declaration of *Gp*, body of *Gp*, instantiation *Np*

◇◇◇◇◇

For both cases, the legality of the units is implementation dependent. In the first, an implementation may

  • successfully compile all three units, but not allow the instantiation to be elaborated,
  • accept the declaration and instantiation, but reject the body, or
  • accept the declaration and body, but reject the instantiation.

In the second case, an implementation may

  • successfully compile all three units, but not allow the instantiation to be elaborated, or
  • accept the declaration and body, but reject the instantiation.

Clearly, the language provides much leeway here.

This example illustrates the difficulty in assessing the legality of a compilation unit with respect to other units. [Ada83, §10.3] would seem to indicate that the instantiation of *Gp* is dependent only on the declaration, and not the body, of *Gp*. Likewise, the body of *Gp* would seem to be dependent only on its declaration, and not the instantiation. These are the only dependencies created by some implementations. Other implementations may, and are allowed to, define a dependency between the body of a generic unit and any units in which that generic unit is instantiated.

The creation of a dependency between *Np* and the body of *Gp* is a double-edged sword. On the one hand, a clever implementation can allow recompilation of the body of *Gp* without the subsequent recompilation of *Np*. On the other hand, checking the legality of *Np* against the body of *Gp* can be quite difficult. The language allows an implementation flexibility in performing this complex legality check by creating a dependency between complete bodies of generic units and instantiations thereof.

An implementation may require that the declaration and the complete body of a generic unit be compiled in a single compilation. If an instantiation and a generic body appear in the same compilation, an implementation is not allowed to reject the instantiation solely because it appears lexically before the complete body of the generic unit.

Consider an implementation that imposes no restrictions on either separate compilation or order of compilation for generic units and instantiations. In case number 1 specified above, an implementation may take one of two actions. First, when the body of *Gp* is compiled, the instantiation becomes illegal. An implementation may handle illegal units in a number of ways. It may simply not allow *Np* to be elaborated. Alternatively, it may mark *Np* as obsolete and remove it from the library. The second possible action is that the body of *Gp* is rejected because it is illegal with respect to a unit already in the library.

Case number 2 above is very similar to case number 1. An implementation may successfully compile all three units, but not allow elaboration of *Np*. (A common method of preventing elaboration is to issue an error message when linking a main program that is dependent on *Np*.) Alternatively, the compilation of *Np* can be rejected, since it is illegal with respect to the previously compiled body of *Gp*.

In writing a generic package specification, if one foresees the need for declaring hidden variables of a generic formal private type, then one may circumvent the dependency issues discussed here simply by declaring such a variable within the specification of the generic unit. An example would be if the declaration of *Gp* were altered as follows:

```
generic
   type T is private;
package Gp is
   procedure P;
private
   Renegotiate : T;
end Gp;
```

A Related Problem: If one compiles a declaration of a generic unit that does not require a body, and then an instantiation of the unit, must the instantiation be accepted?

[Ada83]   10.3; 10.4(2); 12.3.2(4)
[ARG]   AI-00256/23, 06-16-88; AI-00257/04, 07-23-86; AI-00328/08, 03-16-87;
             AI-00408/11, 08-20-87; AI-00506/07, 06-12-90; AI-00602/01, 07-10-89

20.6.4 Dependencies for Generic Units

difficulty: designer

Compile the following units in the given order:

```
generic
procedure Gp;

with Text_Io;
procedure Gp is
begin
   Text_Io.Put_Line ("Alpha");
end Gp;

with Gp;
procedure Main is
   procedure P is new Gp;
begin
   P;
end Main;

with Text_Io;
procedure Gp is
begin
   Text_Io.Put_Line ("Beta");
end Gp;
```

Without any further compilation, can *Main* be elaborated and executed? If so, what will it print?

◇◇◇◇◇

The answer to this question is implementation dependent.

Suppose an implementation imposes no restrictions regarding separate compilation for generic units and instantiations. (If it does, see Section 20.6.3 for an answer.) An implementation is allowed to create a dependency between the body of a generic unit and a unit that instantiates the generic unit. That is, when the body of a generic unit is compiled, an implementation is allowed to remove from the program library any units that instantiate this generic unit. Note that the creation of such a dependency is allowed, but not required.

Now consider the case where a dependency between the body of *Gp* and *Main* is created. Then execution of the program is not allowed until the body of *Main* has been recompiled. Next, consider the case where no such dependency exists. Then the recompilation of *Main* cannot be required. However, in this case, the elaboration of the instantiation of *Gp* must create a subprogram (the instance of *Gp*) that corresponds to the body of *Gp* currently in the library. In either case, when *Main* is executed, *Beta* must be printed.

[Ada83]   10.3(6, 8)
[ARG]   AI-00408/11, 08-20-87; AI-00530/04, 06-16-88

20.7 ELABORATION OF PROGRAM UNITS

The elaboration of a program unit must occur before the unit is executed. Elaboration can be thought of as the process of registering the effect of declarations. The effects of elaboration include the evaluation of initialization expressions and the execution of the sequence of statements at the end of a package body. This section is concerned with the order in which elaborations occur, rather than the actual effects of elaboration, which are discussed in other chapters.

20.7.1 Order of Elaboration

difficulty: programmer

Compile the following units in the order specified:

```
package  P  is  end  P;
package  Q  is  end  Q;

with  Text_Io;
pragma  Elaborate  (Text_Io);
package body  P  is
   function  "="  (L,  R  :  in  Text_Io.Count)  return  Boolean
      renames  Text_Io."=";
begin
   if  Text_Io.Col  /=  1  then
      Text_Io.Put  (",  ");
   end  if;
   Text_Io.Put  ("Top  of  the  world");
end  P;
with  Text_Io;
pragma  Elaborate  (Text_Io);
package body  Q  is
   function  "="  (L,  R  :  in  Text_Io.Count)  return  Boolean
      renames  Text_Io."=";
begin
   if  Text_Io.Col  /=  1  then
      Text_Io.Put  (",  ");
   end  if;
   Text_Io.Put  ("Ma");
end  Q;

with  P,  Q,  Text_Io;
procedure  Main  is
begin
   Text_Io.Put_Line  ("!");
end  Main;
```

What will the program print?

◇◇◇◇◇

The program may print either

    Ma, Top of the world!

or

    Top of the world, Ma!

The units directly needed by a library unit are those which are

- named in a with-clause of the declaration of the library unit,
- named in a with-clause of the body of the library unit,
- named in a with-clause of a subunit for which the library unit is the ancestor, and
- part of the complete body of the library unit.

In addition, the units indirectly needed by the library unit are those which are directly or indirectly needed by the foregoing units. (*Needed by* defines a transitive relation.)

The units needed by a main program must be elaborated before the execution of the main program begins. The focus of the preceding program is the order in which these units are elaborated. Since the pragma *Elaborate* appears before the bodies of *P* and *Q*, *Text_Io* must be elaborated before either of these packages is. However, the order in which *P* and *Q* are elaborated is indeterminate. If *Q* is elaborated before *P*, then the first line above will be printed. Otherwise, the second line will be printed. Because *P* and *Q* are elaborated in some order not defined by the language, and because the effect of the program depends on this order, the program contains an incorrect order dependency. An implementation may raise Program_Error if it is able to detect this dependency.

Note that *P* and *Q* cannot be elaborated in parallel. This restriction assures that some lines, such as the following, cannot be printed:

    Top of the Maworld!

The use of the *Elaborate* pragma naming a predefined library unit cannot be ignored. This is not true for user-defined library units. For example, naming the package *P* in such a pragma may have no effect. Generic units are one way of removing an indeterminate order of elaboration. For example, if packages *P* and *Q* were made generic, and the procedure *Main* were rewritten as

```
with  P, Q, Text_Io;
procedure Main is
   package Np is new P;
   package Nq is new Q;
```

```
begin
   Text_Io.Put_Line  ("!");
end  Main;
```

then execution of the program would always print

Top of the world, Ma!

The elaboration of an instantiation includes the elaboration of the created unit, including its body. Since elaboration within a single declarative region is linear, the body of *Np* is elaborated before the body of *Nq* is.

[Ada83]   1.6(8 .. 10); 10.5
[ARG]   AI-00354/03, 12-01-86; AI-00355/06, 12-01-86

20.7.2 Elaboration of Subunits

difficulty: novice

Compile the following units in the order specified:

```
package Outer is
   type Text is access String;
   T : Text := new String'("");
   package P is end P;
end Outer;

package body Outer is
   package body P is separate;
begin
   T := new String'(T.all & " pac Outer;");
end Outer;

separate (Outer)
package body P is
   package Q is end Q;
   package R is end R;
   package body Q is separate;
   package body R is separate;
begin
   T := new String'(T.all & " pac P;");
end P;

separate (Outer.P)
package body Q is
begin
```

```
      T := new String'(T.all & " pac Q;");
   end Q;


   separate (Outer.P)
   package body R is
   begin
      T := new String'(T.all & " pac R;");
   end R;


   with Text_Io, Outer;
   procedure Main is
      T : Outer.Text := new String'(Outer.T.all & " proc Main;");
   begin
      Text_Io.Put_Line (T.all);
   end Main;
```

What will the program print?

◇◇◇◇◇

The program will print

```
      pac Q; pac R; pac P; pac Outer; proc Main;
```

The subunits of a unit are elaborated in the order in which their body stubs appear in the parent unit. If a body stub were replaced with an actual body, the effect of the program would be the same. As this example indicates, when nesting units, elaboration occurs from innermost to outermost scope, i.e., in a postorder fashion.

[Ada83]   10.2(7); 10.5(1 .. 2)

20.7.3 Handling Elaboration Exceptions

difficulty: programmer

Compile the following units in a legal order:

```
package P1 is                       package body P1 is
   function F return Integer;           function F return Integer is
end P1;                                 begin
                                           return 42;
                                        end F;
                                     end P1;


                                     with P1;
package P2 is                        package body P2 is
```

```
      function F return Integer;        X : constant Integer := P1.F;
      end P2;                           function F return Integer is
                                        begin
                                           return X;
                                        end F;
                                        end P2;
```

```
   with P2, Text_Io;
   procedure Main is
   begin
      Text_Io.Put_Line (Integer'Image (P2.F));
   exception
      when Program_Error => Text_Io.Put_Line ("Program_Error");
      when others        => Text_Io.Put_Line ("Not 11.6 again!");
   end Main;
```

What will the program print?

◇◇◇◇◇

The program will print either nothing or *42*.

    The elaboration of the declaration of the object X could raise Program_Error. The body of *P1* need not be elaborated before the body of *P2* is. In such a case, the function *P1.F* would be called before its body has been elaborated, and Program_Error would be raised. If Program_Error were raised during the elaboration of X, the main program could not be elaborated. The reason for this is that the exception is propagated to the environment task, which calls the main program, and *P2* is never completely elaborated; the main program cannot begin until *P2* has been elaborated.

    Several attempts have been made to eliminate the possibility that Program_Error is propagated. First, one might handle Program_Error internally:

```
   package body P2 is
      X : Integer;
      ⋮
   begin
      loop
         begin
            X := P1.F;
            exit;
         exception
            when Program_Error => delay 0.1;
         end;
      end loop;
   end P2;
```

But this method will not work, because units cannot be elaborated in parallel. If Program_Error is raised during the first iteration, it will be raised in every subsequent iteration.

Then one might use pragma Elaborate:

```
pragma Elaborate (P1);
package body P2 is ...
```

But this method is not guaranteed to work either: since *P1* is not a predefined library unit, an implementation is free to ignore the pragma.

Or, one could use generic units. One might make the package *P1* generic and instantiate it within the body of *P2*. This method is guaranteed by the language to prevent Program_Error from being raised and propagated.

Finally, one could eliminate *X* and have the function *P2.F* simply return *P1.F* directly. Such a method, however, will not work if *P1.F* returns a different value every time it is called.

As an aside, notice the subtle error in [Ada83, §10.5(1)]. A strict reading of this paragraph would indicate that the body of the main program is not elaborated before it is called by the environment task. Such a situation, of course, would result in Program_Error being raised by every program. Clearly, this was not the intent of the language: the main program is understood to be elaborated after the elaboration of all needed units, but before it is called.

[Ada83]   1.6(9); 3.9(3 .. 8); 10.5(1 .. 4)
[ARG]   AI-00158/05, 05-23-88

chapter 21

Scope and Visibility

Leave the beaten path occasionally and dive into the woods. You are certain to find something that you have never seen before.
Alexander Graham Bell

The scope of an entity in Ada is defined by the location of its declaration. A scope is a textual region where an entity has meaning. Within its scope, an entity may or may not be visible. Visibility defines a region where an entity can be named. An entity is visible only within its scope; thus, the visibility of an entity is a proper subset of its scope.

In Figure 21.1, the scope of each integer object begins at the start of its declaration and ends at the end of the innermost enclosing declarative region. Note that the scope of the outer object includes that of the inner one—that is, the two overlap. The direct visibility of the outer object comprises two disjoint regions:

1. the region immediately after the declaration of the outer object to the beginning of the declaration of the second object
2. the region immediately after the block statement to the end of the subprogram.

The direct visibility of the inner object is the same as its scope, except that it does not include the object declaration itself.

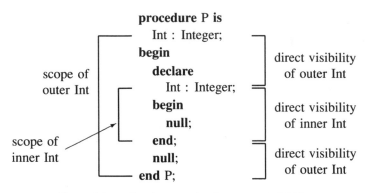

Figure 21.1 Simple example of scope and visibility.

21.1 SCOPE OF DECLARATIONS

Ada defines the scope of all declarations precisely. Typically, the scoping rules are intuitive, and programmers need not be too concerned with their intricate semantics. Programs in previous chapters all relied on Ada's scoping rules in order to present various semantics, but never really precisely defined the concepts of scope, immediate scope, and extended scope. In this section, we make the intuitive notion of scope more explicit and provide a basis for understanding the visibility rules presented in Section 21.2.

21.1.1 Scope Bindings

difficulty: designer

Can a predefined or basic operation ever have a scope that differs from that of its corresponding type declaration?

◇◇◇◇◇

No two entities in Ada have the same scope. Typically, the scope of an entity begins at the start of its declaration and continues throughout the declarative region enclosing the declaration. The basic and predefined operations associated with a type are implicitly declared immediately after the type declaration and thus do not include the type declaration itself. Private types can be used to emphasize this point:

```
package P is
   type T is private;
   ⋮
private
```

```
   type T is (Xyzzy, Qqsv);
end P;
```

The private type declaration and corresponding full declaration have the same scope; they are considered to be parts of a single declaration. Lexically, the scope of *T* starts at the beginning of the private type declaration. However, operations such as equality and membership are implicitly declared after the private type declaration, whereas other operations, such as enumeration literals, are declared after the corresponding full declaration.

A Related Problem: For the preceding enumeration type, do the scopes of its six relational operators differ? Do the scopes of both literals differ?

[Ada83]   3.3.3; 8.2(1 .. 2)

21.1.2 Kinds of Scope

difficulty: programmer

List the immediate and extended[1] scopes of the entities named in the following procedure. Also, name all the declarative regions present.

```
procedure P is
   type T is range 1 .. 2;

   task Tsk is
      entry E (Int : in Integer);
   end Tsk;

   procedure Q (J : in Integer) renames Tsk.E;

   task body Tsk is
   begin
      accept E (Int : in Integer);
   end Tsk;
begin
   L: loop null; end loop L;
end P;
```

◇◇◇◇◇

Figure 21.2 lists the immediate and extended scope of each explicitly named entity. The declarations of *P*, *Tsk*, *E*, and *Q* form declarative regions.

---

[1][Ada83, §8.2(2)] refers to this as a scope that extends beyond the immediate scope.

Entity	Immediate Scope	Extended Scope
P	From the beginning of its declaration until the end of the declarative region formed by package Standard.	None.
T	From the beginning of its declaration until the end of the declarative region formed by *P*.	None.
Tsk	From the beginning of its declaration until the end of the declarative region formed by *P*.	None.
E	From the beginning of its declaration until the end of the task declaration, and throughout the task body.	Those parts of the scope of *Tsk* which occur after the declaration of *E* and are not in the immediate scope of *E*.
Int	From the beginning of its declaration to the end of the entry declaration, and throughout all accept statements for *E*.	Those parts of the scope of *E* which occur after the declaration of *Int* and are not in the immediate scope of *Int*.
Q	From the beginning of its declaration until the end of the declarative region formed by *P*.	None.
J	From the beginning of its declaration to the end of the renaming declaration.	Those parts of the scope of *Q* which occur after the declaration of *J* and not are in the immediate scope of *J*.
L	From the beginning of its implicit declaration to the end of the declarative region formed by *P*.	None.

Figure 21.2   Immediate and extended scopes.

In order to understand scope, one must first understand the concept of a declarative region. A declarative region is a possibly noncontiguous portion of a program. Declarative regions are formed by (1) package, subprogram, task, and generic unit declarations together with their bodies and subunits; (2) entry declarations together with all corresponding accept statements; (3) block and loop statements; (4) renaming declarations that include formal parts; (5) generic parameter declarations that include formal or discriminant parts; and (6) record type declarations together with any corresponding private or incomplete declarations and representation clauses.

The scope of a declaration can be either *immediate* or *extended*. The immediate scope of a declaration starts at the beginning of the declaration and continues to the end of the innermost enclosing declarative region. Only certain kinds of declarations have an extended scope associated with them, namely, those appearing immediately within the visible part of a package; entry, component, and generic parameter declarations; and discriminant and parameter specifications. Each of these types of declaration appears immediately within an enclosing declaration:

- A package declaration encloses declarations appearing within its visible part.
- A task declaration encloses entry declarations.
- A record type declaration encloses component declarations.
- A generic unit declaration encloses generic parameter declarations.
- A record or private type declaration encloses discriminant declarations.
- A subprogram, entry, or renaming declaration encloses parameter declarations.

The extended scope of a declaration *d* is defined as those parts of the scope of its enclosing declaration which

- appear after *d* and
- are not included in the immediate scope of *d*.

The scope of a declaration is then the union of its immediate scope and its extended scope. Note that for the purpose of clarity, the preceding definition assumes that the immediate and extended scopes of a declaration are disjoint. A careful distinction between the immediate and the extended scope is made in order to define the language's visibility rules more accurately. For example, the extended scope is required to define the semantics of selected components, expanded names, and named associations. Also, note that the definition of extended scope is transitive in that the scope of a declaration is a function of the scope of its enclosing declaration. To illustrate, the use of the entry parameter *Int* in

```
Tsk.E (Int => 3);
```

is legal even outside the immediate scope of *E*, since the extended scope of *Int* includes portions of the extended scope of *E* and, thus, portions of the scope of *Tsk*.

A Related Problem: What is the difference between the uses of the terms *immediate* in [Ada83, §8.2(2)] and *immediately* in [Ada83, §9.7.2(1)]?

[Ada83]   8.1(1 .. 7, 9); 8.2(2 .. 9)
[ARG]   AI-00865/04, 12-13-90

21.1.3 Naming Scopes

difficulty: novice

Is the following code legal?

```
procedure P is
begin
  declare
    X : Integer;
  begin
    P.X := 4;
  end;
end P;
```

◇◇◇◇◇

The left-hand name used in the assignment statement is illegal.

An *expanded name* is formed by a prefix and a selector, separated by a dot. The prefix denotes the name of the declarative region in which the selector is declared. For example, in the name "Standard.Integer," "Standard" is the prefix and "Integer" is the selector. Note that the definition of a prefix is recursive, since the prefix may itself denote an expanded name. Conceptually, an expanded name is a list of names separated by dots. All but the last name in the list must denote declarative regions.

In this example, both the procedure and the block statement form declarative regions. The procedure is named, but the block statement is not. The name $P.X$ is illegal, as there does not exist an entity named X immediately within the scope formed by P. The expanded name could be made legal by naming the block and changing the prefix to include this name. Note that the prefix need not begin with the name of a library or compilation unit; it may begin with any directly visible declarative region. By uniquely naming (or renaming) all declarative regions, one is assured that each entity can be named anywhere within its scope.

[Ada83]   4.1.3(1 .. 2, 13 .. 18); 8.2(1 .. 2)

21.1.4 Subprogram Hiding

difficulty: programmer

Is the following code legal?

```
procedure Hide is
  procedure P (Int : in Integer) is ... end P;
begin
  declare
```

```
    procedure P (J : in Integer) is ... end P;
begin
    P (Int => 33);
    P (J  => 44);
end;
end Hide;
```

◇◇◇◇◇

The first subprogram call is illegal.

Since both procedures have the same parameter profile, within the scope of the inner *P*, the outer subprogram is hidden. The use of *Int* in the first call is illegal, since the call must conform to the specification of the inner subprogram. The outer subprogram can be called within the scope of the inner subprogram by using an expanded name:

```
Hide.P (Int => 33);
```

A Related Problem: Is the parameter *Int* visible at the point of the first subprogram call?

[Ada83]   6.6(1 .. 2); 8.3(1 .. 4, 14 .. 15)

21.1.5 Homographs

difficulty: programmer

Is the following package declaration legal?

```
package P is
    procedure P;
    generic procedure P (Int : in Integer);
end P;
```

◇◇◇◇◇

The declarations of the procedure and the generic subprogram form an illegal homograph.

A declaration is a *homograph* of another if both have the same identifier, operator symbol, or character literal, and

- Overloading is allowed for only one or neither of the declarations, or
- Overloading is allowed for both declarations, and both have the same parameter and result type profile.

Homographs appearing immediately within the same declarative region are illegal, unless one of them is the implicit declaration of a predefined operation or a derived subprogram. In the foregoing code, the subprogram is overloadable but the generic unit is not; thus, the two declarations form an illegal homograph. If the generic unit were removed, then the package *P* and the subprogram *P* would not form an illegal homograph, since they are declared in different declarative regions.

There are many forms of legal homographs, most of which involve one of the two declarations being hidden by the other. Section 21.1.4 gives an example of such a homograph. Another example is shown in the following:

```
with  Text_Io;
package  P  is
   use  Text_Io;
   Text_Io : File_Type;                     -- Legal.
   Mode    : Text_Io.Mode_Type;             -- Illegal.
   Open    : Boolean := Is_Open (Text_Io);  -- Legal.
end  P;
```

Within the immediate scope of the object *Text_Io*, the library unit by the same name is hidden. Nevertheless, the use clause makes those declarations appearing immediately within the visible part of package *Text_Io* directly visible inside package *P*.

Consider yet another example involving visibility within a context clause:

```
package  Q  is end  Q;
package  body  Q  is
   Text_Io : Integer;
   procedure R  is  separate;
end  Q;

with  Text_Io;
separate  (Q)
procedure R  is  ...
```

The compilation units are legal. The library package *Text_Io* is visible within the context clause associated with the body of *R*. However, within the declarative region formed by the body of *R*, the library package is hidden by the declaration *Q.Text_Io*.

A Related Problem: In what case can the declaration of two character literals form an illegal homograph? Can they ever form a legal homograph?

[Ada83]   6.6(1 .. 2); 8.3(15, 17); 10.1(3, 5)

21.1.6 Hiding Package Standard

difficulty: designer

What will the following program print?

```
package Standard is
   type Positive is new Integer;
   function "+" (Left, Right : in Positive) return Positive;
end Standard;

package body Standard is
   function "+" (Left, Right : in Positive) return Positive is
   begin
      return Right − Left;
   end "+";
end Standard;

with Text_Io, Standard;
procedure Main is
begin
   Text_Io.Put_Line (Standard.Positive'Image (Standard."+" (1, 2)));
   Text_Io.Put_Line (Standard.Standard.Positive'Image (
                  Standard.Standard."+" (1, 2)));
end Main;
```

◇◇◇◇◇

The program will not print anything, because the names *Standard.Standard.Positive'Image* and *Standard.Standard*."+" are illegal.

Within the scope of the user-defined package *Standard*, the predefined package by the same name is hidden. Since the user-defined package is named in a with-clause of procedure *Main*, it is directly visible within the declarative region formed by *Main*. As a consequence, *Main* is a part of the scope of the user-defined package *Standard*.

Within *Main*, the prefix *Standard* refers to the user-defined package. The prefix *Standard.Standard* is illegal, since no entity named *Standard* is declared within the user-defined package. The first name used in a prefix must be directly visible. For this reason, the first *Standard* in the prefix *Standard.Standard* does not refer to the predefined package.

The first call to *Put_Line* is legal and will print *1*, because the user-defined addition is called. Predefined addition could have been called as follows:

```
Text_Io.Put_Line (Positive'Image (1 + 2));
```

A Related Problem: In what declarative region is the predefined package Standard declared?

[Ada83]   4.1.3(13 .. 15); 8.3(15); 8.6(2 .. 3); 10.1.1(5)

21.1.7 Nesting

difficulty: novice

Is the following code legal?

```
function Int return Integer is
  Int : Float := 2.0;
begin
  return Int + 2;
end Int;
```

◇◇◇◇◇

The expression used in the return statement is illegal.

The function and the object form a legal homograph. Thus, within the scope of the object declaration, the name of the function is hidden. Since the return statement appears within this scope, the use of *Int* in the expression names the floating point object, and not the function. Following are two legal return statements:

```
return Standard.Int + 2;
return Integer (Int) + 2;
```

A Related Problem: Why is the last use of *Int*, as the ending designator, in the code at the beginning of this subsection legal?

[Ada83]   8.3(15)

21.1.8 Nested Accept Statements

difficulty: designer

Is the following code legal?

```
procedure Nested_Accepts is
  task T is
    entry X (Int : in out Integer);
    entry Y (Int : in out Integer);
    entry Z (Int : in out Integer);
  end T;
```

```
task body T is
begin
  accept X (Int : in out Integer) do
    accept Y (Int : in out Integer) do
      accept Z (Int : in out Integer) do
        Int := Y.Int;                      -- 1.
        Int := X.Y.Int;                    -- 2.
        Int := T.Y.Int;                    -- 3.
        Int := Nested_Accepts.T.X.Int;     -- 4.
      end Z;
    end Y;
  end X;
end T;
begin
  null;
end Nested_Accepts;
```

◇◇◇◇◇

Assignment statement number 2 is illegal.

Recall that the declarative region formed by an entry declaration includes its declaration and all corresponding accept statements. Furthermore, regardless of the positions of any accept statements in the body of a task, entries are declared immediately within the declarative region formed by the task declaration. As a consequence, nested accept statements form nested declarative regions, but naming of entities does not follow "normal" nested scope rules. For example, in the foregoing code, the name Y is not declared within the declarative region formed by X, even though a portion of the declarative region formed by Y overlaps a portion of the declarative region formed by X.

The preceding assignment statements are within the immediate scopes of all three entries. The left-hand names all denote the parameter associated with entry Z, since the declarative region formed by Z is the innermost region. At the point of the assignments, the other two parameters are hidden.

The right-hand expression of the first assignment is legal, since it appears within the scope of Y at a point where Y is not hidden and there exists an *Int* declared immediately within the declarative region formed by Y. The second right-hand expression is illegal, because Y is not declared within the declarative region formed by X. The third expression is legal, since there exists an *Int* declared immediately within Y and Y is declared immediately within T. The fourth expression is legal for a similar reason.

A set of special rules handles entry families used in expanded names. In the code

```
task T is
  entry E (Boolean) (Int : in out Integer);
end T;

task body T is
begin
```

```
    accept E (True) (Int : in out Integer) do
       Int := E (True).Int;   -- Illegal.
       Int := E.Int;          -- Legal.
    end E;
 end T;
```

the first assignment statement is illegal because an entry index cannot appear within the prefix of an expanded name.

A Related Problem: In the preceding example, what is the declarative region formed by *E (True)*?

[Ada83]   4.1.3(16 .. 17); 8.2(2, 4); 8.3(6, 13 .. 15); 9.5(1, 7 .. 8)
[ARG]   AI-00865/04, 12-13-90

21.2 GENERAL VISIBILITY RULES

Ada's visibility rules are based on those of other block-structured languages, such as Algol and Pascal. The Pascal-like rules are associated with the concept of *direct visibility*. Ada also defines the concept of *visibility by selection*. This section concentrates on the more complex visibility rules and presents the differences between direct visibility and visibility by selection.

21.2.1 Self-seeing

difficulty: programmer

Is the following package specification legal?

```
package Beauty_Within is
   type T1 is access T1;
   type T2 is access Beauty_Within.T2;
   type T3 is private;
   subtype S3 is T3;
private
   type T3 is access S3;
end Beauty_Within;
```

◇◇◇◇◇

The declarations of *T1* and *T2* are illegal.
    Within all declarations, except those of packages and generic packages, the identifier used to name a declared entity hides all other occurrences of the identifier; furthermore, the identifier is not visible within its own declaration.

Similarly to the concept of scope, visibility can be divided into two notions: *direct visibility* and *visibility by selection*. An entity is directly visible if it can be named without the use of an expanded name. If an entity can be named using an expanded name, the entity is said to be visible by selection.

T1 is not visible within its own declaration. Thus, the second occurrence of *T1* within the first type declaration is illegal. For a similar reason, the declaration of *T2* is illegal: inside this declaration, *T2* is visible neither directly nor by selection.

The declarations of *T3* and *S3* are legal. Subtypes of private types may be declared before the corresponding full declaration of the private type. Also, there is no language rule that prevents the full declaration of a private type from being an access type whose designated subtype is a subtype of itself. Note that there are specific language rules that prevent the full declaration of *T3* from being a composite type that includes components of the subtype *S3*.

The hiding that can occur within a declaration is emphasized in the following example:

```
package P is
   Int : constant := 434;
   type J is range 0 .. 10;
   package Q is
      type Int is range 0 .. Int;     -- Illegal.
      procedure J (X : in P.J);       -- Illegal.
   end Q;
end P;
```

A Related Problem: In what cases can an entity be directly visible, but not visible by selection?

[Ada83]   3.3(8); 8.3(5, 16, 22)
[ARG]   AI-00385/05, 11-04-88; AI-00392/06, 06-16-88

21.2.2 End Game

difficulty: novice

Is the following package legal?

```
package P is
   P : Boolean;
end P;
```

◇◇◇◇◇

The package is legal. At issue is the legality of the last use of the identifier *P*. This use is within the scope of the Boolean variable. Thus, does the third use of the *P* denote the Boolean variable or the package? While the Ada visibility rules are not defined accurately enough to answer this question, it is clearly the intent that the last use of *P* denote the package.

A Related Problem: What meaning do the visibility rules associate with the following use of the identifier *X*?

```
    X : Integer;
```

[Ada83]   8.1; 8.2(2); 8.3(1 .. 4)
[ARG]   AI-00253/01, 03-07-89

21.2.3 Tricky Expanded Names

difficulty: designer

Give the expanded names, beginning with package Standard, for the identifiers *Int* and *X* in the following program.

```
        procedure P is
        begin
          For_Loop:
          for Int in Integer loop
            Declare_Block:
            declare
              X : Integer;
            begin
               .
               .
               .
            end Declare_Block;
          end loop For_Loop;
        end P;
```

◇◇◇◇◇

The expanded names are *Standard.P.For_Loop.Int* and *Standard.P.Declare_Block.X*.

Statement labels and the names of loop and block statements are implicitly declared. The point of this program is to examine where these declarations occur. The declarations occur at the end of the declarative part of the innermost enclosing block statement or program unit body containing the statement name or label.

In this example, *For_Loop* and *Declare_Block* are declared at the end of the declarative part of procedure *P*. Therefore, to name these entities in an expanded name, the prefix must denote *P*. Note the distinction between the declaration of the entities and the use of the entities: although *Declare_Block* is used within the declarative region formed by *For_Loop*, it is declared within the declarative part of *P*.

A Related Problem: Where does the implicit declaration of *Int* occur in the above program?

[Ada83]   4.1.3(13, 16 .. 17); 5.1(3); 8.3(6, 13)

21.2.4 Visibility of Block Names and Labels

difficulty: designer

Is the following code legal?

```
procedure Labels is
   B : Boolean;
begin
   for L1 in Integer loop
      << L1 >> goto L1;
   end loop;

   for L2 in Integer loop
      declare
         X : Integer := L2;          -- 1.
      begin
         X := L2 + X;                -- 2.
         << L2 >> null;
      end;
   end loop;

   for L3 in Boolean loop
      B := L3;                       -- 3.

      begin
         B := L3;                    -- 4.
         L3: begin null; end L3;
         B := L3;                    -- 5.
      end;

      B := L3;                       -- 6.
   end loop;
end Labels;
```

◇◇◇◇◇

The goto statement and assignment statements 2, 4, and 5 are illegal.

The label *L1* is declared at the end of the declarative part of *Labels*. Since the loop index *L1* is declared in an inner declarative region, it hides the label. Thus, the name used in the goto statement denotes an integer object, not a label. The goto statement could be made legal by using an expanded name, e.g., *Labels.L1*.

The label *L2* is declared at the end of the declarative part of the block statement. Thus, within assignment 2, this name denotes the label rather than the loop index. For a similar reason, within the second block statement, the block name *L3* hides the loop index *L3*. Hence, assignments 4 and 5 are illegal.

This code illustrates some of the nonintuitive scoping rules of Ada. Assignments 2 and 4 are made illegal by subsequent code. This is one of the few areas of the language where one must read beyond a piece of code to determine the legality and meaning of that piece.

A Related Problem: In what other areas of the language must one read subsequent code in order to determine the legality of a prior piece of code?

[Ada83]   5.1(3); 8.1(1, 6); 8.3(15)

21.2.5 Hide-and-seek

difficulty: designer

Is the following code legal?

```
package P is
   type Color is (Red, Blue, Green, Yellow);
   function F return Color;

   generic procedure Proc;
end P;

with P;
package Q is
   function Color return P.Color;

   function F return P.Color;

   package Inner is
      generic
         X : in P.Color := F;
         Y : in P.Color := P.F;
         function F (Z : in P.Color := P.F) return Boolean;
      end Inner;
```

```
procedure Proc is new P.Proc;

function Func return Integer;
function Func (Par : in Integer := Q.Func) return Integer;
end Q;
```

◇◇◇◇◇

The declarations of function *Color*, the generic formal object *X*, the subprogram parameter *Z*, the instantiation *Proc*, and the subprogram parameter *Par* are illegal.

Within the specification of a subprogram, the designator of the subprogram hides all other uses of the designator. This semantics is intuitive, since the specification of a subprogram is a part of the declaration of the subprogram. The language, however, strengthens the effect of the hiding by also stating that, within the subprogram specification, other uses of the designator are not visible even by selection. The same rules hold for a generic instantiation that forms a subprogram. For these reasons, the declarations of the function *Color*, the instantiation *Proc*, and the second function *Func* are illegal.

The generic function *F* offers a considerably more interesting situation. The declaration of *F* includes its generic formal part. Throughout its declaration, *F* directly hides other entities named *F*. The declaration of the generic formal object *X* is illegal, since its default expression names the generic function itself. The declaration of *Y* illustrates how to name the function *P.F* within the generic formal part. This declaration may name *F*, since the declaration is within the generic formal part, but not within the specification, of the generic unit *F*. Finally, the declaration of the generic function *F* includes a subprogram specification. This specification must adhere to the aforementioned hiding rules. Specifically, the default expression for the subprogram parameter *Z* is illegal, since it names *F*.

The code

```
with Text_Io, P;  -- Package P is from the previous code.
package Few_More is
   function F return P.Color renames P.F;

   generic
      with procedure Put (C : in Character) is Text_Io.Put;
   procedure Get (C : out Character);

   package Integer_Io is new Text_Io.Integer_Io (Integer);
end Few_More;
```

is legal. The use of *P.F* in the renaming declaration is allowed, since *P.F* does not appear within the subprogram specification. Similarly, *Text_Io.Put* does not appear in the specification of the generic formal subprogram. Finally, the instantiation *Integer_Io* is legal, since it defines a package and is not restricted by the hiding rules associated with subprogram specifications.

[Ada83]   8.3(5, 16)
[ARG]   AI-00286/11, 06-18-87; AI-00370/06, 01-13-87

21.2.6 Names in Operations

difficulty: programmer

Is the following package specification legal?[2]

```
package P is
   package Inner is
      type T is new Integer;
      type A is access T;

      T_Obj : constant T := Inner.Mod (3, 4);
      A_Obj : constant A := Inner.Null;
   end Inner;

   X1 : constant Inner.T := T'(3);
   X2 : constant Boolean := 3 in T;
   X3 : constant Inner.A := null;
end P;
```

◇◇◇◇◇

All of the object declarations except that of *X3* are illegal.

Although reserved words are identifiers, they can never be used as declared identifiers. If the selector of an expanded name is a simple name, then the selector is required to be a declared identifier. The notions of scope and visibility simply do not apply to reserved words. For these reasons, the uses of *Mod* and *Null* in the first two declarations are illegal.

Qualification and membership are basic operations of every type. Basic operations are always directly visible. However, in order to formulate an expression using these operations, it is often necessary to name the corresponding type. The type marks used in the initialization expressions of *X1* and *X2* are not directly visible, even though the basic operations of the type *Inner.T* are.

The use of the reserved word **null** in the declaration of *X3* is not that of a declared identifier. The literal **null** is a basic operation of the type *A*, directly visible at the point of this declaration. In contrast, the use of *Null* in the declaration of *A_Obj* is that of a declared identifier, not that of a basic operation. Even though the literal **null** is implicitly

---

[2]This code was adapted from code presented by Dr. John B. Goodenough.

declared immediately after the declaration of *A*, it cannot be named using an expanded name. The same is true for all basic operations. For example, the following declaration is also illegal:

```
X4 : constant Inner.T := Inner.T'Inner.First;   -- Illegal.
```

[Ada83]   2.9(3); 3.3.3(6); 4.1(3); 4.4(2); 8.3(1, 18)
[ARG]   AI-00027/07, 06-18-87

21.2.7 In Search of Character Literals

difficulty: designer

Is the following program legal?

```
package Strings is
   type Char is ('a', 'b', 'c', 'd');
   type Str is array (Positive range <>) of Char;
end Strings;

with Strings;
package User is
   S : constant Strings.Str := Strings.Str'("abcd");
end User;
```

◇◇◇◇◇

The declaration of the object *S* is illegal: the character literals used are not directly visible.

There is a variety of ways in Ada to achieve direct visibility of entities declared within the visible part of a package. However, none of these methods, except the use clause, will work in the foregoing example.

String literals are basic operations and thus are always directly visible. Character literals are not basic operations; thus, the characters used inside a string literal must be directly visible. Note that the characters used in a string literal must be literals rather than identifiers. For example, in the following code, the declaration of *S* is also illegal:

```
function a return Strings.Char renames Strings.'a';   -- Legal.
S : constant Strings.Str := Strings.Str'("aaa");       -- Illegal.
```

A use clause is the only method of "importing" character literals and, thus, string literals. This example is often cited in defense of the use clause.

[Ada83]   3.3.3(3 .. 7); 4.2(3, 5); 8.3(14); 8.4(1)

21.3 THE USE CLAUSE

The package is Ada's fundamental unit of abstraction. The designers of the language felt that some succinct mechanism was required to import the entities exported by a package. The use clause was designed to serve this purpose. The use clause represents Ada's most general importation mechanism. This section presents some of the more complex semantics associated with this seemingly simple construct.

21.3.1 What to Use

difficulty: programmer

Is the following code legal?

```
procedure Library (A : in Boolean) is ... end Library;

with Library;
use Ascii;
package Peek_A_Boo is
   use Library, Text_Io, Peek_A_Boo, Standard, Standard.Ascii;
   use Ascii, Standard.Ascii, Ascii;
end Peek_A_Boo;
```

◇◇◇◇◇

The first two use clauses are illegal.

The use clause may appear either

- within the context clause of a compilation unit, or
- as a declarative item.

When appearing in a context clause, the use clause may list only the simple names of library packages that have been previously named in a with-clause of the same context clause. For this reason, the first use clause is illegal.

When appearing as a declarative item, a use clause may name any visible package. The naming of *Library* in the second use clause is illegal simply because *Library* is not a package; the naming of *Text_Io* is illegal because no package with this name is visible. The naming of *Peek_A_Boo* and *Standard* are legal, but have no semantic effect. Also, the naming of *Standard.Ascii* illustrates the use of an expanded name in a use clause.

Any number of use clauses may appear within a context clause or declarative part. The same package may be named multiple times within the same or different use clauses. Naming a package within multiple use clauses of a single scope has the same semantic effect as naming the package the first time. For this reason, the third use clause is legal, though redundant.

[Ada83] 8.4(1 .. 3); 10.1.1(2 .. 3)

21.3.2 Scope of a Use Clause

difficulty: novice

Is the following unit legal?

```
with Text_Io;
package Unit is
   X : Text_Io.Positive_Count := Col;
   use Text_Io;
   Y : Text_Io.Positive_Count := Col;
end Unit;
```

◇◇◇◇◇

The declaration of *X* is illegal. At the point of this declaration, the function *Col* is not directly visible. The scope of the use clause begins immediately after the clause and continues to the end of the immediately enclosing declarative region. Note that there exists no extended scope for a use clause. The declaration of *Y* is legal since it appears within the scope of the use clause, making *Col* directly visible.

A Related Problem: If, in another library unit, the package *Unit* is named in a use clause, would *Col* become directly visible?

[Ada83]   8.2(1); 8.4(3)

21.3.3 Counterintuitive Semantics

difficulty: designer

What will the following program print?

```
package P is
   subtype S is Integer range 1 .. 10;
   function "+" (L, R : in S) return S;
end P;

package body P is
   function "+" (L, R : in S) return S is
   begin
      return L;
   end "+";
end P;
```

```
with  P,  Text_Io;
procedure  Main  is
   X,  Y  :  P.S  :=  2;
begin
   declare
      use  P;
   begin
      Text_Io.Put_Line  (
         "The  answer  is"  &  P.S'Image  (X  +  Y)  &  '.');
   end;
end  Main;
```

◇◇◇◇◇

The program will print *The answer is 4*.

　　The intended use of the use clause is to make entities declared immediately within the visible parts of packages directly visible. However, the use clause makes entities only *potentially visible*, and not always directly visible. Other visibility rules must be considered in order to determine which potentially visible declarations are made directly visible.

　　If an entity is made directly visible by means other than a use clause, then the presence of a use clause can never result in the hiding of the entity. This is one of the essential differences between potential and direct visibility: declarations that are to be made visible by means of a use clause are considered only *after* all the other visibility rules are considered, no matter how "local" the scope is in which a use clause appears.

　　The resolution of the situation rests solely on determining which "+" operator is named. Note that P."+" forms a homograph with the predefined addition declared in package Standard. Even though the use clause appears in an inner declarative region, the declarations in package *P* are at first considered to be only potentially visible. Direct visibility to the operator P."+" cannot be achieved, because it would result in the hiding of a directly visible operator declared in package Standard, namely, "+" of the type Integer. Thus, the operator P."+" is not made directly visible in this case. The use clause in the preceding program, in fact, has no semantic effect—it could be removed, with no change in the program's behavior.

　　If the intent of the program was to invoke the operator declared in package *P*, the use clause should be replaced with the renaming declaration

```
function  "+"  (L,  R  :  in  P.S)  return  P.S  renames  P."+";
```

With this replacement, the program would then print *The answer is 2*, since the renaming declaration hides the "+" defined in package Standard.

　　Another example illustrating that the visibility rules of the use clause are considered last when determining the meaning of a name is the following:

```
package P is
  function F return Integer;
end P;

package R is ... end R;
package body R is
  ⋮
  procedure S is separate;
end R;

with P; use P;
separate (R)
procedure S is
  X : Integer := F;
begin
  ⋮
end S;
```

The function *P.F* is being called during the initialization of the object *R.S.X*. The function is made directly visible by the use clause. Now suppose that the following declaration is inserted in the body of package *R*:

```
package body R is
  F : constant := 3;
  ⋮
  procedure S is separate;
end R;
```

Then the body of *R* and the subunit *S* are still legal and can be recompiled. After recompilation, however, the semantics of the declaration of *X* has been changed: the function *P.F* is no longer called.

[Ada83]   8.3(15); 8.4(4 .. 6)
See also   [Mendal88] and [Rosen87]

21.3.4 Clash of the Clauses

difficulty: designer

Is the following code legal?

```
package Colors is
  type Color is (Red, Yellow, Green);
end Colors;
```

```
with Colors;
package Traffic is
   Red : constant Colors.Color := Colors.Red;
   function Yellow return Colors.Color renames Colors.Yellow;
end Traffic;

with Colors, Traffic;
use Colors;
package Winwood is
   use Traffic;
   Stop        : Colors.Color := Red;
   Accelerate : Colors.Color := Yellow;
   No_Op       : Colors.Color := Green;
end Winwood;
```

◇◇◇◇◇

The declarations of the objects *Stop* and *Accelerate* are illegal.

If two potentially visible declarations are homographs of each other, then neither declaration is made directly visible unless both represent overloadable entities. In the preceding example, *Colors.Red* and *Traffic.Red* are not made directly visible by the use clauses. The reason for this is that *Traffic.Red* is a nonoverloadable entity. A more subtle semantics exists for the declarations *Colors.Yellow* and *Traffic.Yellow*. Both declarations are made directly visible, since both represent overloadable entities. However, since they have the same parameter and result type profile, the name *Yellow* in the declaration of *Accelerate* is ambiguous.

Note that whether the scope of a use clause is local is not a factor in determining which potentially visible declarations are made directly visible. Even though the two use clauses in the preceding code have different scopes, both scopes include the declarations of *Stop*, *Accelerate*, and *No_Op*.

Consider another example with declarations that form a legal homograph:

```
package P1 is
   procedure P (Int : in Integer);
end P1;

package P2 is
   procedure P (J : in Integer);
end P2;

with P1, P2;
use P1, P2;
procedure Name_Em is
begin
   P (Int => 32);   -- Legal.
```

```
    P  (44);              -- Ambiguous.
end Name_Em;
```

Both of the procedures *P* are made directly visible within the scope of the use clause. The first subprogram call is legal, since the formal parameter name is used to disambiguate the call. The second call, however, is ambiguous for the same reason that the declaration of *Accelerate* in the previous code is illegal.

[Ada83]   6.6(3); 8.3(15); 8.4(4 .. 6)
See also   [Mendal88] and [Rosen87]

chapter 22

Renaming Declarations

> *The renaming is not allowed if the subtype of the variable, as defined in a corresponding object declaration, component declaration, or component subtype indication, is an unconstrained type; or if the variable is a generic formal object (of mode* **in out***).* [Ada83, §8.5(5:2)]

This chapter presents the syntax, semantics, and use of renaming declarations. Renaming declarations are a unique feature of Ada. Renaming is used to introduce new names for existing entities. As this chapter describes, renaming declarations can be used to resolve name conflicts, provide more meaningful names than currently exist, or make subprograms more usable than they would otherwise be.

Ada provides many ways of creating aliases, renaming being only one method. Others, discussed in previous chapters, are the following:

- Subprogram parameters passed by reference
- Subtypes
- Access values
- Generic formal parameters.

22.1 RENAMING OBJECTS AND PACKAGES

An object (variable or constant) may be renamed as an object. A (nongeneric) package may be renamed as a package. This section presents the two classes of renaming declarations that accomplish these tasks. The semantic issues involved in the renaming of components of objects are covered in depth.

22.1.1 Syntax and Simple Static Semantics

difficulty: novice

Is the following compilation unit legal?

```
with  Text_Io;
procedure  Simple_Renaming  (A  :  in  Integer)  is
    B  :  constant  Integer  renames  A;

    task  T;
    Another_T  :  T'Base  renames  T;

    Line_Length  :  constant  :=  80;
    Last           :  Integer  renames  Line_Length;

    package  Int_Io  renames  Text_Io.Integer_Io;

    Lc  :  Text_Io.Type_Set  renames  Text_Io.Lower_Case;
begin
    ⋮
end  Simple_Renaming;
```

◇◇◇◇◇

All of the renaming declarations are illegal.

An object must be renamed as an object. The syntax for the renaming declaration of an object is

    identifier : type_mark **renames** *object*_name;

For this reason, the declaration of *B* is syntactically illegal. The object being renamed, *A*, is a constant, and thus, any identifier that renames *A* denotes a constant. The declaration of *B* could be made legal simply by removing the reserved word **constant**.

The syntax of a declaration that renames an object requires a type mark. Any object whose type is anonymous cannot be renamed. The language provides no mechanism to rename the task object *T*; hence, the declaration of *Another_T* is syntactically illegal.

Another example of an object whose type is anonymous and thus may not be renamed is the following array:

```
Arr : array (1 .. 10) of Integer;
```

Line_Length is a named number, and not an object. It therefore cannot be renamed as an object; thus, the declaration of *Last* is semantically illegal.

The language defines no mechanism for renaming a generic unit. Specifically, a generic package cannot be renamed as a package, and thus, the declaration of *Int_Io* is illegal. Other entities that cannot be renamed are statement labels and loop and block names. Of course, statement labels can be aliased simply by providing multiple labels for a single statement.

Enumeration literals may be renamed only as functions. Hence, the declaration of *Lc* is semantically illegal, but one may rename *Text_Io.Lower_Case* as follows:

```
function Lc return Text_Io.Type_Set renames Text_Io.Lower_Case;
```

A Related Problem: Can the task denoted by *T* be aliased?

[Ada83]   3.2.1(1 .. 3); 8.5(2, 6, 9, 15)

22.1.2 Transitivity

difficulty: programmer

Are the following renaming declarations legal?

```
X : Integer;
Y : Integer renames X;
Z : Integer renames Y;
```

◇◇◇◇◇

Both renaming declarations are legal. *Y* is not itself an object, but rather denotes the object *X*. In turn, *Z* is not an object, but denotes *Y*, which denotes the object *X*. Thus, there exists only one object in the foregoing code.

After an entity has been renamed, the original name is not hidden. That is, one could use any of the identifiers *X*, *Y*, or *Z* to name the integer object.

A Related Problem: If Proc1 denotes a subprogram, and Proc2 renames Proc1, can Proc3 rename Proc2?

[Ada83]   8.5(1, 3 .. 4, 13)

22.1.3 Subtype Constraints

difficulty: designer

What will the following program print?

```
with Text_Io;
procedure Different_Constraints is
   type T is range -20 .. 20;
   subtype S is T range 1 .. 20;

   A : T;
   B : S renames A;

   C : S;
   D : T renames C;
begin
   begin
      B := -10;
      Text_Io.Put ("B assigned the value " &
                   S'Image (B) & "; ");
   exception
      when Constraint_Error | Numeric_Error =>
         Text_Io.Put ("B assignment failed; ");
   end;

   D := -10;
   Text_Io.Put_Line ("D assigned the value " & T'Image (D));
exception
   when Constraint_Error | Numeric_Error =>
      Text_Io.Put_Line ("D assignment failed.");
end Different_Constraints;
```

◇◇◇◇◇

The program will print *B assigned the value −10; D assignment failed.*

The type mark provided in a renaming declaration is used only to check the legality of the declaration; it does not affect the run-time constraints of the entity itself. In the case of a renaming of an object, the type mark provided must be of the same base type as the object being renamed. The declarations of B and D meet this requirement.

The assignment to B executes without exception, since the subtype (T) of the object includes the value −10. Also, the evaluation of *S'Image (B)* does not raise an exception, since the constraint check is against the base type of S, not the subtype S.

The assignment to D will raise an exception, since D denotes the object C and C is constrained by the subtype S. The fact that the declaration of D names the type T does not affect the constraint checks of the assignment to the object.

[Ada83]   3.5.5(10); 8.5(4)

22.1.4 Components and Slices

difficulty: programmer

Are the following declarations legal?

```
W : String (1 .. 10);
X : String renames W;
Y : String renames W (1 .. 5);
Z : Character renames W (6);
```

◇◇◇◇◇

All of the declarations are legal.

Similarly to formal parameters, a renaming declaration can specify an unconstrained type. In this case, the constraints are those of the object being renamed, e.g., the constraints of *X* are those of *W*.

A slice of a variable is a variable, a component of a variable is a variable, a slice of a constant is a constant, and component of a constant is a constant. Thus, the identifiers *X*, *Y*, and *Z* all denote variables. Consider the following uses of these variables:

```
W := (others => 'w');
X := (others => 'x');
Y := (others => 'y');
Z := 'z';
```

After execution of these assignments, the value of *W* (and *X*) will be "yyyyyzxxxx".

The declarations of *Y* and *Z* are examples of a common use of renaming: to give a more notationally convenient, and possibly more readable and understandable, alias for another name. Some further examples are the following:

```
type Bit is range 0 .. 1;
type Word is array (Natural range <>) of Bit;

Instruction : Word (0 .. 15);
Op_Code : Word renames Instruction (0 .. 3);
Register : Word renames Instruction (4 .. 7);
Address : Word renames Instruction (8 .. 15);

type Taxpayer is
  record
    Name      : String (1 .. 100);
    Lip_Reader : Boolean;
    ⋮
  end record;
```

```
John_Q_Public : Taxpayer;
First_Initial      : Character renames John_Q_Public.Name (1);
Republican      : Boolean   renames John_Q_Public.Lip_Reader;
```

The semantics of renaming declarations should not be interpreted as simple textual substitution. Similar to subtype declarations, they are aliases that are elaborated only once. In the program

```
with Text_Io, Calendar;
procedure Only_Once is
    S : String (1 .. Integer (Calendar.Day_Duration'Last));
    A : String renames S (1 .. Integer (
            Calendar.Seconds (Calendar.Clock)));
begin
    Text_Io.Put_Line (Integer'Image (A'Length));
    delay 5.0;
    Text_Io.Put_Line (Integer'Image (A'Length));
end Only_Once;
```

the length of the object denoted by *A* is determined during the elaboration of the renaming declaration; it does not change during execution of the sequence of statements. This program will print the same value twice.

A Related Problem: How many variables are declared in the code at the beginning of this subsection?

[Ada83]   3.9(3); 8.5(2 .. 4, 13)

22.1.5 Dynamically Created Objects

difficulty: designer

What will the following program print?

```
with Text_Io;
procedure Dynamic_Renaming is
    type Text is access String;

    T : Text := new String'("abcd");
    S : String renames T.all;
begin
    Text_Io.Put (S & ' ');        -- 1.

    T.all := "efgh";
    Text_Io.Put (S & ' ');        -- 2.
```

```
    S  :=  "ijkl";
    Text_Io.Put  (T.all  &  ' ');  -- 3.

    T  :=  null;
    Text_Io.Put  (S  &  ' ');      -- 4.

    T  :=  new  String'("wxyz");
    Text_Io.Put_Line  (S);         -- 5.
exception
  when  Constraint_Error  =>
      Text_Io.Put_Line  ("Constraint_Error  was  raised.");
end  Dynamic_Renaming;
```

◇◇◇◇◇

The program will print *abcd efgh ijkl ijkl ijkl*.

An object renaming declaration defines a new name for an object. Previously, the identifier and *object*_name used in a renaming declaration always denoted the same object, throughout the scope of the renaming declaration. The use of access types to dynamically create objects illustrates the distinction between an object name and the object itself.

Immediately after the elaboration of the renaming declaration, the names S and T.**all** denote the same object, namely, that created by the allocator during the initialization of T. Throughout the scope of the renaming declaration, S will always denote this dynamically created object. However, as the following table indicates, S and T.**all** do not denote the same object throughout this scope:

Statement	S	T.**all**
1.	"abcd"	"acbd"
2.	"efgh"	"efgh"
3.	"ijkl"	"ijkl"
4.	"ijkl"	N/A
5.	"ijkl"	"wxyz"

At statements 1, 2, and 3, the two names denote the same object. The assignment before statement 4 causes the name T.**all** to denote no object. This assignment, however, does not affect the object denoted by S. (In particular, the object denoted by S will not be collected as garbage.) Likewise, the assignment before statement 5 does not affect the object denoted by S. At statement 5, the names S and T.**all** denote distinct objects. This problem illustrates that it is insufficient for an implementation to implement the renaming declaration merely by textually substituting T.**all** for each occurrence of S.

Finally, suppose the third assignment statement were replaced by a call to an instance of Unchecked_Deallocation. Then the object denoted by *S* would be subject to the semantics of unchecked programming, and later attempts to read the value of the object denoted by *S* would be erroneous, with Program_Error possibly being raised.

[Ada83]   8.5(3 .. 4, 13)
[ARG]   AI-00028/05, 12-13-90

22.1.6 Subprogram Formal Parameters

difficulty: programmer

Is the following subprogram legal?

```
procedure Proc (Int1 : in        Integer;
                 Int2 : in out Integer;
                 Str  :        out String) is
   subtype Int is Integer range 1 .. 0;
   X : Integer renames Int1;
   Y : Int       renames Int2;
   Z : String  renames Str;
begin
   X := 3;
   Y := Y + Z'Length;
   Z := Z (Str'Range);
end Proc;
```

◇◇◇◇◇

The assignment statements for *X* and *Z* are illegal. *X* renames a constant and, thus, denotes a constant. One may not assign anything to a constant. *Z* renames a parameter of mode out and, thus, denotes a write-only variable. One may not read the value of a write-only variable.

The assignment to *Y* is legal. *Y* denotes a parameter of mode in out and can both be read from and written to. The use of *Z'Length* is legal here, since it is always possible to read the subtype of a mode out parameter. The constraints of *Z* are the same as those of *Str*. Note that although the type mark used in the declaration of *Y* denotes a null range, the subtype of the object denoted by *Y* is *Integer*. Thus, the assignment to *Y* is equivalent to the following assignment to *Int2*:

```
Int2 := Int2 + Str'Length;
```

[Ada83]   6.2(1 .. 5); 8.5(4)

22.1.7 Evaluating Names

difficulty: programmer

What will the following program print?

```
with  Text_Io;
procedure  John_B  is
   procedure  Proc  (S  :  in  String)  is
      C  :  Character  renames  S  (S'First);
   begin
      Text_Io.Put_Line  ("Renaming  good  enough.");
   end  Proc;
begin
   declare
      Int1  :  Integer;
      Int2  :  Integer  renames  Int1;
   begin
      null;
   end;

   Proc  ("");
exception
   when  Program_Error  =>
      Text_Io.Put_Line  ("Renaming  erroneous  enough.");
   when  Constraint_Error  =>
      Text_Io.Put_Line  ("Renaming  not  good  enough.");
end  John_B;
```

◇◇◇◇◇

The program will print *Renaming not good enough.*

    This program highlights the difference between the evaluation of an object and the evaluation of a name of an object. During the elaboration of the declaration of *Int2*, the name *Int1*, but not the value of *Int1*, is evaluated. Similarly, during the elaboration of *C*, the object name *S (S'First)* is evaluated. It is the evaluation of this name that causes Constraint_Error to be raised. (Constraint_Error can also be raised when evaluating record component names; see Section 22.1.10.)

    Suppose the declarations of *Int2* and *C* were changed as follows:

```
Int2  :  Integer     :=  Int1;
C     :  Character  :=  S  (S'First);
```

In these cases, an attempt is made to evaluate both object names and object values. The elaboration of *Int2* would be erroneous, since the object *Int1* has an undefined value.

The elaboration of *C* would raise Constraint_Error for the same reason as it does in the program.

A Related Problem: If, in the preceding program, a nonnull string with an undefined value were passed to *Proc*, would the elaboration of the renaming declaration of *C* be erroneous?

[Ada83]   4.1.1(4); 8.5(3)

22.1.8 Implicit Importation

difficulty: designer

Provide a rationale for the renaming declaration in the following code:

```
with Calendar;
package Activity_Manager is
   package Clock renames Calendar;

   function Is_Done_Or_Do (... ) return Clock.Time;
     ⋮
end Activity_Manager;
```

◇◇◇◇◇

The renaming declaration, in some limited sense, abstracts the dependency on a specific implementation of the type *Time*. If later, during development, it was decided that *Activity_Manager* should use a different implementation of time—one that has a better resolution than that offered by package *Calendar*—then the effect of this change could be minimized by the renaming declaration. That is, the with-clause and the renaming declaration would be the only code that would require changes to name the new package. In fact, users of *Activity_Manager* need not even be affected by such a change. The user in

```
with Activity_Manager;
procedure User is
   T : Activity_Manager.Clock.Time :=
          Activity_Manager.Is_Done_Or_Do (... );
     ⋮
```

makes all references to the clock through the interface of the package *Activity_Manager*, rather than by explicitly creating a dependency on a specific clock, e.g., the one provided by package *Calendar*.

This renaming concept is also applicable to smaller scopes, such as package bodies. Suppose that the specification of *Activity_Manager* abstracted the dependency on

Calendar. In such a case, the body of *Activity_Manager* would still need to import some implementation of time. Within the body, the renaming declaration could be used as it was in the earlier program to minimize the effect of changing to a different time implementation.

[Ada83]   8.5(1, 6, 13)

22.1.9 Prefixes of Expanded Names

difficulty: programmer

Is the following package legal?

```
package Pac is
   package Repac renames Pac;
   V : Integer := 1;
private
   P : Integer := 0;

   R1 : Integer := Repac.V;
   R2 : Integer := Repac.P;
end Pac;
```

◇◇◇◇◇

The declaration of *R2* is illegal.

A name declared by a renaming declaration can be used as the prefix of an expanded name only when the selector denotes an entity declared in the visible part of a package. The expanded name in the declaration of *R2* denotes an entity *P* declared in the private part of a package. The prefix of this expanded name, *Repac*, is declared by a renaming declaration. Thus, the declaration of *R2* is illegal.

Consider another declaration inside the private part of the preceding package:

```
R3 : Integer := Repac.Repac.V;
```

This declaration is legal, since the named entity, *V*, is declared in the visible part of a package. The prefix *Repac.Repac* is itself an expanded name and is legal, since the selector *Repac* is declared in the visible part of the package denoted by the prefix *Repac*. Note that *Repac.Repac* is legal, even though *Repac* is not declared within *Repac*. (Such prefixes are discussed further later.) This convention illustrates an interesting aspect of renaming packages, namely, that arbitrarily long expanded names can be generated to refer to entities declared in the visible part of a package. This type of name is similar to those that can be created by record and access type declarations; as in the following code:

```
declare
  type R;
  type Acc is access R;
  type R is
    record
      Data : Integer := 0;
      Next : Ptr;
    end record;

  Ptr : Acc := new R;
begin
  Ptr.Next := Ptr;
  Ptr.Next.Next.Next.Data := 1;
end;
```

The variable name in the last assignment statement may be specified more simply as Ptr.Data.

The entity denoted by an expanded name that includes a prefix declared by a renaming declaration must be declared in the visible part of a package. Yet, one may question whether the renaming declaration itself must appear in the visible part of the package. Consider the following example:

```
package New_Pac is
  N : Integer := 1;
private
  package Npac renames New_Pac;

  R4 : Integer := Npac.N;
  R5 : Integer := New_Pac.Npac.N;
  R6 : Integer := Npac.Npac.N;   -- Illegal.
end New_Pac;
```

Here, *R4* is legal, since *Npac* denotes a package and *N* is declared within the visible part of this package. For a similar reason, *R5* is legal. In considering the legality of *R5*, one must consider two expanded names and thus two sets of prefixes and selectors:

Expanded Name	Prefix	Selector
New_Pac.Npac.N	New_Pac.Npac	N
New_Pac.Npac	New_Pac	Npac

Clearly, the first expanded name is legal. The second expanded name is legal also, since its prefix is not a name declared by a renaming declaration and the selector is declared immediately within the prefix.

Now consider the declaration of *R6*. In the (inner) expanded name *Npac.Npac*, although the prefix denotes a package, the selector is not declared within the visible part of this package. Further, the selector is not declared immediately within the prefix. (*Npac* is not declared within *Npac*.) Compare this semantics to that for the declaration of *R3*: only when the renaming declaration is not declared within a visible part need one be concerned with whether the selector is declared within the prefix.

Finally, the following code shows the use of renaming declarations as prefixes of expanded names that denote entities other than packages:

```
procedure Proc (A : in out Integer) is
    procedure Subpgm (B : in out Integer) renames Proc;
    Int : Integer;
begin
    Proc.Int          := Proc.A;
    Subpgm.Int        := Proc.A;   -- Illegal.
    Subpgm.B          := 5;        -- Illegal.
    Proc.Subpgm.Int := Proc.A;   -- Illegal.
end Proc;
```

These examples further illustrate that an expanded name whose prefix includes a name declared by a renaming declaration and whose selector does not denote an entity defined in the visible part of a package is illegal. Rules like this are intended to eliminate the complexity inherent in determining that a name such as *Subpgm.B* denotes the same object as does *Proc.A*.

A Related Problem: Name all the prefixes and selectors of the expanded name X.Y.Z.

[Ada83]   4.1(2); 4.1.3(2, 13 .. 18)
[ARG]   AI-00016/10, 08-05-86; AI-00119/06, 07-06-90; AI-00187/06, 09-12-87; AI-00468/04, 08-06-87

22.1.10 Renamable

difficulty: language lawyer

Is the following code legal?

```
package Rename is
    type R1 (D : Integer) is
    record
        S : String (1 .. D);
        case D is
            when 0      => null;
            when others => N : Integer;
        end case;
    end record;
```

```
    type R2 (D : Integer := 1) is
       record
          S : String (1 .. D);
          case D is
             when 0       => null;
             when others => N : Integer;
          end case;
       end record;

    Obj1 : R1 (5);
    Obj2 : R2;
    Obj3 : R2 (0);

    S1 : String  renames Obj1.S;
    S2 : String  renames Obj2.S;
    N1 : Integer renames Obj2.N;
    N2 : Integer renames Obj3.N;
end Rename;
```

◇◇◇◇◇

The declarations of *S2* and *N1* are illegal. The elaboration of *N2* would raise Constraint_Error.

The types *R1* and *R2* are both unconstrained; however, only *Obj2* is of an unconstrained subtype. An unconstrained variable (e.g., *Obj2*) may have components or slices that are dependent on discriminants. Such components and slices cannot be renamed, because, at run time, it would be possible for the renamed component or slice to become nonexistent. Suppose if the following assignment were made to *Obj2* :

```
    Obj2 := (0, "");
```

If the declaration of *N1* were allowed, then after this assignment, *N1* would denote a nonexistent object. Similarly, if the declaration of *S2* were allowed, it would not be clear after the assignment which string object *S2* denoted. That is, would *S2* denote the original string object of length 1 or the new string object of length 0? This example highlights the difference between renaming a designated object (see Section 22.1.5) and renaming a dependent object.

Consider further cases of attempts to rename parts of *Obj2* :

```
    C1 : Character renames Obj2.S (1);       -- Illegal.
    S3 : String    renames Obj2.S (1 .. 1);  -- Illegal.
```

C1 is much like the declaration of *N1* : it attempts to rename an object that may not exist later. Although a strict reading of [Ada83, §8.5(5)] would allow the declaration of *S3*, the clear intent of the standard was to disallow *S3* for the same reasons *C1* is disallowed.

The preceding package illustrates the most simple cases of renaming dependent components. Formal parameters of unconstrained record types offer more complicated examples. Consider the following subprogram formal parameters (assume visibility to the type *R2* from the earlier code):

```
procedure Proc (X : in     R2;
                Y :      out R2) is
  S1 : String  renames X.S;
  S2 : String  renames Y.S;  -- Illegal.
  N1 : Integer renames X.N;
  N2 : Integer renames Y.N;  -- Illegal.
begin
  null;
end Proc;
```

The declarations of *S1* and *N1* are legal. The formal parameter *X* is a constant—its subtype is constrained by the actual parameter. Because the subtype of *X* may not change, *S1* and *N1* are legal. However, for some values of *X*, the component *N* will not exist. In such cases (when the discriminant is 0), the elaboration of *N1* will raise Constraint_Error.

The declarations of *S2* and *N2* are illegal. The formal parameter *Y* is a variable, and its subtype may be unconstrained. If the actual parameter for *Y* is a variable of an unconstrained subtype, then *Y* would itself be unconstrained. For this reason, renaming the components of *Y* is subject to the same rules as renaming the components of *Obj2*.

Now suppose the declaration of the formal parameter *Y* named the type *R1* instead of *R2*. Then the declarations of *S2* and *N2* would be legal. The difference between the use of *R1* and that of *R2* in defining subprogram parameters is that with *R2*, it would be possible to change the discriminant of *Y* and, thus, change the existence of the component *N* and the subtype of the component *S*, whereas with *R1* this is impossible.

Now consider the following examples using generic formal parameters:

```
generic
  X : in     R1;
  Y : in out R1;
package Gp is
  S1: String  renames X.S;
  S2: String  renames Y.S;  -- Illegal.
  N1: Integer renames X.N;
  N2: Integer renames Y.N;  -- Illegal.
end Gp;
```

The declarations of *S2* and *N2* are illegal. *X* is a constant—its subtype is constrained by the actual parameter. Since *X* denotes a constant, the renamings of its components are legal. As previously described, the elaboration of *N1* may raise Constraint_Error.

For all instances of *Gp*, *Y* will be of a constrained subtype, since all objects of the type *R1* are constrained. It would appear that renamings of dependent components of *Y* would be legal. The elaboration of such renamings would either succeed or raise Constraint_Error. If the elaboration succeeded, one would be assured that the component would always exist, since the discriminant of *Y* could never change. Suppose that the declaration of *N2* were allowed. Then, for some instances of *Gp*, the elaboration of this declaration would raise Constraint_Error, as in the code

```
Sans_N  :  R1  (0);
With_N  :  R1  (1);

package  P1  is new  Gp  (With_N, Sans_N);
package  P2  is new  Gp  (With_N, With_N);
```

If allowed, the elaboration of *P1.N2* would raise Constraint_Error. Nevertheless, the language does not allow renaming a dependent component of a generic formal variable (a parameter of mode in out).

Note this apparent asymmetry between the rules for subprogram formal parameters and those for generic formal parameters: the rules for subprogram parameters allow renaming dependent components of variables of the type *R1*, while those for generic units do not. This is because the rules for generic units do not distinguish between unconstrained record types without default discriminant values and unconstrained record types with default discriminant values.

A Related Problem: Provide the rationale for having the aforementioned asymmetry.

[Ada83]   3.2.1(1 .. 3); 3.7.1(7); 4.1(4, 9 .. 10); 4.1.3(1 .. 3, 6 .. 8); 6.2(5); 8.5(5)
[ARG]   AI-00170/07, 06-13-88; AI-00502/05, 05-23-88; AI-00738/04, 10-30-89;
           AI-00845/01, 01-10-90

22.2 RENAMING OPERATIONS AND EXCEPTIONS

Subprogram renaming declarations offer the user a number of ways to change the semantics of invoking a subprogram. This section focuses on the diverse subtleties of using subprogram renaming declarations. The semantics of renaming exceptions, like that of renaming packages, is not complicated. The section presents a common error that occurs when using renamed exceptions.

22.2.1 Changing Subprogram Formal Parameters

difficulty: designer

Is the following package legal?

```
package Different_Strokes is
  procedure P1 (X       : in Integer);
  procedure P2 (X, Y : in Positive := 3);
  procedure P3 (A       : in Integer; B : in out Float);

  procedure R1 (Y : Integer) renames P1;
  procedure R2 (X : out Integer) renames P1;
  procedure R3 (X : in Positive := −3) renames P1;
  procedure R4 (X : Positive := 1; Y : in Integer) renames P2;
  procedure R5 (B : in out Float; A : in Integer) renames P3;

  function "∗" (L, R : in Integer := 1) return Positive
    renames Standard."/";
end Different_Strokes;
```

◇◇◇◇◇

The renaming declarations *R2*, *R5*, and "∗" are illegal.

A surprisingly wide latitude is allowed for renaming subprograms. One can do any of the following:

- Provide a different subprogram name.
- Change, add, or remove default expressions.
- Not follow the conformance rules.
- Provide different but compatible type marks for formal parameters and result types.

The declaration of *R1* is legal and illustrates that a renaming declaration can change the subprogram and formal parameter names and provide an implicit mode where the explicit one was used in the original subprogram.

The declaration of *R2* is illegal because it attempts to change the mode of a formal parameter, and the declaration of *R5* is illegal because it does not preserve the parameter profile of the original subprogram. The declaration of *R3* is legal and illustrates that the type mark of a parameter specification can be changed, as well that a default expression may be added.

The declaration of *R4* is legal and illustrates that a renaming declaration can change the parameter specification's type name, change the value of a default expression, remove a default expression, and change a single parameter specification that uses an identifier list to one that uses separate parameter specifications. When a default expression is changed, it still must be of the same base type as the type mark of the parameter specification. When the type mark of a parameter specification is changed, it still must be of the same base type as that of the corresponding renamed parameter, thus preserving the parameter profile of the subprogram.

The declaration of "∗" is illegal because it attempts to provide a default expression for a parameter specification of an operator. This declaration illustrates that a renaming declaration of a function can specify a different designator as well as different formal parameter names. It also shows that a type mark can be replaced by one that is of the same base type as that of the corresponding parameter specification of the renamed subprogram.

When one provides a different type mark for a parameter specification in a renaming declaration, confusion is likely to occur. For example, the call

        R3;

will not raise an exception, even though the value of the default expression is not a member of the subtype *Positive*, the type mark specified in the renaming declaration. That is, even though *Positive* was specified in the renaming declaration, the subtype used for all calls is that of the original parameter, namely, *Integer*. A further example illustrates these semantics:

```
package A is
   type Int is range 1 .. 40;
end A;

with A;
package B is
   subtype S is A.Int range 1 .. 10;
   function "−" (L, R : in S) return S renames A."+";

   Obj : A.Int := 20 − 11;   −− No Constraint_Error.
end B;
```

Although the subtype *S* is provided as the type mark for the operands in the renaming declaration, the type *Int* is used at run time for constraint checking. Thus, the operands *20* and *11* will not cause Constraint_Error to be raised. Further, the result of the operation, 31, will not raise an exception, as again, the type *Int* is used as the result subtype.

There are three common uses for renaming subprograms:

1. To achieve direct visibility to a subprogram declared in a different scope, e.g., "−" in the example.
2. To give new identifiers to subprograms and to provide different names for formal parameters to increase understandability.
3. To modify, add, or remove default expressions that make the subprogram more usable in a specific context.

An example of the third use is the following:

```
function Center (S              : in  String;
                 Within_Length  : in  Positive;
                 Padding        : in  Character) return String;
```

```
function Make_Title (Text       : in String;
                     Of_Length : in Positive := 75;
                     Filler    : in Character := '*') return String
  renames Center;
```

[Ada83]   6.6(1); 8.5(2, 7 .. 8, 13)

22.2.2 Renaming Entries

difficulty: designer

What will the following program print?

```
with Text_Io;
procedure Entry_Rename is
   task T is
      entry E1;
      entry E2 (Boolean);
   end T;

   procedure R1 renames T.E1;
   procedure R2 renames T.E2;

   task body T is
   begin
      accept E2 (False);
      accept E2 (True);
      accept R1;
   end T;
begin
   Text_Io.Put ("1, ");

   for B in Boolean loop
      declare
         procedure R3 renames T.E2 (B);
      begin
         R3;
      end;
   end loop;

   Text_Io.Put ("2, ");
   R1;
   Text_Io.Put_Line ("3.");
exception
   when Tasking_Error => Text_Io.Put_Line ("Boom!");
end Entry_Rename;
```

◇◇◇◇◇

The program is illegal and thus will not print anything.

An entry family cannot be renamed as a procedure, although individual members of the family may. Thus, the declaration of *R2* is illegal and the declaration of *R3* is legal. *R3* illustrates that, in a renaming declaration, the name of an entry family member need not be static.

An accept statement must specify the name of an entry. A declaration that renames an entry cannot be named in an accept statement. Thus, the accept statement for *R1* is semantically illegal.

If the declaration of *R2* were removed and the accept statement naming *R1* were replaced by

```
accept E1;
```

then the program would be legal and would print *1, 2, 3*.

Timed and conditional entry calls must also specify the names of entries. Thus, the following statements are also illegal:

```
select                    select
   R1;   -- Illegal.         R1;   -- Illegal.
or                        else
   delay  1.0;               null;
end  select;              end  select;
```

Using a procedure as an alias for an entry is something that the reader has seen before; recall that an actual parameter for a generic formal subprogram may be an entry.

[Ada83]   8.5(2, 7, 9, 14); 9.5(4, 7)

22.2.3 Attributes

difficulty: programmer

Is the following package legal?

```
package Attribute_Renaming is
   task T is
      entry E;
   end T;

   function "+" (B : in Boolean) return Boolean
      renames Boolean'Succ;
   function "−" (Int : in Integer) return Integer
      renames Integer'Pred;
   function Image_Of (C : in Character) return String
      renames Character'Image;
```

```
    function A_to_B (S : in String) return Integer
       renames Integer'Value;
    function Pos_Of (Int : in Integer) return Integer
       renames Integer'Pos;
    function Val_Of (Int : in Integer) return Boolean
       renames Boolean'Val;
    function Last return Integer renames Integer'Last;
    function Queue_Depth return Natural renames T.E'Count;
  end Attribute_Renaming;
```

◇◇◇◇◇

The declarations of *Pos_Of*, *Val_Of*, *Last*, and *Queue_Depth* are illegal.

Only attributes defined as functions can be renamed. There are six such attributes: Image, Value, Pos, Val, Succ, and Pred. However, only four of these attributes—Image, Value, Succ, and Pred—have parameter and result type profiles that may be specified in a renaming declaration. The profiles of Pos and Val use anonymous types and therefore cannot be renamed.

A Related Problem: Which attributes may be used as generic actual subprograms?

[Ada83]   8.5(2, 7, 9, 13)

22.2.4 Equality

difficulty: programmer

Is the following package legal?

```
    with Text_Io, Calendar;
    package Equals is
       function "=" (L, R : in Text_Io.File_Type)      -- 1.
          return Boolean renames Text_Io."=";
       function "=" (L, R : in Calendar.Time)           -- 2.
          return Boolean renames Calendar."=";
       function "=" (L, R : in Calendar.Time)           -- 3.
          return Boolean renames Calendar."<";
       function "=" (L : in Calendar.Time;              -- 4.
                     R : in Duration)
          return Calendar.Time renames Calendar."+";
       function Is_Equal (L, R : in Integer)            -- 5.
          return Boolean renames Standard."=";
    end Equals;
```

◇◇◇◇◇

Declarations number 1, 3, and 4 are illegal.

   A renaming declaration whose designator is the equality operator may only rename another equality operator. Inequality may never be the designator of a renaming declaration. Declaration 1 is illegal because no subprogram named *Text_Io*."=" exists with the specified parameter and result type profile. Declaration 2 is legal, since it renames the equality operation for *Calendar.Time*, providing the same parameter and result type profile. Declarations 3 and 4 are illegal because equality cannot be used to rename any operator other than equality. Declaration 5 is legal and simply illustrates that an equality operation may be renamed using any designator.

[Ada83]   6.7(4 .. 5); 8.5(2, 7, 9)

22.2.5 Name versus Entity

difficulty: programmer

Is the following program legal?

```
with  Text_Io,  Sequential_Io;
procedure  Rosebud  is
   package  Seq_Io  is  new  Sequential_Io (Integer);
   use  Text_Io,  Seq_Io;
begin
   raise  Data_Error;
exception
   when  Text_Io.Data_Error  |  Seq_Io.Data_Error  =>  null;
end  Rosebud;
```


◇◇◇◇◇

The raise statement and the exception handler are illegal.

   A renaming declaration forms a new declaration, although the new declaration denotes the renamed entity. *Data_Error* is declared in both *Text_Io* and *Seq_Io*. The semantics of the use clause does not cause *Data_Error* to become directly visible. The fact that both *Text_Io.Data_Error* and *Seq_Io.Data_Error* denote the same exception is irrelevant insofar as the semantics of the use clause is concerned. The raise statement is illegal simply because the identifier *Data_Error* is not directly visible.

   The exception handler specifies two different names for the same exception. Recall that a renaming declaration forms a new name for an entity, but it does not declare a new entity. The rules for exception handlers state that an exception may not be specified more than once in the handlers for a given frame. Thus, the use of both *Text_Io.Data_Error* and *Seq_Io.Data_Error* in the handler is illegal.

The raise statement may be made legal by using an expanded name, e.g., Text_-Io.Data_Error or Seq_Io.Data_Error. Similarly, the exception handler could be made legal by using only one of these expanded names.

[Ada83]   8.4(3 .. 6); 8.5(1 .. 3, 6); 11.2(5); 11.3; 14.3.10; 14.4(1)

22.2.6 Overload Resolution

difficulty: programmer

Given direct visibility to the declarations

```
function Random return Integer;
function Random (Seed : in Integer := 123) return Integer;
```

show how one can invoke each function. (Use default parameter association when invoking the second function.)

◇◇◇◇◇

Rename each declaration of *Random* using different designators:

```
function Unseeded_Random return Integer renames Random;
function Seeded_Random (Seed : in Integer := 123)
   return Integer renames Random;
```

The declarations of the *Random* functions have different parameter profiles. This allows one to rename both functions without the renaming declarations being ambiguous. That is, overload resolution will determine which *Random* function is being named in each renaming declaration.

Renaming allows a "call" to *Unseeded_Random* to "invoke" the first *Random* function. Likewise, a call to *Seeded_Random* will invoke the second function. This situation and that in Section 22.2.5 illuminate the difference between an entity and the name of an entity.

[Ada83]   6.4(1); 6.6; 8.5(2, 7 .. 8, 13)

22.2.7 On Being Static

difficulty: language lawyer

Is the following program legal?

```
with Calendar;
procedure Static_Tests is
    Int1 : constant Integer := 15;
    Int2 : Integer renames Int1;
    type Int is range Int1 .. Int2;
    function Okay return Boolean renames True;
    function Error return Boolean renames False;
begin
    case Calendar.Day (Calendar.Clock) < Int1 is
        when Okay => ...
        when Error => ...
    end case;
end Static_Tests;
```

◇◇◇◇◇

The program is legal.

A declaration that renames a static entity creates a new name for that entity. Any use of the new name denotes the static entity and thus is itself static. A reading of [Ada83, §4.9] would clearly indicate that the uses of *Int2*, *Okay*, and *Error* are nonstatic. However, the Ada Rapporteur Group has interpreted the intent of the designers of the language as allowing any name that *denotes* a static entity to be used in an expression that is required to be static. This situation illustrates one of the few areas where the Ada Rapporteur Group has recommended (and effected) changes to the standard, rather than simply interpreting the existing semantics.

[Ada83]   4.9; 8.5(4)
[ARG]   AI-00001/10, 07-23-86; AI-00438/09, 06-16-89

22.2.8 Type Conversions

difficulty: designer

What will the following program print?

```
with Text_Io;
procedure Convert is
    Int : Integer := −9;

    procedure P (Int : in out Integer);
    procedure Q (J  : in out Positive) renames P;
    procedure P (Int : in out Integer) is
    begin
        null;
    end P;
begin
```

```
    Q (Positive (Int));
    Text_Io.Put_Line ("Is done or do?");
exception
   when Constraint_Error =>
      Text_Io.Put_Line ("Type conversion failed.");
end Convert;
```

◇◇◇◇◇

The program is illegal and will not print anything.

The call to *Q* is illegal. When calling a subprogram declared by a renaming declaration and using an actual parameter that is a type conversion to a formal parameter of mode out or mode in out, one must name the type mark of the original, denoted subprogram parameter declaration. The call to *Q* could be made legal by replacing *Positive* with *Integer*.

If the foregoing call to *Q* where allowed, then the semantics of the call would seem to indicate that Constraint_Error should be raised during evaluation of the actual parameter. But there is only one subprogram here, and the constraints of the parameters of that subprogram are not affected by any renaming declarations. To ensure the proper constraint checks for the type conversion, the language requires that one specify the original type mark.

A Related Problem: Is the following subprogram call legal?

```
procedure R (K : in Natural);
   ⋮

R (Positive (Int));
```

[Ada83]   6.4.1(3 .. 4); 8.5(7 ..8)
[ARG]   AI-00245/08, 05-23-88

chapter 23

The Predefined I/O
Packages

The Ada I/O interface was thrown in almost as an afterthought.
Anonymous Ada student

Ada predefines I/O utilities via two packages and two generic units. The predefined package Io_Exceptions simply contains the declarations of the exceptions common to the three other units. The package Text_Io contains routines for reading and writing ASCII images. Contained within Text_Io are generic packages that facilitate I/O for scalar types. The generic packages Sequential_Io and Direct_Io are used to read and write binary images of any nonlimited type.

The package Io_Exceptions is shared by the other units so that similar exceptional conditions are reported by the same exception, regardless of whether the condition occurred while using a text, sequential, or direct file. This arrangement has the drawback of occasionally making it more difficult to pinpoint the cause of an exception. The advantage is that the simple model of common conditions across kinds of files often directly corresponds to the model employed by operating systems.

The detailed semantics of the predefined I/O units are voluminous and complex. This chapter concentrates on the semantics that most users will require, as well as some of the semantics that most users find baffling. The goal of the chapter is to provide readers with a foundation from which they can assimilate the entire I/O model. The chapter makes no attempt to present every feature of the model. Specifically, a presentation of low-level I/O is omitted.

For notational convenience, the use clause is employed in many of the program examples.

23.1 FILE MANAGEMENT

File management includes the creation, opening, resetting, closing, and deleting of files. File management performs the critical operation of associating an Ada file object with an "external" file. The file management model and operations are shared between the text, sequential, and direct I/O units.

23.1.1 Roses

difficulty: programmer

Will the following subprogram raise an exception?

```
with Text_Io;   use Text_Io;
procedure Rose is
   F1, F2 : File_Type;
   C        : Character;
begin
   Open (File => F1, Mode => In_File, Name => "xyzzy");
   Open (File => F2, Mode => In_File, Name => "xyzzy");
   Delete (F1);
   Get (F2, C);
end Rose;
```

◇◇◇◇◇

Both calls to *Open* may propagate Name_Error or Use_Error. The call to *Delete* may propagate Use_Error. The call to *Get* may propagate End_Error.

Ada defines the concepts of a *file* and an *external file*. A file is simply a value of one of the File_Type types defined in Text_Io, instances of Direct_Io, or instances of Sequential_Io. An external file is defined by the environment in which an Ada program executes. These two concepts are distinct and form the basis of understanding the semantics of I/O in Ada.

I/O in any language is inherently system dependent. This is not to say that many aspects of I/O cannot be standardized across many implementations. The designers of Ada made the distinction between a file and an external file so that standardized behavior could be associated with a file and system-dependent behavior could be isolated in the concept of an external file.

Opening a file requires that a corresponding external file already exist. If the environment cannot identify an external file with the given name, *Open* will propagate Name_Error. Name_Error could be propagated on the second call to *Open* if another user of the environment were to move, delete, or rename the external file after the first call, but before the second call, to *Open* has executed.

Use_Error is raised if the external file can be identified, but cannot be opened for other reasons. One reason might be that the user does not have read access to the external file. Another reason might be that the environment does not support multiple opening of a single external file. This second possibility explains why the second call to *Open* in the foregoing subprogram may propagate Use_Error.

Yet another reason why either call to *Open* may propagate Use_Error is that an external file of the given "form" cannot be identified. Note that Create and Open define four parameters, the last being a parameter of mode in of the type String named Form. The intent of this parameter is to provide system-dependent information beyond Name and Mode that might be required for identifying the external file and its intended use. For example, in some environments, the Form parameter might be used to specify that the external file is to be read as eight-bit characters, treating the high-order bit as of even parity. Other environments might use the Form parameter to indicate that a file is being opened for write-append—a capability not predefined in Ada. It is legal for an implementation always to propagate Use_Error in the presence of a nonnull Form parameter. (A null string for the Form parameter specifies the use of the implementation's default options.)

If both *Open* calls execute without exception, then the call to *Delete* may propagate Use_Error if the environment does not support deletion of an external file that is open multiple times. Neither call to *Open* or *Delete* may raise Status_Error. On a call to Open, Status_Error is propagated only if the file (not the external file) is already open. Similarly, a call to Delete will propagate Status_Error only if the file is not open.

Each I/O package defines a function named Is_Open that is used to determine whether a file is currently open. This function and the exception Status_Error together define and enforce one aspect of file management in Ada—that a file can be associated with only one external file at a time. The following table illustrates the relationship between Is_Open and Status_Error:

Operation	*Precondition*	*Error*	*Postcondition*
Create	**not** Is_Open	Status_Error	Is_Open
Open	**not** Is_Open	Status_Error	Is_Open
Close	Is_Open	Status_Error	**not** Is_Open
Delete	Is_Open	Status_Error	**not** Is_Open

Note that no corresponding Is_Open function exists for external files.

In the preceding program, the call to *Get* may raise End_Error for two reasons:

1. The original external file identified by the name "xyzzy" was empty.
2. The original external file was not empty, but the call to *Delete* in effect caused it to become empty.

Alternatively, the call to *Get* may execute without exception and simply return the first character of the original external file.

At this point, it might be useful to distinguish between properties of a file and properties of an external file. The following table provides a few examples of whether a property belongs to an internal or external file:

Property	File	External File
Is_Open	✓	
End_Of_File	✓	
Name		✓
Form	✓	✓
Mode	✓	
Direct_Io.Index	✓	
Direct_Io.Size		✓
Text_Io.Column	✓	
Text_Io.Line	✓	
Text_Io.Page	✓	

One may question the stability of these properties in the presence of multiple tasks. If two tasks operate concurrently on different files associated with different external files, then the files behave as prescribed by [Ada83, §14], that is, as one would expect. If a file is shared between tasks, then the semantics of shared variables [Ada83, §9.11] governs the file's behavior like any other shared object. Finally, external files are not considered objects that are governed by the semantics of shared variables. If multiple tasks operate on different files associated with the same external file, then side effects may occur.

A Related Problem: Under what cases can a call to Open propagate Mode_Error?

[Ada83]   14.1(1 .. 2, 6); 14.2.1(2 .. 6, 11 .. 13, 26 .. 27); 14.3.5(10);
             14.4(2, 4 .. 5, 7)
[ARG]   AI-00278/06, 06-16-89; AI-00320/06, 07-23-86; AI-00544/00, 08-08-87;
             AI-00574/04, 12-13-90; AI-00591/03, 07-07-90

23.1.2 Name Dropping

difficulty: programmer

What will the following program print? (Assume that the file can be opened.)

```
with Text_Io;   use Text_Io;
procedure Expanded is
   F : File_Type;
begin
   Create (F, Mode => Out_File, Name => "x");
   Put_Line (Name (F));
end Expanded;
```

◇◇◇◇◇

The answer to the question is implementation dependent.

The *Name* function returns a string that "uniquely" identifies the external file and thus may be used in a subsequent call to Create or Open. The degree to which files can be uniquely named is, of course, implementation dependent. For example, the string returned may include a directory name, a disk name, a version number, or a host name.

Examples of the output of the preceding program include the following:

```
PD2:<ADA.PD>X..1
DISK2:[BRYAN]X.LIS;1
/u/mendal/book/vol2/examples/x
c:x
C:X
```

[Ada83]   14.2.1(20 .. 21)

23.1.3 Reset

difficulty: designer

What will the following program print? (Assume that the external file can be created and reset.)

```
with Sequential_Io, Text_Io;
procedure Resetting is
   package Int_Io is new Sequential_Io (Integer);
   F : Int_Io.File_Type;
   X : Integer;
begin
   Int_Io.Create (F, Name => "x");
   for Int in 1 .. 5 loop
      Int_Io.Write (F, Int);
   end loop;

   Int_Io.Reset (F);
   for Int in 1 .. 2 loop
      Int_Io.Write (F, Int);
   end loop;

   Int_Io.Reset (F, Int_Io.In_File);
   while not Int_Io.End_Of_File (F) loop
      Int_Io.Read (F, X);
      Text_Io.Put (Integer'Image (X));
   end loop;
   Text_Io.New_Line;
end Resetting;
```

◇◇◇◇◇

The program will print *1 2*.

Reset changes the position within a file to the beginning of the file. For example, a call to Text_Io.Reset would set the line, column, and page counters of the file to 1. *Reset* operates on an open file and may be used to change the mode of a file. The following table illustrates the behavior of *Reset* on sequential and text files:

Old Mode	New Mode	File Size
In_Mode	In_Mode	unchanged
In_Mode	Out_Mode	0
Out_Mode	In_Mode	unchanged
Out_Mode	Out_Mode	0

The effect of the *Reset* operation on a direct file is quite different: *Reset* never changes the size of the file. If the foregoing program made use of Direct_Io instead of Sequential_Io, the output would be *1 2 3 4 5*.

[Ada83]   14.2.1(14 .. 16); 14.3.1(1, 4)
[ARG]   AI-00357/05, 06-18-87

23.1.4 Temporary Files

difficulty: programmer

Will the following program execute without raising an exception?

```
with Text_Io;   use Text_Io;
procedure Temp is
   type Text is access String;
   N : Text;
   F : File_Type;
begin
   Create (F);
   N := new String'(Name (F));
   Close (F);
   Open (F, In_File, N.all);
end Temp;
```

◇◇◇◇◇

The answer to the question is implementation dependent.

The last three parameters of the *Create* procedure have default expressions. The default for the Name parameter is a null string, signifying that the external file to be created is temporary. The name of the external file actually created is not specified by the language. Specifically, the value returned by the *Name* function need not be a null string. The intent is that temporary, external files not be accessible—e.g., they are automatically deleted after completion of the main program.

Ada allows an implementation a wide degree of latitude in the handling of temporary files. The association of a file to a temporary external file is implementation dependent. Since the *Name* function returns an identifier for an external file, its semantics is also implementation dependent. In fact, the function *Name* can propagate Use_Error.

Once a file associated with a temporary external file is closed, the association between the two is severed. Nothing prevents the implementation from deleting the external file as soon as this association is lost. In such a case, the call to *Open* in the preceding program would raise Name_Error.

The program might be made less implementation dependent by replacing the first call to *Close* and the subsequent call to *Open* by the call

```
    Reset (F, In_File);
```

Note that *Reset* may raise Use_Error. However, by using *Reset* instead of *Close* and *Open*, the association between the temporary file and the external file is not severed.

A Related Problem: If a main program and a library task share a temporary file, and the main program is completed before the library task terminates, can the temporary file be deleted before the library task has finished using it?

[Ada83]   14.2.1(2 .. 10, 14 .. 16, 20 .. 22); 14.4(1, 4 .. 5)
[ARG]   AI-00046/06, 07-23-86

23.1.5 Side Effects Associated with Files

difficulty: programmer

What will the following program print?

```
    with Text_Io;   use Text_Io;
    procedure Status is
      F : File_Type;
    begin
      Create (F);
      Open (F, Out_File, Name (F));
      Close (F);

      Put_Line ("It works.");
    exception
      when others =>
        begin
          Put_Line (Boolean'Image (Is_Open (F)));
```

```
        exception
          when others => Put_Line ("Just not my day.");
        end;
    end Status;
```

◇◇◇◇◇

The program will print *TRUE*.

The call to *Open* will propagate Status_Error, since *F* is already open. This exceptional call to *Open* does not affect the value of the file parameter *F*. Thus, within the exception handler, *F* is still open.

This requirement is a fairly strong constraint on the implementation of the I/O packages. Because of it, an implementation of *Open* cannot, for example, reset the line, column, and page of a file to 1 before propagating Status_Error.

Finally, note that the program does not close the file *F*. The language does not define the effect on an external file whose associated file is never closed.

A Related Problem: What other cases in the language are there where one can return from a subprogram exceptionally and guarantee that the "out" state of parameters of mode in out is the same as the "in" state?

[Ada83]   14.2(6 .. 7); 14.2.1(2 .. 7); 14.4(1 .. 2)
[ARG]   AI-00501/04 06-16-89

23.1.6 Exception Pecking Order

difficulty: designer

Suppose that in a given environment *dir/file* identifies an external file named *file* in directory *dir*. If an attempt is made to open this file for output, and write access is provided for *dir* but not for *file*, is the exception Mode_Error, Name_Error, or Use_Error propagated?

◇◇◇◇◇

Use_Error is propagated.

Most I/O operations can fail for a variety of reasons. Unlike other cases in the language where a single exception such as Constraint_Error can be raised for several different reasons, the I/O operations attempt to define distinct exceptions for each of the various failure conditions. The language explicitly defines an ordering for these conditions:

1. Status_Error
2. Mode_Error

3. Name_Error
4. Use_Error
5. Device_Error
6. End_Error
7. Data_Error
8. Layout_Error

At first glance, it would seem most likely that either Mode_Error or Name_Error would be raised in the situation described. But Mode_Error cannot be raised by Open, unless the file parameter is serving as current input or current output. Also, Name_Error is not raised, since the external file can be identified. Thus, Use_Error is raised, since the external file cannot be written to.

[Ada83]   14.4; 14.5
[ARG]   AI-00604/00, 11-08-88

23.1.7 Propagation of Predefined Exceptions

difficulty: programmer

For each of the exceptions predefined in package Standard, state whether a call to a Text_Io.Put_Line procedure may propagate the exception.

◇◇◇◇◇

Tasking_Error	No.
Numeric_Error	Only on evaluation of parameters.
Constraint_Error	Only on evaluation of parameters.
Program_Error	Yes.
Storage_Error	Yes.

The intent of the designers of Ada is that, upon beginning execution of an I/O subprogram, only the exceptions defined in package Io_Exceptions may be propagated. Constraint_Error and Numeric_Error may be raised during the evaluation of subprogram parameters—that is, before execution of the subprogram begins when copying in parameters, or after normal subprogram completion when copying out parameters. Program_Error may be raised upon an attempt to invoke *Put_Line* before the body of Text_Io has been elaborated, or if the execution of *Put_Line* is erroneous (say, if the string parameter passed is uninitialized). Therefore, Program_Error can only be raised due to a user's error. The raising of Storage_Error is completely system dependent. It may be raised at any time and, thus, may be propagated from the I/O routines.

A Related Problem: Explain why the following call will raise Constraint_Error:

```
S : String (−1 .. −2);   −− A null string.
L : Natural;
  ⋮
Get_Line (S, L);
```

[Ada83]   11.1(2 .. 9); 14.3.6(16 .. 17); 14.4(1)
[ARG]   AI-00279/09, 12-01-86

23.2 BINARY INPUT AND OUTPUT

Binary files are usually more efficient than text files in terms of both the size of the files and the execution of operations performed on them. Binary files are not intended to be humanly readable; rather, they are files containing data in a representation that is most easily operated on by the machine. Ada predefines two kinds of binary files: sequential and direct. Both kinds of files may be thought of as heterogeneous sequences of data (in that records whose components are of different types may be read and written). The data of a sequential file are read and written in a linear order (much like a linked list), while a direct file allows for random access (much like arrays).

23.2.1 Random Access

difficulty: programmer

What will the following program print?

```
with Direct_Io, Text_Io;
use Text_Io;
procedure Shuffle is
   package Dio is new Direct_Io (Character);
   F : Dio.File_Type;
   C : Character;
begin
   Dio.Create (F);
   for Char in 'A' .. 'E' loop
      Dio.Write (F, Char);
   end loop;

   Dio.Write (F, 'Z', 3);

   Dio.Read (F, C, 2);   Put (C);
   Dio.Read (F, C, 1);   Put (C);
   Dio.Read (F, C, 3);   Put (C);
```

```
Dio.Read  (F,  C);        Put  (C);
Dio.Read  (F,  C);        Put  (C);

New_Line;
end Shuffle;
```

◇◇◇◇◇

The program will print *BAZDE* and illustrates the use of direct files to read and write data in nonsequential order.

Upon opening or resetting a direct file, the file index is set to 1. Calling *Read* or *Write* without an index value causes the operation to be performed at the current index, and the current index is then incremented by one. Calling *Read* or *Write* with an index parameter has the effect of setting the current index to the value supplied and then calling the corresponding operation that has no index parameter.

Unlike the other predefined I/O packages, one can use Direct_Io to read from an uninitialized portion of a file. In the code

```
Dio.Create  (F);
Dio.Write   (F,  'A',  3);
Dio.Read    (F,  C,   1);
```

the call to *Read* may raise Data_Error. If Data_Error is not raised, then the code will execute without exception and the value read into *C* will be implementation dependent.

If one attempts to read beyond the current size of a direct file, as in the following code, the exception End_Error is raised:

```
Dio.Create  (F);
Dio.Write   (F,  'A',  3);
Dio.Read    (F,  C,   Dio.Size  (F)  +  1);
```

Note that the call to *Size* need not return the value 3; the value must be *at least* 3.

[Ada83]   14.2(1, 3 .. 4); 14.2.4; 14.2.5

23.2.2 Access Values

difficulty: designer

What will the following program print? (Assume that the files are opened and reset without exception.)

```
with Text_Io, Sequential_Io;
procedure Pickle is
   type Text is access String;
```

```
    package T_Io is new Sequential_Io (Text);
    V1, V2 : Text;
    F        : T_Io.File_Type;
begin
    T_Io.Open (F, T_Io.Out_File, "fto");
    V1 := new String'("one");
    T_Io.Write (F, V1);
    V1.all := "uno";

    T_Io.Reset (F, T_Io.In_File);
    T_Io.Read (F, V2);
    Text_Io.Put_Line (V2.all);
end Pickle;
```

◇◇◇◇◇

The program might print *uno*.

Before the call to *Reset*, *V1* designates a string object whose value is *uno*. It is possible that the call to *Read* will assign the value of *V1* to *V2*, and thus, both access objects will designate the same string object.

The effect of reading and writing access values is implementation dependent. Some implementations may disallow the foregoing instantiation of *Sequential_Io*, others may raise an exception on any of the calls to *T_Io*, and still others may simply output a random sequence of characters.

Although Ada is a strongly typed language, it does not strongly type the data in files. Conceptually, the data in a file is untyped and may be written and read using different types. Consider the following example:

```
declare
    type Int is range −2 ** 15 .. 2 ** 15 − 1;
    for Int'Size use 16;

    type Word is array (0 .. 15) of Boolean;
    for Word'Size use 16;

    package Seq_Io1 is new Sequential_Io (Int);
    package Seq_Io2 is new Sequential_Io (Word);

    F1 : Seq_Io1.File_Type;
    F2 : Seq_Io2.File_Type;
    W  : Word;
begin
    Seq_Io1.Create (F1, Seq_Io1.Out_File, "convert");
    Seq_Io1.Write  (F1, −1);
    Seq_Io1.Close  (F1);

    Seq_Io2.Open (F2, Seq_Io2.In_File, "convert");
```

```
      Seq_Io2.Read  (F2,  W);
      Seq_Io2.Close  (F2);
   end;
```

This code can have the effect of using a file to perform a checked type conversion between *Int* and *Word*. Such a method of conversion is different from employing an instance of Unchecked_Conversion, since the call to *Read* may include constraint checks on the value of *W*. If the value read is not of the type *Word*, Data_Error may be propagated; as described in Section 23.1.7, Constraint_Error may not be propagated. The language allows, but does not require, an implementation to check that the value read is of the subtype *Word*: such checks may be omitted if they are deemed by an implementation to be "too complex." Thus, the possible mechanics of the call to *Read* are:

1. The value read is not of the subtype *Word*, but no check is performed. The resulting value of *W* is implementation dependent, but the execution is not erroneous.
2. The value read is not of the subtype *Word*, a check is performed, and the exception Data_Error is propagated.
3. The value read is of the subtype *Word* and is returned as the value of *W*.

[Ada83]   14.1(7); 14.2(2); 14.2.2(1 .. 7)

23.2.3 Heterogeneous Files

difficulty: designer

How can one create a sequential file that contains both character and Boolean values?

◇◇◇◇◇

Two methods of creating such files are by using Ada's typing mechanism to create a heterogeneous type, i.e., a record type with a variant part, and by converting the different types to a single common type.

In the first approach, one simply defines a record type that may contain either a character value or a Boolean value:

```
      type Heterogeneous (Is_Char : Boolean := True) is
        record
          case Is_Char is
             when True   => C : Character;
             when False  => B : Boolean;
          end case;
        end record;

      package H_Io is new Sequential_Io (Heterogeneous);
```

This method can easily be extended to write strings as sequences of record values whose variant supports a character:

```
procedure Write (File  :  in  H_Io.File_Type;
                           Item  :  in  String) is
begin
  for Index in Item'Range loop
    H_Io.Write (File, (True, Item (Index)));
  end loop;
end Write;
```

This subprogram can be thought of as part of a transparent layer on top of *H_Io*: users can either call *H_Io* directly or call the foregoing operation.

Reading strings involves a bit more mechanics. Suppose one wants the semantics to be that characters are read until the string actual parameter is filled or a Boolean value is encountered. Such semantics involves look-ahead to see whether the next value to be read is of the type Character. An opaque layer must be used to preserve the state of the file so that the state is not corrupted by inadvertent calls to *H_Io*. The following code is illustrative:

```
with Sequential_Io;
package Opaque_Io is
  type File_Type is limited private;
    :
    :
  procedure Read (File  :  in       File_Type;
                         Item  :       out String;
                         Last  :       out Natural);
private
    :
    :
  type Look (Ahead : Boolean := False) is
    record
      case Ahead is
        when False  =>  null;
        when True   =>  H : Heterogeneous;
      end case;
    end record;

  type File_Rec is
    record
      F : H_Io.File_Type;
      L : Look;
    end record;

  type File_Type is access File_Rec;
end Opaque_Io;
with Io_Exceptions;
```

```
package body Opaque_Io is
   :
   :
procedure Read (File : in       File_Type;
                    Item :      out String;
                    Last :      out Natural) is
begin
   if File = null then
      raise Io_Exceptions.Mode_Error;
   end if;

   Last := 0;

   if not File.L.Ahead then
      File.L := (True, (True, Ascii.Nul));
      H_Io.Read (File.F, File.L.H);
   end if;

   for Index in Item'Range loop
      exit when not File.L.H.Is_Char;
      Item (Index) := File.L.H.C;
      Last := Index;
      H_Io.Read (File.F, File.L.H);
   end loop;
end Read;
end Opaque_Io;
```

The second method involves the use of a homogeneous file and conversion of character and Boolean values to a common type:

```
type Common is range 0 .. 127;
package Common_Io is new Sequential_Io (Common);

procedure Write (File : in Common_Io.File_Type;
                     Item : in Character) is
begin
   Common_Io.Write (File, Character'Pos (Item));
end Write;

procedure Read (File : in       Common_Io.File_Type;
                    Item :      out Boolean) is
   Temp : Common;
begin
   Common_Io.Read (File, Temp);
   Item := Temp /= 0;
end Read;
```

This implementation does not preserve the type of the data in an external file. For example, one can write the Character value 'A' and read it as the Boolean value True.

A worthwhile application of using a common type for writing values of multiple types involves Text_Io.[1] For example, one might want to write a string, a number, and another string on the same line. This can be accomplished by multiple calls to Put and a call to Put_Line, but such code is often viewed as unreadable. Instead, one could use String as a common type and generate the desired output with one call:

```
package Flt_Io is new Text_Io.Float_Io (Float);
function "+" (Item : in Float) return String is
   Str : String (1 .. Flt_Io.Default_Fore + Flt_Io.Default_Aft +
                       Flt_Io.Default_Exp  + 2);
begin
    Flt_Io.Put (Str, Item);
    return Str;
end "+";
   .
   .
Flt_Io.Default_Fore := 5;
Flt_Io.Default_Aft  := 2;
Flt_Io.Default_Exp  := 0;
Put_Line ("Total is " & (+10.0) & " dollars.");
```

A Related Problem: Rewrite Opaque_Io.Read so that if a file contains only three characters and the user passes an *Item* of length 5, then the three characters are returned instead of End_Error being propagated.

[Ada83]   14.2(2); 14.2.2; 14.2.3

23.3 TEXT INPUT AND OUTPUT

The package Text_Io is large and contains many features. The package includes 4 type declarations, 3 named subtype declarations, 70 constructors, 34 selectors, 8 exceptional conditions, and 4 generic units. It is not difficult to understand a given feature in isolation, but the sheer number of features and the semantic interactions between them can become overwhelming.

The goal of this section is to highlight a few key concepts that form the foundation for understanding Text_Io. Each concept involves a number of package features.

[1]This approach is adapted from one presented by Dr. Paul Hilfinger.

23.3.1 Extensions

difficulty: programmer

Is it legal for an implementation to extend the declaration of Text_Io given in [Ada83, §14.3.10] by adding more subprograms?

◇◇◇◇◇

No new declarations to the visible part of Text_Io or any of its generic units may be added. Such extensions would decrease the portability of Ada code. Consider the following example:

```
with  Text_Io;
package  My_9X  is
   Standard_Error : Text_Io.File_Type;
end  My_9X;

with  Text_Io, My_9X;
use  Text_Io, My_9X;
procedure  Potentially_Portable  is
begin
   Put_Line (Standard_Error, "Sorry, a system error occurred.   ID=02");
end  Potentially_Portable;
```

Given the definition of *Text_Io* in [Ada83], this program would compile without error, and the naming of *Standard_Error* denotes My_9X.Standard_Error. If an implementation had extended the visible part of Text_Io with

```
function  Standard_Error  return  File_Type;
```

then the foregoing procedure would be semantically illegal.

As an alternative to extending Text_Io, an implementation is allowed to extend the visible part of package System. (An implementation is also allowed to provide implementation-defined attributes and pragmas.)

[Ada83]   1.1.2; 13.7(2); 14.3.10; F(10)
[ARG]   AI-00248/05, 12-13-90

23.3.2 Buffering Output

difficulty: designer

Suppose that standard input and output are associated with an interactive device such as a terminal. Must the string in the call to Put in the following program appear on the terminal before Get_Line is executed?

```
with Text_Io;   use Text_Io;
procedure Q is
   Id   : String (1 .. 100);
   Last : Natural;
begin
   Put ("Enter your name: ");
   Get_Line (Id, Last);
   Put_Line ("Your name is " & Id (1 .. Last) & '.');
end Q;
```

◇◇◇◇◇

The string need not appear before Get_Line is executed.

Clearly, the intent of the program is that the prompt (*Enter your name:*) appear before the user begins typing a name. But the semantics of Text_Io does not guarantee this behavior. In general, effects on an external file need not be observable until the associated (internal) file has been closed. These lenient semantics allow, for example, an implementation to buffer input and output for reasons of efficiency.

An execution of the program could display the prompt only after the user enters a name followed by a line terminator. Or, the prompt could be displayed while the user is entering a name. In fact, the prompt might never appear on the terminal, since standard output is never closed: [Ada83] does not define whether or, if so, when the standard input and output files are closed.

A Related Problem: Could the desired effect of the program be achieved by inserting the following code between *Put* and *Get_Line*?

```
declare
   Stdout : constant String := Name (Standard_Output);
   F      : File_Type;
begin
   Open (F, Out_File, Stdout);
   Close (F);
   Open (F, Out_File, Stdout);
end;
```

[Ada83]   14.1(7); 14.3(5); 14.3.2(1, 8 .. 16)

23.3.3 Resetting Default Streams

difficulty: designer

What will the following program print?

```
with Text_Io;   use Text_Io;
procedure Set_And_Reset is
   F : File_Type;
begin
   Open (F, In_File, "abc");

   begin
      Set_Input (F);
   exception
      when others =>
         Put ("Set failed... ");   raise;
   end;

   begin
      Reset (F, Out_File);
   exception
      when others =>
         Put ("Reset failed... ");   raise;
   end;
exception
   when Status_Error => Put_Line ("status.");
   when Name_Error   => Put_Line ("name.");
   when Mode_Error   => Put_Line ("mode.");
end Set_And_Reset;
```

◇◇◇◇◇

Assuming the call to Open executes without exception, the program will print *Reset failed... mode.*

Text_Io defines four files that determine the semantics of I/O operations that do not include a file parameter: standard input, standard output, current input, and current output. (Functions returning a *File_Type* value are provided for each of these.) Input routines that do not supply a file parameter read from current input. Output routines without file parameters write to current output. Initially, standard input and current input refer to the same file, and similarly for standard output and current output. The association of standard input and standard output to external files is predefined by an implementation and may not be changed by calls to Text_Io subprograms. Current input and current output, however, may be changed. The call to *Set_Input* has the effect of changing the "current input" file to *F*. Subsequent calls to Get without a file parameter will read from the file *F*.

Reset may be invoked to change the mode of a file (from input to output or vice versa). However, one may not change the mode of a file that is serving as current input or current output.

Current input and current output are simply aliases of other files. As the preceding program illustrates, these other files may be declared by users and may be created, opened, closed, or deleted. Thus, a call to Get without a file parameter can propagate Status_Error when current input is closed.

A Related Problem: Can Text_Io.Open ever raise Mode_Error?

[Ada83]   14.2.1(1, 14 .. 16); 14.3(4 .. 5); 14.3.1(1, 4 .. 5);
               14.3.2(1 .. 4, 8 ,, 16)
[ARG]   AI-00048/12, 02-23-87; AI-00546/04, 08-15-90

23.3.4 Closed Default Files

difficulty: programmer

To which internal file is the following call to Put writing? To which external file is the call writing?

```
with Text_Io;   use Text_Io;
procedure Trade_Winds is
  F : File_Type;
begin
  Create (F, Name => "x");
  Set_Output (F);
  Close (F);
  Put ("Now what?");
end Trade_Winds;
```

◇◇◇◇◇

The call to *Put* will raise Status_Error.

After the call to *Set_Output*, the internal files *F* and the one returned by Current_Output are aliases for each other. Thus, the call to *Close* has the side effect of closing the internal file returned by Current_Output. *Put* then attempts to write to current output, a closed file, causing Status_Error to be raised.

[Ada83]   14.1(6); 14.2.1(8 .. 10); 14.3(5); 14.3.2(1, 5 .. 7); 14.3.5(9);
               14.4(2)
[ARG]   AI-00048/12, 02-23-87

23.3.5 Nonexistent Default Files

difficulty: language lawyer

Explain the semantics of the following program when reading from standard input is not supported:

```
with Text_Io;   use Text_Io;
procedure P is
   B : constant Boolean := Is_Open (Standard_Output);
   package Int_Io is new Integer_Io (Integer);
   Item, Last : Integer;
begin
   Int_Io.Get (" 123", Item, Last);   -- "Get" from a string.
end P;
```

◇◇◇◇◇

The program will execute without exception.

The standard input and output files are *open* at the beginning of program execution. [Ada83], however, does not specify how these files get *opened*. Associating external files with standard input and output is an environment issue that is outside the scope of the language. If the association fails (e.g., if the files cannot be opened with the correct modes), then the program cannot begin execution.

Implementations that do not support any I/O with external files must still support the Get and Put routines that do not involve files. This stipulation may appear to introduce an inconsistency into the semantics of Text_Io: on the one hand, the standard files must be open before the operations of Text_Io can be invoked, yet on the other hand, some implementations need not support opening of external files. The intent is that the standard files somehow become open, and then any subsequent reading from or writing to these files raises an exception. Since the preceding program never manipulates the state of the standard files, it can be executed without exception on all implementations.

[Ada83]   14.1(6); 14.2.1(26 .. 27); 14.3(3, 5); 14.3.7(13 .. 17);
           14.3.8(17 .. 21); 14.3.9(10 .. 14)
[ARG]   AI-00575/00, 07-06-88; AI-00576/04, 12-13-90

23.3.6 Parsing with Enumeration_Io

difficulty: programmer

Suppose a program is to read commands from Current_Input using the following syntax:

```
command::= direction [ number ] color
             | quit
direction ::= up | down | left | right
number   ::= 1 | 2 | 3 | 4 | 5
color     ::= red | green | blue
```

Show how the program can be written to read commands using instantiations of Enumeration_Io and Integer_Io.

◇◇◇◇◇

The following program illustrates how to read one command:

```
with Text_Io;   use Text_Io;
procedure Parser is
   type Direction is (Up, Down, Left, Right, Quit);
   type Number  is range 1 .. 5;
   type Color   is (Red, Green, Blue);

   package Dio is new Enumeration_Io (Direction);
   package Nio is new Integer_Io (Number);
   package Cio is new Enumeration_Io (Color);

   No_Number : Boolean;
   N         : Number;
   D         : Direction;
   C         : Color;
begin
   Dio.Get (D);

   if D /= Quit then
      begin
         Nio.Get (N);
         No_Number := False;
      exception
         when Data_Error => No_Number := True;
      end;

      Cio.Get (C);
   end if;

   Skip_Line;

   :  -- Process the command.
exception
   when Data_Error => Skip_Line;
                      Put_Line ("Bad command.");
end Parser;
```

The first call to *Get* tries to read a direction. If a legal direction is not entered, then *Data_Error* is raised and an error message is issued. If the direction entered is not *Quit*, then a check is performed to see whether an optional number has been entered; the call to *Nio.Get* and the enclosing block perform this check. Finally, *Cio.Get* reads the color. If an invalid color is entered, *Data_Error* is again raised and an error message is issued.

This program can recognize the following valid commands:

```
uP        ReD
QUIT
left  2#11#  blue
down     02  blue
```

It can also detect the following invalid commands:

```
xy  4  green
left
up  9099
down02  blue
```

A Related Problem: The preceding code recognizes "down green language". Show how to modify the code so that extra tokens following a valid command sequence are not ignored.

[Ada83]   14.3(2 .. 3); 14.3.5(5 .. 6, 10); 14.3.7(2, 5 .. 8); 14.3.9(5 .. 7); 14.4(8)

23.3.7 Nongraphic I/O

difficulty: programmer

What will the following program print?

```
with Text_Io;
procedure Imaging is
   package Char_Io is new Text_Io.Enumeration_Io (Character);
begin
   Text_Io.Put  (Ascii.Nul);
   Char_Io.Put  (Ascii.Nul);
   Text_Io.New_Line;
end Imaging;
```

◇◇◇◇◇

The use of Text_Io with nongraphic characters is implementation dependent. One might expect that, when writing characters using Text_Io, the characters would be written without interpretation. However, when writing to devices such as terminals, it is common for certain character sequences that include nongraphic characters to be interpreted. For example, writing Ascii.FF (form feed) to a terminal may cause the terminal to clear its screen.

The call to *Char_Io.Put* prints the enumeration literal corresponding to the first value of the type Character. The problem is that the standard does not define the literals of nongraphic characters. The Ada Rapporteur Group has provided literals for such characters: the literals are simply the names given in italics in [Ada83, §C(13)]. This interpretation by the Ada Rapporteur Group is nonbinding: not all implementations need to conform to it. An implementation that accepts such an interpretation will print *NUL* on the call to *Char_Io.Put*.

Reading nongraphic characters by using Text_Io is equally problematic. Consider a file that contains Ascii.Nul, Ascii.Soh, and Ascii.Stx, followed by a line, page, and file terminator. Reading this file using Get_Line may yield zero characters. Alternatively, only the Ascii.Soh may be returned.

The difference between the preceding two *Put* calls goes beyond the use of graphic characters. For example, in

```
Text_Io.Put ('f');
Char_Io.Put ('f');
```

the first call will print one character, f, while the second call will print the image of the enumeration literal, 'f', including the single quotes.

The generic formal parameter of *Enumeration_Io* can be any discrete type. This means that an integer subtype may be used as the generic actual parameter. However [Ada83, §14.3.9(15)] states explicitly that the use of *Enumeration_Io* with integer sub-types is implementation dependent.

[Ada83]   14.3(7); 14.3.5(5, 7 .. 8); 14.3.9
[ARG]   AI-00239/11, 02-23-87

23.3.8 Invalid Data

difficulty: programmer

What will the following program print if an asterisk is entered in the input stream?

```
with Text_Io;   use Text_Io;
procedure Recovery is
   package F_Io is new Float_Io (Float);
   R : Float;
begin
   loop
     begin
       Put ("Enter a number: ");
       F_Io.Get (R);
       exit;
     exception
       when Data_Error => Put_Line ("Get real!");
     end;
   end loop;
end Recovery;
```

◇◇◇◇◇

The following line will be printed an infinite number of times:

    Enter a number: Get real!

Only those characters conforming to the syntax of the specified type are input. When the call to *Get* encounters the asterisk, Data_Error is raised since an asterisk does not conform to the syntax of a real number. The asterisk is never input by the call to *Get*, even though it has been examined by *Get*. The exception is handled, and "Get real" is output. Upon each iteration, *Get* encounters the same invalid asterisk character, raises Data_Error, and so on ad infinitum.

Suppose the user entered "1.2*". Then *R* would obtain the value 1.2, the asterisk would never be input, and the program would terminate normally.

Suppose the user entered "123.45E*". In this case, *Get* would again read up to the asterisk. Since the preceding sequence of characters (123.45E) does not form a real number, Data_Error would be raised and the asterisk would not be input. The sequence preceding the asterisk, however, would be input; only the asterisk would remain.

In general, the Get routines of the four generic packages in Text_Io begin by skipping preceding blanks, tabs, line, and page terminators. A sequence of characters is then read until the syntax of values of the target type is no longer satisfied or a line terminator is encountered. The character sequence read is then checked to see that it is a syntactically legal value and a value of the target subtype. If either check fails, then Data_Error is raised.

The original program could be modified as follows to eliminate the infinite loop:

```
declare
    C : Character;
begin
    Put ("Enter a number: ");
    F_Io.Get (R);
    exit;
exception
    when Data_Error => Put_Line ("Get real!");
                        Get (C);
end;
```

This modification might not be the most user-friendly solution, since it would issue an error message for each invalid character entered. When the user enters "* * *", three lines are output.

Another solution would be to invoke Skip_Line, to bypass illegal character sequences:

```
begin
    Put ("Enter a number: ");
    F_Io.Get (R);
    Skip_Line;
```

```
      exit;
exception
  when Data_Error => Skip_Line;
                        Put_Line ("Get real!");
  end;
```

The calls to *Skip_Line* have the effect of flushing the input, up to and including the next line terminator.

A third solution is to use only Get_Line. The string read can then be analyzed using the Get subprograms that read from strings.

A Related Problem: How would the semantics of the original program be affected if a nonzero value were supplied for the Width parameter in the call to *Get*? Is Data_Error raised by the following code?

```
declare
   type Int is range 1 .. 10;
   pragma Suppress (Range_Check, Int);
   L : Positive;
   N : Int;
   package Int_Io is new Text_Io.Integer_Io (Int);
begin
   Int_Io.Get ("11", N, L);
end;
```

[Ada83]   14.3.5(1 .. 2, 5 .. 6, 10); 14.3.8(8 .. 11, 17 .. 19); 14.4(8)

23.3.9 Parsing Integer Literals

difficulty: programmer

What will the following program print?

```
with Text_Io;   use Text_Io;
procedure Lex is
  package Int_Io is new Integer_Io (Integer);

  procedure Test (From : String) is
     Item, Last : Integer;
  begin
     if Text_Io.Col > 1 then
        Put ("; ");
     end if;
     Int_Io.Get (From, Item, Last);
     Put (Integer'Image (Item) & Integer'Image (Last));
  exception
```

```
      when Data_Error =>
         Put ("Data_Error");
   end Test;
begin
   Test ("Hello world.");
   Test (' ' & Ascii.Ht & "4.3");
   Test ("0E-3");
   Test ("20#A#");
   New_Line;
end Lex;
```

◇◇◇◇◇

The program will print *Data_Error; 4 3; Data_Error; Data_Error*.

The semantics of reading from a file and reading from a string are operationally equivalent. The first execution of *Test* will raise *Data_Error* because the first character of the input, 'H', is not syntactically a part of an integer value.

The second call involves the skipping of white space. When the period is encountered, input ceases, the characters read are determined to represent an integer value, and Item is returned with the value 4. Since three characters were successfully read from the string, *Last* is returned as 3.

The third and fourth invocations of *Test* raise Data_Error. Both string parameters syntactically form integer values. Thus, the entire strings are read. However, neither string represents a legal integer value. The first and third invocations of *Test* illustrate the syntactic and semantic reasons, respectively, for why Data_Error can be raised.

A Related Problem: Identify the typographical error in [Ada83, §14.3.8(20)].

[Ada83]   14.3(3, 8); 14.3.4(26, 41 .. 42); 14.3.5(5 .. 6); 14.3.7(2, 13 .. 15);
             14.4(8)
[ARG]   AI-00051/07, 07-23-86; AI-00215/05, 07-23-86

23.3.10 Real Imaging

difficulty: programmer

What will the following program print?

```
with Text_Io;
procedure Image is
   type R is digits 6;
   package R_Io is new Text_Io.Float_Io (R);
   use Text_Io, R_Io;
   Pi : constant R := 3.14159_26535;
   S  : String (1 .. 10);
```

```
begin
    Put  (Pi);                                              New_Line;   -- 1.
    Put  (Pi,  Fore  =>  5,  Aft   =>  10,  Exp  =>  5);    New_Line;   -- 2.
    Put  (Pi,  Fore  =>  0,  Exp  =>  0);                   New_Line;   -- 3.
    Put  (-Pi  *  10.0,  0,  0,  1);                        New_Line;   -- 4.

    Put  (S,  Pi);   Put_Line  (S);                                     -- 5.
exception
    when  Layout_Error  =>  Put_Line  ("Squeezed  dry.");
end  Image;
```

◇◇◇◇◇

The program will print

```
3.14159E+00
     3.1415925026E+0000
3.14159
-3.14E+1
Squeezed  dry.
```

(The second literal printed is implementation dependent.)
    The parameters Fore, Aft, and Exp of the *Put* routines in *Float_Io* determine the layout of real-number output. Fore determines the number of characters preceding the decimal point, Aft determines the number of digits following the decimal point that appear before the 'E' that begins the exponent, and Exp determines the number of characters in the exponent. These three parameters have default expressions defined by the following objects declared in the visible part of *Float_Io*:

```
Default_Fore  :  Field  :=  2;
Default_Aft   :  Field  :=  Num'Digits  -  1;
Default_Exp   :  Field  :=  3;
```

Thus, in the first call to *Put*, Fore is 2, Aft is 5, and Exp is 3. Note that the generic package Fixed_Io provides the same three subprogram parameters, as well as the three variables with similar semantics.
    The program illustrates that

- The *fore* field may constrain leading spaces, followed by a minus sign for negative numbers.

- The *aft* field does not include the character used for the decimal point, and similarly, the *exp* field does not include the 'E' character.

- The *exp* field, if present, always includes a sign (+ or -) and may include leading zeros.

The following illustrates the fields of the second call to *Put*:

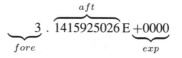

$$\underbrace{}_{fore}\ 3\ .\ \overbrace{1415925026}^{aft}\ \text{E}\ \underbrace{+0000}_{exp}$$

Calls 3 and 4 indicate that the value zero applied to the *Fore* parameter causes the number to be output with a minimum number of characters before the decimal point, i.e., with no leading blanks. The minimum number of characters is a function of the value being output, the value of *Aft*, and the value of *Exp*.

The value of *Aft* may also be zero, in which case *Aft* is reinterpreted as the number one. If *Exp* is zero, then no exponent field is output; e.g., for values greater than or equal to 10.0, an *Exp* of zero will cause multiple digits to be output before the decimal point.

If *Exp* is nonzero, its value is not always interpreted as the exact number of characters to output after the 'E'. Consider the value of *Exp* in call number 4. If *Exp* is less than the number of characters needed to represent the exponent (including the sign), then the actual parameter is "overridden" by as many characters as are needed.

Call number 5 illustrates outputting a real value to a string variable. This overloading of *Put* has *Aft* and *Exp* parameters, but no *Fore* parameter. The fore field is interpreted as the number of characters needed to fill the string variable, given the real value and the layout specified by the *Aft* and *Exp* parameters. If the layout generates more characters than the string parameter's length, the exception Layout_Error is raised. (Layout_Error is never raised by calls to Put that operate on files.)

One might question the output of the second call to *Put*. The number printed is not the same as the literal given in the initialization of *Pi*. Further, more digits are output than are specified in the accuracy constraint of *R*. There are many possible explanations for this behavior:

- The accuracy of R'Base could be greater than that of R.
- The number in the initialization of *Pi* may not be a model number of *R*, and thus, any number in the minimal model interval surrounding the value is assigned to the object.
- Digits beyond the accuracy of R (or R'Base) are generated arbitrarily.

A Related Problem: Output the value 1.1 such that the only digit before the decimal point is zero. Output a real value in a base other than decimal.

[Ada83]   14.3.(3); 14.3.8(2 .. 6, 12 .. 16, 20 ..21)

23.3.11 Skipping Lines

difficulty: designer

Suppose that the external file identified by the name "x" contains "abcde" as its first line and "fghij" as its second line. What will the following program print?

```
with Text_Io;   use Text_Io;
procedure Skippy is
   F : File_Type;
   S : String (1 .. 5);
   L : Natural;
begin
   Open (F, In_File, "x");
   Get_Line (F, S, L);
   Put_Line ('>' & S (1 .. L) & '<');
   Get_Line (F, S, L);
   Put_Line ('>' & S (1 .. L) & '<');
end Skippy;
```

◇◇◇◇◇

The program will print

```
>abcde<
><
```

Get_Line reads characters until

1. The string actual parameter is filled, or
2. A line terminator has been reached.

Note that the order in which these conditions are checked affects the output.

Suppose the check for a line terminator is performed first. Then the first call to *Get_Line* would read "abcde", encounter the line terminator, invoke Skip_Line, and return.

If the check for filling the string parameter is performed first, then *Get_Line* would read "abcde", realize that the string is full, and return; *Get_Line* would never cause the skipping of the subsequent line terminator. The second call to *Get_Line* would then immediately encounter the line terminator and return no characters.

The Ada Rapporteur Group has stipulated that filling the string is checked first. This semantics is outlined by the following code:

```
Last := Item'First − 1;
for Int in Item'Range loop
   if line terminator next then
```

```
        Skip_Line;
            exit;
        end if;

        Get (Item (Int));
        Last := Int;
    end loop;
```

A Related Problem: How can one tell whether a call to Get_Line caused the skipping of a line terminator?

[Ada83]   14.3.6(12 .. 14)
[ARG]   AI-00050/11, 12-01-86

23.3.12 Turn the Page

difficulty: designer

What will the following program print? (Assume that Text_Io.Count'Last is at least 6.)

```
            with Text_Io;   use Text_Io;
            procedure Pager is
              F : File_Type;
            begin
              Create (F);
              for Page in 1 .. 2 loop
                for Line in 1 .. 3 loop
                  Put_Line (F, "hi");
                end loop;
                New_Page (F);
              end loop;

              Reset (F, In_File);

              while not End_Of_Page (F) loop
                Skip_Line (F);
              end loop;
              Put_Line (Positive_Count'Image (Page (F)) &
                        Positive_Count'Image (Line (F)));
            end Pager;
```

◇◇◇◇◇

The program will print *3 1*.

Before the call to *Reset*, the file contains

```
hi←
hi←
hi←¶
hi←
hi←
hi←¶
⊥
```

where ← represents a line terminator, ¶ represents a page terminator, and ⊥ represents
a file terminator.

    End_Of_Page returns True if a line terminator followed by a page terminator is
next or if a file terminator is next. The first two calls to *Skip_Line* skip the first two
lines of the file. The third call to *Skip_Line* skips the third line *and* the following page
terminator. After skipping the page terminator, the page count is incremented and the
line count is reset to 1. The sixth call to *Skip_Line* skips the sixth physical line and the
second page terminator, increments the page count, and resets the line count to 1. At
that point, *End_Of_Page* will yield True since a file terminator is next.

[Ada83]   14.2.1(14 .. 15); 14.3(6, 8); 14.3.1(1, 4);
               14.3.4(6, 8, 14 .. 15, 20 ..21)
[ARG]   AI-00605/00, 11-22-88

23.3.13 The Disappearing Line Trick

difficulty: designer

What will the following program print? (Assume that the file can be opened and reset.)

```
with Text_Io;   use Text_Io;
procedure Ullage is
   F  : File_Type;
   Int : Natural := 0;
begin
   Create (F);
   New_Line (F, 2);
   Reset (F, In_File);

   while not End_Of_File (F) loop
      Int := Int + 1;
      Skip_Line (F);
   end loop;

   Put_Line (Integer'Image (Int) & Count'Image (Line (F)));
exception
```

```
   when End_Error => Put_Line ("Dry cork.");
end Ullage;
```

◇◇◇◇◇

The program will print *1 2*.

   After the call to *Reset*, the file contains

↩
↩¶
⊥

where ↩ represents a line terminator, ¶ represents a page terminator, and ⊥ represents a file terminator.

   Reset has the effect of calling *New_Page*, since the current page had not been terminated prior to calling *Reset*. If the current line were not terminated, *New_Page* would output a line terminator as well as a page terminator.

   End_Of_File returns True if a file terminator is next or if the sequence ↩¶⊥ is next. The first call to *End_Of_File* will thus return False, and *Skip_Line* will read past the first line terminator. At this point, the file is positioned at the second line terminator. The second call to *End_Of_File* then returns True, since the sequence ↩¶⊥ is next.

   This program illustrates an anomaly of using Text_Io to read a file in which the last "line" is of length zero. Consider reading the following files using Get_Line or Skip_Line:

File 1	*File 2*	*File 3*
↩	Hello↩	Hello↩¶
Hello↩¶	↩¶	⊥
⊥	⊥	

   Two lines can be read from the first file, but only one line can be read from files 2 and 3. Since Skip_Line reads past the next line terminator and an immediately following page terminator (if it exists), End_Of_Page will never yield True when reading from files 2 and 3 with Get_Line.

   Both Reset and Close ensure that the last line and page of a file are always terminated. All files written with Text_Io will end with the ↩¶⊥ sequence. Text_Io files cannot contain the sequence ↩⊥. Also, it is not possible to position a file at the sequence ¶⊥.

   One can determine the difference between files 2 and 3 by reading each file a character at a time and attempting to predict the file terminator, as in the following code:

```
declare
   C : Character;
```

```
begin
  while not End_Of_File (F) loop
    Get (F, C);
  end loop;
  Put_Line ("Survey says... file 3.");
exception
  when End_Error => Put_Line ("Survey says... file 2.");
end;
```

When reading file 2, *End_Of_File* never returns True, and yet *End_Error* is raised. The reason for this anomaly is that *Get* skips past adjacent line and page terminators, looking for the next character. When reading file 3, *End_Of_File* becomes True after reading the fifth character, 'o'.

A Related Problem: Describe how to read a file twice, once using Get_Line and once using Get with a character parameter, in order to determine whether the last n lines of a file are of length zero.

[Ada83]   14.2.1(8 .. 9, 14 .. 15); 14.3(6, 8); 14.3.1(1, 3 .. 4);
             14.3.4(2 .. 4, 6, 8, 20 .. 21, 23 .. 24, 44 .. 45); 14.3.5(3, 10);
             14.3.6(2 .. 4, 12 .. 13); 14.4(7)

chapter 24

Machine Representations

When an instance of Unchecked_Deallocation is applied to a task object designating a terminated task, a good compiler will reclaim the storage occupied by the task. Not all compilers are good. Norman H. Cohen, Internet message, February 27, 1990

At the request of then-congressman Bill Chappell, the GAO was directed to conduct an investigation into why the Army was spending money collecting Ada metrics on the AFATDS program. The investigator went into the program manager's office and demanded to know why the customer and the Army were spending so much money converting Ada to the metric system. Ralph E. Crafts, at the Bay Area SIGAda meeting, July 17, 1990

Representation clauses allow one to specify more exactly the implementation of types, objects, subprograms, packages, tasks, and entries. Representation clauses can be used to define the physical implementation of data; the address at which objects, subprograms, packages, and tasks are located; and the interpretation of entries. All of these aspects of Ada entities are low-level concerns that, for the most part, do not affect the operational semantics of a program. In most programming, it is acceptable to provide no representation clauses and thus allow an implementation to select default representations for Ada entities. Mainly, these low-level representation issues become important only when binding language features to a particular target architecture.

The language provides four kinds of representation clauses:

1. length clauses, which specify the accuracy of fixed point types and the size of types, collections, and task activations
2. enumeration representations, for specifying the internal codes used for values of an enumeration type
3. record representations, which specify the physical layout of record values
4. address clauses, which specify the physical addresses at which entities are to be located.

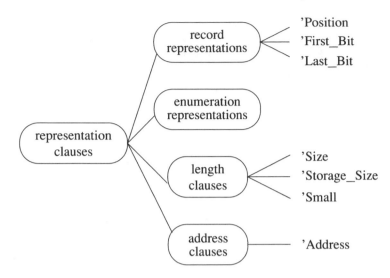

Figure 24.1   Categories of representation clauses with attributes.

The various kinds of clauses are categorized in Figure 24.1, along with the attributes they affect.

Because these clauses are used to bind entities to a specific representation, it should not be surprising that *all* representation clauses are implementation dependent. Thus, even the most innocent representation clause, e.g.,

```
type T is   (A, B, C);
for   T use (0, 1, 2);
```

may be illegal. Although the standard defines the syntax and the semantics of representation clauses, it does not require an implementation to support any representation clause.[1] However, if an implementation cannot support a representation clause, it cannot simply ignore it. Rather, the implementation must declare the clause illegal at compilation time. Each implementation of Ada is required to supply *Appendix F* of the standard to document the restrictions it places on the use of representation clauses.

Because representation clauses are optional, the answers to almost all of the questions posed in the first five sections of this chapter are implementation dependent. Thus, many of these questions include a qualifying assumption that an implementation can support the clauses under discussion, so that the effect of the clauses, when supported, may be discussed.

The last two sections present two additional implementation-dependent and optional language features: machine code insertion and unchecked programming.

---

[1] AI-00361/08, 02-10-87.

24.1 SCALAR TYPES

The representation clauses discussed in this section are those used to define the internal codes of enumeration values, the model numbers of a fixed point type that are not multiples of a power of two, and the size of scalar types and objects.

24.1.1 Internal Codes versus Position Numbers

difficulty: programmer

Suppose an implementation supports all forms of representation clauses. What will the following program print?

```
with  Text_Io;
procedure  Ic  is
   type  T  is  (A,  B,  C);
   for  T  use  (C  =>  25,  B  =>  20,  A  =>  10);
begin
   Text_Io.Put_Line  (Integer'Image  (T'Pos  (B)));
end  Ic;
```

◇◇◇◇◇

The program will print *1*.

The *Pos* and *Val* attributes operate on position numbers, while enumeration representation clauses specify internal codes. (Internal codes given in a representation clause must be static and of the type *universal_integer*.) The only relationship between position numbers and internal codes is that, for all values *X* and *Y* of an enumeration type *E*,

$$X < Y = E'Pos (X) < E'Pos (Y) =$$
$$internal{-}code(X) < internal{-}code(Y)$$

An example of an enumeration representation clause that violates this relationship and is thus illegal is

```
for  T  use  (2,  3,  2);   --  Illegal.
```

In the absence of an enumeration representation clause, the internal codes for an enumeration type are implementation dependent. That is, the language does not require that the default internal codes be the position numbers.

Internal codes are not observable within the language. In fact, internal codes are intended to be useful only when interfacing with non-Ada code. One cannot obtain the internal code of an enumeration value without making use of unchecked programming, e.g., unchecked conversion, pragma Interface, or I/O conversions.

[Ada83]   13.1(5); 13.3
[ARG]   AI-00564/00, 10-11-88

24.1.2 The Predefined Type Character

difficulty: language lawyer

The definition of the type Character, as given in [Ada83, §C(13)], includes a representation clause. Suppose an implementation does not support any representation clauses. Is package Standard then illegal?

◇◇◇◇◇

It is meaningless to consider whether package Standard is legal or illegal. Package Standard is never compiled: it is not a compilation unit, and it exists prior to any compilation. Annex C of the standard is intended to convey concisely the facilities within package Standard, but it cannot be taken as actual Ada code.

Similarly, not all implementations support pragma Pack. Nonetheless, this does not mean that the definition of the predefined type String is illegal.

A Related Problem: Explain the difference between an annex of the standard and an appendix to the standard.

[Ada83]   13.1(10 .. 13); C(13, 17)

24.1.3 The Cost of Internal Codes

difficulty: designer

Consider:

```
type E1 is (A, B, C);
type E2 is new E1;
for E2 use (10, 20, 22);

type A1 is array (E1) of Boolean;
type A2 is array (E2) of Boolean;
```

Explain why it may be that the indexing operation of *A2* takes more time to execute than the indexing operation of *A1*.

◇◇◇◇◇

It is common for the default internal codes of an enumeration type to be contiguous and for arrays to be implemented as contiguous storage units. Thus, indexing can be performed as addressing relative to the beginning address of the array. Conceptually, this can be understood as

$$A \ (N) = contents-of-address \ (A \ (A'First)'Address \ +$$
$$Index\_Subtype'Pos \ (N) \ - \ Index\_Subtype'Pos \ (A'First))$$

It is also common for an implementation to represent enumeration values as their integer internal codes. For types where these codes are contiguous, the evaluations of the Pos attribute in the foregoing relation can be eliminated. This simplification of the relation fails for index subtypes with noncontiguous internal codes.

There are two common methods of implementing indexing with noncontiguous internal codes. One is to allocate sufficient storage units for the array such that internal codes can be used directly for indexing. Thus, in the preceding example, 22 components could be created for objects of the type *A2*, but only components 10, 20, and 22 would ever be used.

Another method is to use a more complex implementation of the Pos attribute. When internal codes are used to represent enumeration values, the Pos attribute maps internal codes onto position numbers. For noncontiguous internal codes, this mapping may be nontrivial. For example, the Pos attribute for type *E2* might search, at run time, the aggregate given in the representation clause. Thus, the difference between the indexing operations of *A1* and *A2* reduces to the difference between the Pos attributes of *E1* and *E2*. For *E1*, the Pos attribute can essentially be eliminated. For *E2*, the Pos attribute can be a searching function.

A Related Problem: Must the internal codes of an integer type be the same as the integer values?

[Ada83]   13.3

24.1.4 Changing Model Numbers

difficulty: language lawyer

Suppose an implementation supports all forms of representation clauses. What will the following program print?

```
with  Text_Io;
procedure  Modeling_Change is
   type  F  is  delta 2.0 range  0.0 .. 10.0;
   for  F'Small  use  1.0;

   package  F_Io  is  new  Text_Io.Fixed_Io  (F);
begin
   F_Io.Put  ((1.0  / 3)  * 2);
   Text_Io.New_Line;
end  Modeling_Change;
```

◇◇◇◇◇

The answer to the question is implementation dependent. In the absence of the length clause, the program would print some value between zero and four; with the length clause, it may print any value between zero and two.

The model numbers of a fixed point type are determined by the *small* of the type, not by its *delta*. In the absence of the length clause, *small* for the type F would be 2.0, and thus, its model numbers would be multiples of two. The length clause forces *small* to be 1.0 and, thus, the model numbers to be multiples of one. Setting *small* using a length clause simply determines the model numbers of the type; it does not, however, constrain an implementation to use a base type that represents only the model numbers. Thus, the preceding type may be implemented by a base type with a precision much greater than that specified by the length clause.

For the type F, the Delta attribute will yield 2.0 and the Small attribute will yield 1.0. (Also, F'Base'Small will be 1.0.) When providing a length clause, *small* must be less than or equal to *delta*, but *small* need not be a power of two. (The value of *small* given in a length clause must be static.) An implementation must use exactly the value of the expression given in the length clause. For example, if the following clause is legal, then the model numbers of *Pennies* will be multiples of 0.01:

```
type Pennies is delta 0.01 range 0.0 .. 100.0;
for Pennies'Small use 0.01;
```

Since a length clause affects the model numbers of a type (and thus the precision of arithmetic operations), it can change the effect of a program. Such a statement may seem to contradict [Ada83, §13.1(10)], which states that representation clauses do not alter the "net effect" of a program. Without the length clause, the program will print a value between zero and four. With the length clause, it still prints a value between zero and four. Has the "net effect" been changed? Clearly, the effect has changed, since without the length clause, the program can print four and with the length clause it cannot print four. [Ada83, §13.1(10)] states an intent that was not met by the language and thus cannot be taken literally.

Using address clauses to install interrupts is another form of a representation clause that changes the net effect of a program. If an interrupt handler prints "hello world", then, in computations that include interrupts, a program without an interrupt handler will have a different result than a program with a handler.

A Related Problem: If a program raises Storage_Error when no length clauses are specified, but does not raise Storage_Error when a length clause is given, has the "net effect" of the program been changed by the length clause?

[Ada83]   13.1(10); 13.2(11 .. 12)
[ARG]   AI-00341/15, 09-26-89; AI-00523/06, 06-16-89
See also   *Exploring Ada, Volume 1*, §7.1.2

24.1.5 Conflicting Representations

difficulty: designer

Suppose an implementation supports all forms of representation clauses. Is the following code legal?

```
type T is delta 1.0 range −7.0 .. 7.0;
for T'Size  use 4;
for T'Small use 0.5;
```

◇◇◇◇◇

The code is illegal on all implementations.

In the absence of the second length clause, the specification of *Size* may be legal: three bits are needed to represent the value 7.0 given a *small* of 1.0, and one bit is used for the sign. However, the second length clause changes *small*, thus requiring four bits to represent the unsigned value 7.0. The two length clauses are incompatible and thus illegal.

[Ada83]   13.1(3, 10); 13.2(4 .. 5, 11 .. 12)

24.1.6 Dynamic Sizes

difficulty: language lawyer

Suppose an implementation supports all forms of representation clauses. What will the following program print?

```
with Text_Io;
procedure Inflammation is
   type T is range −32_000 .. 32_000;
   for T'Size use 16;
   X : T;
   Y : T range 1 .. 100;

   procedure Looky is
   begin
      Text_Io.Put (Integer'Image (T'Size) &
                   Integer'Image (X'Size) &
                   Integer'Image (Y'Size));
   end Looky;
begin
   Looky;
   X := 0;
```

```
     Looky;
     Text_Io.New_Line;
  end Inflammation;
```

◇◇◇◇◇

The answer to the question is implementation dependent. The program will print six integer values. Let v_1 through v_6 denote the values, in the order in which they are printed.

Since the length clause defines $T'Size$, the values v_1 and v_4 will be 16. [Ada83, §13.2(5)] states that the length clause "specifies an upper bound for the number of bits to be allocated to objects of the type." Thus, it would seem that v_3 through v_6 must be less than or equal to 16. The Ada Rapporteur Group has directly contradicted this rule stating that objects are "allocated at least the specified number of bits." Thus, it would seem that v_3 through v_6 must be greater than or equal to 16. The three possible relationships between the size of a type T and the size of an object X of the type T are summarized as follows:

Relationship	*Interpretation*
T'Size > X'Size	[Ada83, §13.2(5)]
T'Size = X'Size	[Ada83, §13.2(5)] and Ada Rapporteur Group in agreement. No padding bits are used.
T'Size < X'Size	Ada Rapporteur Group interpretation that padding bits are used.

If the Ada Rapporteur Group interpretation is accepted, then the utility of the length clause in the foregoing program becomes questionable. If such a length clause cannot be used to bound the memory used by objects of the type, then what means are available for specifying object sizes?

Regardless of this contradiction, it is possible that v_2 and v_5 (and v_3 and v_6) will differ. Suppose that the object X is initially located in memory and has the same size as its type. Suppose also that, during the assignment, X is loaded into a 32-bit register. Then an implementation may interpret v_5 as 32.

A Related Problem: Since 8 bits are sufficient to store all values of the object Y, can $Y'Size$ yield 8?

[Ada83]   13.2(5); 13.7.2(5)
[ARG]   AI-00536/08, 07-06-90

24.1.7 Biased Types

difficulty: language lawyer

An implementation is allowed to reject the following length clause as illegal. Is an implementation allowed to accept the length clause?

```
type T is range 1 .. 256;
for T'Size use 8;
```

◇◇◇◇◇

An implementation is allowed to accept the length clause. This illustrates one method of defining unsigned integer types.

Consider an implementation supporting the following predefined (symmetric) integer types defined in package Standard:

```
type Short_Integer is range −2 ** 7 .. (2 ** 7) − 1;
type Integer       is range −2 ** 15 .. (2 ** 15) − 1;
type Long_Integer  is range −2 ** 31 .. (2 ** 31) − 1;
```

In such an implementation, the declaration of the type T is legal since it can be derived from Integer. In this implementation, T'Base'First would yield $−2^{15}$ and T'Base'Size would likely be 16. The aforesaid length clause simply indicates that T and its base type will have different representations. T is said to be *biased*, because it cannot be represented by a predefined type. The same 8-bit pattern would represent different integer values, depending on whether the bits are interpreted as a value of the type T or as a value of the type Short_Integer. For example, the bit pattern 0000_0000 is likely to represent the value 1 of T, but the value 0 of Short_Integer.

The foregoing predefined type Long_Integer supports 2^{64} values. Yet the following declaration would be illegal:

```
type U is range 1 .. 2 ** 64;   −− Illegal.
for U'Size use 64;
```

The reason the declaration is illegal is that there does not exist a predefined integer type from which U can be derived (a type containing the value 2^{64}); an integer type with any value not in the range of the longest symmetric predefined integer type is illegal.

A Related Problem: Can one bias enumeration, fixed point, and floating point types?

[Ada83]   13.2(4 .. 5)
[ARG]   AI-00597/03, 07-07-90

24.2 COMPOSITE TYPES

This section focuses on the use of representation clauses to define the layout of composite types. Most of the exercises deal with record representation clauses; the layout of arrays is managed using a series of length clauses.

24.2.1 Packing Records

difficulty: programmer

Suppose an implementation supports all forms of representation clauses. Is the following code legal?

```
type R is
   record
      C1, C2 : Character;
   end record;

for R use
   record
      C1 at 0 range 0 .. 6;
      C2 at 0 range 7 .. 13;
   end record;
```

◇◇◇◇◇

The answer to this question is implementation dependent.

All numeric values given in a record representation clause must be static. A record representation clause may specify

- that all values of the type must be allocated at an address that is a multiple of a given number,
- the size of record components, and
- the layout of record components.

The syntax of a record representation clause is as follows:

```
record_representation_clause ::=
   for type_simple_name use
      record [ alignment_clause ]
         { component_clause }
      end record;
```

```
alignment_clause ::= at mod static_simple_expression;
component_clause ::=
    component_name at static_simple_expression range static_range;
```

The optional alignment clause specifies addresses at which values may be located, as, for example, in

```
for R use
    record at mod 4;
    end record;
```

This alignment clause indicates that values must begin at addresses that are multiples of 4. Since "address" is an implementation-dependent concept, alignment clauses will be interpreted differently by different implementations. Specifically, since System.Address need not be an integer type, the modulus of an address need not have an intuitive semantics. The upshot is that one cannot assume that addresses number storage units, and thus, alignment clauses need not align record values at multiples of storage units.

Component clauses specify the bits occupied by components, relative to a storage unit. The storage unit specified in a component clause is relative to the beginning of the record value. The first component clause at the beginning of this subsection indicates that *C1* will occupy the first seven bits of the first storage unit. (The first bit and storage unit are each numbered zero.)

Again, suppose that System.Storage_Unit is 8. Then the component clause for *C2* simply specifies that the component will occupy the 8th through 14th bits of the record—that is, the last bit of the first byte and the first six bits of the second byte. If System.Storage_Unit is 16, then the meaning of the representation clause given in the problem would not change, since all components are specified relative to the beginning of the record value (unit 0).

As with all other forms of representation clauses, an implementation is allowed to place restrictions on the record representations it accepts. For example, an implementation may disallow

- components that do not begin at storage unit boundaries
- components that are allocated fewer bits than are specified by the size of the component type
- components that are allocated more bits than are specified by the size of the component type.

Note that even if the representation clause in the code is accepted, R'Size need not be 14. R'Size will be *greater than or equal to* 14, because an implementation may add padding bits or implementation-dependent components to the record, causing its size to be greater than the sum of its parts. However, if the clause is accepted, the following code would print 7:

```
X : R;
⋮
Text_Io.Put_Line (Integer'Image (X.C1'Size));
```

[Ada83]   13.1(10); 13.4(1 .. 5)
[ARG]   AI-00536/08, 07-06-90; AI-00551/05, 05-04-89

24.2.2 Odd Record Representations

difficulty: language lawyer

Suppose an implementation supports all forms of representation clauses. Given the record type declaration

```
type R is
   record
      A, B : Character;
   end record;
```

which of the following representation clauses are legal?

```
for R use            -- 1.
   record
      A at 0 range 0 .. 7;
   end record;

for R use            -- 2.
   record
      A at 1 range 0 .. 7;
      B at 0 range 0 .. 7;
   end record;

for R use            -- 3.
   record
      A at 0 range 0 .. 7;
      B at 0 range 6 .. 13;
   end record;
```

◇◇◇◇◇

All three clauses are legal.

A record representation clause need not provide a representation for all components. The representation of nonspecified components is implementation dependent.

Clause 3 specifies that two components overlap in memory. If one uses an address clause to overlay objects, then executions of the program are erroneous. However, the language does not state that the overlap of components in a nonvariant part of a record is illegal or that it will lead to erroneous executions. What the language does state is that the overlap of record components belonging to the same variant is illegal. Also, components of distinct variants are allowed to overlap, as the following code shows:

```
type R (B : Boolean) is
   record
      case B is
         when False => C1, C2 : Character;
         when True  => C3       : Character;
      end case;
   end record;

for R use
   record
      C1 at 0 range 0 .. 7;
      C2 at 0 range 0 .. 7;   -- Illegal.
      C3 at 0 range 0 .. 7;   -- Legal.
   end record;
```

[Ada83]   3.7(2); 3.7.3(1 .. 2); 13.4(6 .. 7)

24.2.3 Biased Components

difficulty: designer

Suppose an implementation supports all forms of representation clauses. Consider the following code:

```
type Int is range 4 .. 259;

type Rec is
   record
      A, B : Int;
   end record;

for Rec use
   record
      A at 0 range 0 .. 7;
      B at 0 range 8 .. 15;
   end record;
```

Assume that Int'Size is 16. Is the record representation clause legal?

◇◇◇◇◇

The record representation clause is legal. A record component clause is allowed to specify less memory for a component than is denoted by the size of the type of the component. It is implementation dependent whether the memory allocated for a component is sufficient; if it is not sufficient, the representation clause is illegal.

The type *Int* defines only 256 values. Since eight bits are sufficient to represent 256 values, the clause may be accepted. This clause is a means of supporting biased types, since eight bits cannot represent the value 259 unless the bit pattern 1111_1111 is interpreted as 259 rather than 256. If 1111_1111 is interpreted as 259, then 0000_0000 would be interpreted as the value 4 and the component is said to be biased by four.

If a record component or a subcomponent of a record component has a nonstatic constraint, then an implementation may not be able to determine at compilation time whether a component clause specified sufficient memory. The language requires a constraint on a component to be static if the component is named in a record representation clause. This is one reason why a record representation clause need not give a representation for all components.

[Ada83]   13.4(5, 7)
[ARG]   AI-00132/05, 07-23-86

24.2.4 Record Component Attributes

difficulty: programmer

Suppose that System.Storage_Unit is 8, that Integer'Last is greater than 32_000, and that the following program is legal. What will the program print?

```
with Text_Io;
procedure Magnetic_North is
    type R is
        record
            X : Integer range −32_000 .. 32_000;
            Y : Character;
            Z : Boolean;
        end record;

    for R use
        record
            X at 0 range 0 .. 31;
            Y at 5 range 1 .. 8;
            Z at 5 range 9 .. 9;
        end record;

    A : R;
```

```
procedure Print (I,  J,  K  :  Natural) is
begin
   Text_Io.Put (Integer'Image (I) & Integer'Image (J) &
                    Integer'Image (K));
   end Print;
begin
   Print (A.X'Position, A.X'First_Bit, A.X'Last_Bit);
   Print (A.Y'Position, A.Y'First_Bit, A.Y'Last_Bit);
   Print (A.Z'Position, A.Z'First_Bit, A.Z'Last_Bit);
   Text_Io.New_Line;
end Magnetic_North;
```

◇◇◇◇◇

The program will print *0 0 31 5 18 6 11.*

The *Position*, *First_Bit*, and *Last_Bit* attributes are defined for all record components. The *Position* attribute yields the first storage unit occupied by the component—that is, the unit in which the first bit of the component resides. The *First_Bit* attribute yields the first bit position of the first storage unit used by the component. *Last_Bit* yields the last bit position used by the component, relative to the first storage unit occupied by the component.

Note that these attributes are defined for all record components, regardless of whether a representation clause is explicitly specified for the type.

[Ada83]   13.4(5); 13.7.2(7 .. 10)

24.2.5 Minimizing Array Sizes

difficulty: language lawyer

If a programmer's goal is to minimize the size of the following array type, which of the language features used are redundant?

```
type Bit is (Off, On);
for Bit'Size use 1;

subtype Bit_Pos is Integer range 1 .. 16;
type Word is array (Bit_Pos range <>) of Bit;
pragma Pack (Word);
for Word'Size use 16;
```

◇◇◇◇◇

The answer to this question is implementation dependent. On many implementations, either the pragma or the last length clause is needed, but not both. An implementation may reject the second length clause if the first length clause is not provided. That is, without the first length clause *Bit'Size* may be 8, and the second length clause could be rejected since 16 eight-bit array components cannot be represented in only 16 bits. (Note that if the subtype *Bit_Pos* were nonstatic, then the second length clause would be illegal.)

Pragma *Pack* directs an implementation to remove "space" between components. The pragma need not have the effect of reducing the size of the components themselves. Thus, if only the pragma were specified, then *Word'Size* would likely be *Bit'Size* ∗ 16, or potentially greater than 16. Note that pragma *Pack* may be applied to both array and record types.

The first length clause reduces the size of components, the pragma removes "space" between components, and the second length clause directs the implementation to remove other implementation-dependent overhead associated with the array (e.g., dope vectors). Thus, in the general case, both length clauses and the pragma serve a meaningful purpose in minimizing the size of the array type.

Note that pragma Pack is specified for the predefined type String in Annex C of the standard. Thus, the following object does not contain "space" between components:

```
S : String (2 .. 3);
```

This is not to say that the size of the object must be 14 or even 16 bits. A length clause is not defined for the type Character. Therefore, the size of the object *S* will be at least twice that of Character. Also, the object may contain implementation-dependent data, such as its first index and its length.

[Ada83]   13.1(11 .. 12); 13.2(4 .. 6)
[ARG]   AI-00555/07, 03-19-90; AI-00556/04, 10-11-88

24.3 ACCESS AND TASK TYPES

Length clauses may be used to define statically the collection of an access type or to define the storage used during the activation of a task. These forms of length clauses are discussed in this section.

24.3.1 Dynamic Collection Sizes

difficulty: programmer

Suppose an implementation supports all forms of representation clauses. What will the following program print?

```
with  Text_Io;
procedure  Dyn  is
    type  T1  is access  String;
    type  T2  is access  String;
    for  T2'Storage_Size  use  4_000;
    S1 : constant  Integer :=  T1'Storage_Size;
    S2 : constant  Integer :=  T2'Storage_Size;

    X1 : T1 :=  new  String'("collection  usage");
    X2 : T2 :=  new  String'("collection  usage");
begin
    Text_Io.Put_Line (
        Integer'Image (S1) & Integer'Image (T1'Storage_Size) &
        Integer'Image (S2) & Integer'Image (T2'Storage_Size));
end  Dyn;
```

◇◇◇◇◇

The answer to this question is implementation dependent.

The collection of an access type is the memory used for objects designated by values of the type. The *Storage_Size* attribute yields the number of storage units reserved for the collection of an access type. Using a length clause to set the *Storage_Size* of an access type establishes the minimum size of the collection of the type. The value specified in such a length clause is the number of storage units to be reserved; this value may be of any integer type and need not be static.

The foregoing program may raise Constraint_Error if the size of either collection is greater than Integer'Last. The program may also raise Storage_Error during the elaboration of the length clause if reserving the specified number of storage units exceeds the capacity of the environment. As an example, the length clause

```
    for  T'Storage_Size  use  1E999;
```

attempts to reserve *1E999* storage units during elaboration of a type *T*. If the attempt fails, Storage_Error is raised.

Finally, executions of the program may be erroneous and thus raise Program_Error. Evaluation of *T1'Storage_Size* reads the number of storage units reserved for the collection of *T1*, but since no length clause has defined this value, the value may be undefined. Reading an undefined value is erroneous.

If no exception is raised, the program will print four values. Let us denote these values by v_1 through v_4, in accordance with the order in which they are printed. Then v_1 and v_2 are implementation dependent, and v_1 need not equal v_2, because the reserved size of a collection not specified by a length clause may change at run time. For example, v_1 may be zero, since no allocator of *T1* has been executed prior to the determination of v_1. At the same time, v_2 may be greater than zero, since allocators have been performed by the time the value is computed.

However, v_3 must equal v_4 and must be greater than or equal to 4_000. Since a length clause for a collection specifies the minimum number of storage units reserved, an implementation is allowed to reserve more units than the value given in the length clause. Suppose an implementation rounds collections to the next memory page. Then if a page of memory contains 512 storage units and a length clause specifies 600 storage units, the *Storage_Size* attribute may yield 1024, or two pages.

Finally, suppose a length clause specifies zero or even fewer (a negative number of) storage units to be reserved for a collection. In this case, no storage is reserved, and thus, any attempt to allocate an object from the collection will raise Storage_Error.

[Ada83]   13.2(7 .. 8); 13.7.2 (11 .. 12)
[ARG]   AI-00558/03, 07-06-90; AI-00608/04, 07-06-90

24.3.2 Two Sizes of Tasks

difficulty: programmer

Suppose an implementation supports all forms of representation clauses. What will the following program print?

```
with Text_Io;
procedure Size_2 is
  task type T;
  N : constant := 1_000;
  for T'Size use N;
  for T'Storage_Size use N / 2;

  task body T is

    :

  end T;
begin
  Text_Io.Put_Line (Integer'Image (T'Size) & " bits," &
                    Integer'Image (T'Storage_Size) & " units.");
end Size_2;
```

◇◇◇◇◇

The program will print *1000 bits, 500 units*.

This program involves the difference between the size and the storage size of a task type. The size of a type refers to the number of bits for values of the type. Recall that values of a task type are not themselves tasks, but rather denote tasks. Conceptually, a value of a task type is an address. Thus, specifying the size of a task type to be 1_000 bits is, for most implementations, excessive.

The storage size of a task type denotes the number of storage units reserved for the activation of each task of the type. (The specification of storage size in a length clause may be of any integer type and need not be static.) The intent is to determine the amount of memory needed to activate tasks successfully. On many implementations, this will include the memory needed for all local declarations within a task, as well as the call stack needed for subprogram calls made by a task. The intent is that the storage size does not include the memory needed to store the code implementing the task.

Since length clauses can only be given for namable types, the storage size of a task of an anonymous type cannot be specified by the user. Thus, in the code

```
task T;
for T'Storage_Size use 10_000;   -- Illegal.
```

the length clause is illegal, since it names a task, and not a task type.

A Related Problem: Could an address clause be specified for the preceding task *T*?

[Ada83]   13.2(4 .. 5, 9 .. 10); 13.7.2(4 .. 5, 13 .. 15)

24.4 ADDRESSES AND INTERRUPTS

An address clause is used to define where in memory an entity will reside. Additionally, address clauses are used to interpret entries as interrupt handlers. Addresses are specified as expressions of the type System.Address and need not be static.

The address of an entity can be read using the Address attribute, regardless of whether the address is the default determined by the implementation or whether it was set using an address clause. The Address attribute, like System.Address and address clauses, is implementation dependent. Moreover, an implementation need not yield a meaningful address for all uses of the Address attribute. For example, if pragma Inline is applied to a procedure P, then P'Address is likely to be meaningless.

24.4.1 Visibility of the Address Attribute

difficulty: designer

Suppose System.Address is a nonlimited type. Is the following use of the Address attribute legal?

```
with System;
package P1 is
   X : System.Address;
end P1;

with P1;
procedure P2 is
```

```
    Y : Integer;
begin
    P1.X := Y'Address;
end P2;
```

◇◇◇◇◇

The code is legal.

The context clauses of compilation units define a partial ordering. Conceptually, the compilation units of a library must appear within package Standard in an order consistent with this partial ordering. The use of the *Address* attribute is legal in any unit that is ordered after package *System* within Standard.

In the preceding code, the context clause naming *System* and appearing before the declaration of *P1* is needed to obtain visibility to the type *Address*. Thus, the clause dictates that *P1* follows *System* within package Standard. Similarly, the context clause appearing before the declaration of *P2* indicates that *P2* follows *P1*. Hence, *P2* must follow *System*, and the use of the *Address* attribute is legal.

A ramification of these rules is that all uses of the Address attribute that obey the typing model are legal.

Note that System.Address is implementation dependent and thus may be a limited type. On all implementations, though, the type System.Address defines a new base type.

[Ada83]   13.7(2 .. 3); 13.7.2(2 .. 3)
[ARG]   AI-00043/08, 07-06-90

24.4.2 Address Clause Static Semantics

difficulty: programmer

Suppose an implementation supports all forms of representation clauses. Suppose also that System.Address is an integer type. Which of the following address clauses are legal?

```
with System;
package Library_Unit is
    for Library_Unit use at 16#100#;   -- 1.
end Library_Unit;

with Library_Unit;
package Library_Unit_2 is
    X : Integer := 22;
    for X use at 16#200#;              -- 2.
end Library_Unit_2;

with System;
procedure P is
```

```
   procedure Q;
   for Q use at 16#300#;              -- 3.
   procedure Q is ...
begin
   declare
      procedure Q is ...
      for Q use at 16#400#;           -- 4.
   begin
      null;
   end;
end P;
```

◇◇◇◇◇

Only the third address clause is legal.

An address clause may be specified for an object, package, subprogram, single entry, or task (program) unit. In the case of packages, subprograms, task units, and objects that are not single tasks, the address clause causes the named entity to reside at the specified address. An address clause applied to a single task causes the task unit, and not the task object, to reside at the specified address. There is no means of specifying the address for the object of a single task declaration. For example, the following clause specifies the address for an anonymous task unit:

```
task T;
for T use at 12_345;
```

Finally, an address clause applied to an entry defines the entry to be an interrupt entry. Address clauses that cause different entities to occupy a common area of memory result in erroneous executions.

The first address clause is illegal because it does not appear after the declaration of the entity whose address is being set. Rather, it appears within the declaration of *Library_Unit*. The second address clause is illegal because package System is not named by a context clause that applies to the compilation unit in which the address clause appears. The fourth address clause is illegal simply because Q is overloaded at the point of the clause. It is not possible to apply an address clause to an overloaded entry or subprogram, even by means of a renaming declaration, as, for example, in

```
procedure Q;
procedure Q (C : in Character);
procedure R renames Q;
for R use at 16#100#;   -- Illegal.
```

The fourth address clause is also illegally positioned: address clauses are basic declarative items and, as such, cannot follow a later declarative item such as the procedure body they reference.

A Related Problem: [Ada83, §13.5(8)] says that some programs are erroneous. [Ada83, §1.6(7)] says that executions of programs are erroneous. Are there any other kinds of erroneousness?

[Ada83]   3.9(2); 13.5(3 .. 7)
[ARG]   AI-00043/08, 07-06-90

24.4.3 Component Addresses

difficulty: designer

Assume the following code is legal:

```
S : String (1 .. 2);
for S use at 16#100#;
```


Explain the relationships between each of S'Address, S (1)'Address, and S (2)'Address and the address 16#100#.

◇◇◇◇◇

All of the relationships are implementation dependent.

The languages provides implementations a great deal of leeway in interpreting the meaning of an address given in an address clause. Of course, in this example, it would be intuitive to interpret the address 16#100# as the base address of the array, where S'Address would be 16#100#.

Even if S'Address yields 16#100#, S (1)'Address need not be 16#100# and need not have a value "greater than" S'Address. A common case where S'Address and S (1)'Address are not equal is when implementation-dependent information is stored at the beginning of the memory used by the array object. Such information, commonly called a dope vector, might include the first index and the length of the object.

Further, there need not be any relationship between S (1)'Address and S (2)'Address: although it is common for these addresses to be offset by the component size, it is not required that that be the case.

A Related Problem: In an implementation in which addresses reference 32-bit words and characters are implemented as bytes, S (1) and S (2) may be located in the same word. Would S (1)'Address and S (2)'Address then be equal?

[Ada83]   13.5(2, 4); 13.7.2(2 .. 3)

24.4.4 Overlaying Objects

difficulty: programmer

Suppose an implementation supports all forms of representation clauses. Suppose further that System.Address is an integer type. What will the following program print?

```
with  Text_Io, System;
procedure  Pat_C is
    type  Enum is  (A,  B,  C);
    for  Enum use  (1,  3,  5);
    for  Enum'Size use  8;

    type  Int is range  1 .. 5;
    for  Int'Size use  16;

    X : Enum;
    Y : Int := 3;

    for  X use at  101011;
    for  Y use at  101010;
begin
    Text_Io.Put_Line  (Enum'Image  (X));
end  Pat_C;
```

◇◇◇◇◇

The answer to this problem is implementation dependent, since all executions will be erroneous.

Using address clauses to cause two entities to share memory results in erroneous executions. This is not to say that the preceding program cannot print *B*. An erroneous execution is simply an execution whose effect is not defined by the language. The effects of many kinds of erroneous executions are well defined by a given implementation (in Appendix F). Ada provides no nonerroneous means of overlaying objects.

In this program, Unchecked_Conversion could be employed instead of address clauses. *Y* could be converted to the type *Enum*. Use of Unchecked_Conversion, however, has the disadvantage that, generally, a copy of the value converted is made. For large data structures, this may be unacceptable. Further, it is implementation dependent whether a use of an instance of Unchecked_Conversion is erroneous. Thus, using unchecked programming in this program may be as unsafe as overlaying objects.

Another method that might be used in interpreting *Int* objects as *Enum* values involves indirection by means of access types, as in the following code:

```
type Acc is access Enum;
function Addr2Acc is new
    Unchecked_Conversion (System.Address, Acc);

X : constant Acc := Addr2Acc (Y'Address);
  :

Text_Io.Put_Line (Enum'Image (X.all));
```

This method makes many assumptions about the relationship between the implementation of *Acc* and *System.Address*.

To strictly avoid erroneous executions, one must rely only upon "checked conversions." The following code uses checked conversion from a record value to a floating point value:

```
type Format is
  record
    Sign     : Integer range 0 .. 1;
    Exponent : Integer range 0 .. 255;
    Mantissa : Integer range 0 .. 2 ** 23 - 1;
  end record;

for Format use
  record
    Sign     at 0 range 31 .. 31;
    Exponent at 0 range 23 .. 30;
    Mantissa at 0 range  0 .. 22;
  end record;
for Format'Size use 32;

type Single_Precision is digits 6;
for Single_Precision'Size use 32;

function "+" (F : in Format) return Single_Precision is
  Exp_Bias : constant := 127;
begin
  return ((-1.0) ** F.Sign) * (2.0 ** (F.Exponent - Exp_Bias)) *
         Single_Precision (F.Mantissa);
end "+";
```

A Related Problem: Is it possible to write a checked conversion from *Single_Precision* to *Format*?

[Ada83]   13.5(3 .. 4, 8); 13.10.2(3)

24.4.5 Termination of Interrupt Handlers

difficulty: designer

Suppose an implementation supports all forms of representation clauses. Suppose further that System.Address is an integer type. Will the following task ever terminate?

```
with System;
procedure Dead_Handler is
  task T is
    entry E;
    for E use at 16#20#;
  end T;
  task body T is
  begin
    loop
      select
        accept E;
      or
        terminate;
      end select;
    end loop;
  end T;
begin
  null;
end Dead_Handler;
```

◇◇◇◇◇

The answer to the question is implementation dependent.

An address clause may be provided for an entry, indicating that interrupts generated from the given address will act as entry calls to the entry. Whether such entry calls are normal, timed, or conditional is implementation dependent. The priority of the calling task is greater than that of all user-defined tasks and that of the environment task that calls the main program. That is, the priority is higher than all tasks not generating interrupts. The relative priority of two tasks that both generate interrupts is implementation dependent.

Interpreting the address of an address clause as an interrupt is implementation dependent. The original model used by the designers of the language was that interrupts would be generated by memory-mapped devices. Thus, it was conceptually clear that interrupts originated from addresses. There are, however, many other forms of interrupts that have little or nothing to do with hardware devices or physical memory addresses. For example, on some implementations, the address identifies an operating system signal that is analogous to a software exception or an asynchronous message.

If an entry is overloaded within the specification of a task, an address clause may not be specified for the entry. Also, an address clause may not be provided for a member of an entry family or the entry family as a whole.

An interrupt entry (an entry for which an address clause is specified) may include parameters. The parameters must all be of mode in, but the standard places no restrictions on the types of the parameters. The parameters of an interrupt entry might be used with interrupts that normally establish data in registers before issuing the entry call; instead of using registers, the data could be passed as parameters. An implementation is allowed to place arbitrary restrictions on the use of interrupt entries and interrupt entry parameters.

In the absence of the address clause in the foregoing task, the task would terminate upon completion of the sequence of statements in *Dead_Handler*. However, since E is an interrupt entry, calls to E may originate outside the scope of the master of T, and thus, the terminate alternative may have a semantics different than it would have if E were not an interrupt entry. In such a case, the language allows an implementation to add further requirements to the selection of a terminate alternative than those given in [Ada83, §9.4]. Such a further requirement might be that terminate alternatives are never selected. If the preceding terminate alternative is never selected, then the main program will never return.

A Related Problem: Can one define an interrupt handler that has the effect of accommodating parameters of mode out and mode in out?

[Ada83]   9.4(7 .. 10); 13.5 (3, 6, 8); 13.5.1

24.4.6 Multiple Accepts for One Handler

difficulty: language lawyer

Consider the following program:

```
with Text_Io, System;
procedure Ambiguous_Handling is
  task T is
    entry E;
    for E use at 2;
  end T;

  task body T is
  begin
    accept E do
      Text_Io.Put ('1');
    end E;

    accept E do
      Text_Io.Put ('2');
```

```
      end  E;
    end  T;
begin
  T.E;    T.E;    T.E;
  Text_Io.New_Line;
exception
  when Tasking_Error  =>  Text_Io.Put_Line (" Tasking_Error.");
  when others         =>  Text_Io.Put_Line (" others.");
end Ambiguous_Handling;
```

Suppose that the program is legal and that at some time during its execution a single interrupt at address 2 is generated. What will the program print?

◇◇◇◇◇

The answer to this question is implementation dependent.

The canonical model is that interrupts simply act as entry calls. This is an easily understood model. Under such a model, the program would print *1 2 Tasking_Error*. The language, however, allows other models.

Another possible model is that a call to an interrupt entry, regardless of whether it is generated by an interrupt or it is a normal entry call, has the effect of directly executing the "appropriate" accept statement. In such a model, the normal control structures of the task body are circumvented and an implementation may determine that the "appropriate" accept statement is the second one. In that case, the program would print *2 2 2 2*. A pathological example of this model is the following code:

```
S : String (1 .. 2) := "aa";
 ⋮
accept E do
  S := Character'Succ (S (1)) & Character'Succ (S (2));
end E;
```

Suppose that E is an interrupt entry and that halfway through an assignment to S an interrupt is generated. Assume that when interrupted, $S (1)$ has been updated but $S (2)$ has not. Then the interrupt may directly execute the assignment and then return control back to the original assignment. After the two interleaved assignments have been executed, the value of S would be "cb".

Another example where the actual code executed due to an interrupt is ambiguous has to do with entries of a task type. Consider the following legal code:

```
task type T is
  entry E;
  for E use at 16#20#;
end T;

X, Y : T;
```

Any execution of this code would be erroneous, since two entries (*X.E* and *Y.E*) have been associated with the same interrupt. This situation is similar to that wherein objects are (erroneously) overlaid at the same address. Similarly, executions of programs containing the following task would be erroneous:

```
task T is
   entry E;
   entry F;
   for E use at 16#20#;
   for F use at 16#20#;
end T;
```

Also, the following is illegal simply because multiple address clauses are given for a single entity:

```
type T is
   entry E;
   for E use at 16#10#;
   for E use at 16#20#;   -- Illegal.
end T;
```

Finally, note that an address clause may be applied to a subprogram. In fact, some implementations support the handling of interrupts by means of address clauses for procedures. The following code is illustrative:

```
procedure Interrupt_Proc;
for Interrupt_Proc use at 16#20#;
```

A Related Problem: Does an address clause applied to a package specify where the code is to be located, or where the data are to be located?

[Ada83]   13.1(4); 13.5 (3, 6 .. 8); 13.5.1

24.5 POSITIONING OF CLAUSES

This section deals with static semantic issues that are implementation independent and common to all forms of representation clauses. Also, the relationships between the representations of a type and its subtypes and between a derived type and its parent type are discussed.

24.5.1 The Force

difficulty: designer

Suppose an implementation supports all forms of representation clauses. Suppose further that System.Address is an integer type. Which of the following representation clauses are legal?

```
with System;
package Skywalker is
   type T1 is digits 6;
   subtype S1 is T1;
   Dig : constant := S1'Digits;

   type T2 is array (0 .. 7) of T1;
   procedure P2 (X : in T2);

   type T3 is (A, B);
   type T4 is
      record
         X : T3 := B;
      end record;

   type T5 is private;
   Troo : constant T5;

   type T6 is (X, Y);
   type T7 is array (1 .. 2) of T6;
   Obj1 : T7;

   for T1'Size use 32;          -- 1.
   for T2'Size use 32 * 8;      -- 2.
   for T4'Size use 8;           -- 3.
   for T3'Size use 1;           -- 4.
   for T6      use (1, 3, 5);   -- 5.
private
   type T5 is new Boolean;
   for T5'Size use 1;           -- 6.
   Troo : constant T5 := True;

   Obj2 : Integer;
   Obj3 : Integer := Obj2'Size;
   for Obj2 use at 16#Ada#;     -- 7.
end Skywalker;
```

◇◇◇◇◇

Clauses 2, 3, 4, and 6 are legal.

Certain uses of a type or object require that its representation be previously determined. These uses are called *forcing occurrences*. Representation clauses for an entity are not allowed to appear after a forcing occurrence of the entity.

The declaration of the subtype *S1* names *T1*, but is not a forcing occurrence of *T1*. The use of a type name within a type or subtype declaration is not a forcing occurrence, unless the name of the type appears within an expression. The following is a forcing occurrence of *T1*:

```
subtype S2 is T1 digits T1'Digits;
```

At the beginning of this subsection, *S1* is used within an expression of the declaration of *Dig*. This use is a forcing occurrence of *S1* and, thus, also a forcing occurrence of *T1*. For this reason, the first representation clause is illegal.

The representation clause for *T2* is legal, since no occurrence of *T2* prior to the representation clause constitutes a forcing occurrence. The use of a type as a type mark within a subprogram or entry specification is not a forcing occurrence.

The third and fourth representation clauses are both legal. The types of the components of a composite type are not forced by a representation clause for the composite type. The third representation clause does not affect the legality of the subsequent clause: clauses 3 and 4 could easily have been reversed without any change in semantics.

Clause number 6 is legal. The use of a private type in a deferred constant declaration does not force the representation of the type. Compare this situation with that of the type *T7*. The declaration of *Obj1* forces the representation of *T7*. Any representation clause for *T7* that appears after *Obj1* would be illegal. Because the representation of *T7* has been forced, the types of its components are also forced. For this reason, clause 5 is illegal: the representation of *T6* has been (implicitly) forced.

The expression used in the declaration of *Obj3* forces the representation of *Obj2*. Clause 7 is therefore illegal as well.

A Related Problem: What are the forcing occurrences for the representation of a package?

[Ada83]   13.1(6 .. 8)
[ARG]   AI-00321/02, 07-23-86; AI-00371/05, 07-23-86; AI-00494/02, 01-16-87; AI-00515/01, 01-19-87

24.5.2 Declarative Parts

difficulty: designer

Is the following code legal?

```
package P is
private
```

```
     type Inc;
     type Acc is access Inc;
end P;

package body P is
     type Inc is (A, B, C);
     for Inc'Size use 2;
end P;
```

◇◇◇◇◇

The length clause is illegal.

A representation clause for a type must appear in the same declarative part or package specification as the declaration of the type. Entities declared in a visible part may have corresponding representation clauses that appear in the private part. In the example, the (incomplete) type declaration appears in the private part, while the representation clause appears in the package body. Note that the incomplete type declaration is the declaration; the definition of *Inc* in the package body is a corresponding full declaration that "completes" the declaration of *Inc*, but is not in and of itself the declaration of *Inc*.

A private type declared in a visible part may have a representation clause given in the private part, as, for example, in the following code:

```
package P is
     type T is private;
private
     type T is (A, B, C);
     for T'Size use 2;
end P;
```

Although the type declaration and the length clause appear in different declarative parts, this is allowed because they appear in the same package specification.

[Ada83]   13.1(3 .. 5); 13.2(1 .. 4)

24.5.3 Type versus Subtype

difficulty: programmer

Suppose an implementation supports all forms of representation clauses. Is the following code legal?

```
type T is range 0 .. 33_000;
for T'Size use 32;
```

```
subtype S is T range 0 .. 32_000;
for S'Size use 16;
```

◇◇◇◇◇

The second length clause is illegal.

A length clause or enumeration representation clause may not be given for a subtype that is not a base type or a first named subtype. Thus, the length clause for *S* is illegal. When a size has been specified for a type or first named subtype, this size is also used for all subtypes of the type. That is, if the second length clause were removed, then T'Size and S'Size would both be 32.

If a length clause is not provided for a base type or first named subtype, then an implementation may use different representations for a subtype and its base type. For example, if both of the preceding length clauses were removed, an implementation could yield 32 for T'Size and 16 for S'Size.

[Ada83]   13.1(3); 13.2(3 .. 5)
[ARG]   AI-00536/08, 07-06-90

24.5.4 Parent and Derived Type Representations

difficulty: programmer

Suppose an implementation supports all forms of representation clauses. Which of the following representation clauses are legal?

```
type T1 is access String;
type T2 is new T1;
for T2'Storage_Size use 1_000;      -- 1.

type T3 is (A, B, C);
type T4 is new T3;
for T4 use (−3, −2, −1);            -- 2.

package P is
   type T5 is (A, B, C);
   procedure Q (X : in T5);
end P;

type T6 is new P.T5;
for T6 use (0, 1, 2);               -- 3.

type T7 is new P.T5;
for T7'Size use 2;                  -- 4.
```

◇◇◇◇◇

Clauses 2 and 4 are legal.

A derived access type shares the collection of its parent type. For this reason, a derived type cannot provide a length clause specifying the size of its collection, and clause 1 is illegal.

A derived type may have a different representation than its parent type. However, if the parent type of a derived type has (user-defined) derivable subprograms, then only length clauses (e.g., clause 4) may be defined for the derived type. Since clause 3 is not a length clause, it is illegal.

A Related Problem: Since an implementation must support type conversion between a derived type and its parent, even when the types have different representations, what could be the rationale for disallowing clause 3?

[Ada83]   13.1(3); 13.2(7 .. 8); 13.6

24.5.5 Derived Sizes

difficulty: programmer

Consider the following code:

```
type T1 is (A, B, C);
for T1'Size use 2;
type T2 is new T1;

type T3 is (A, B, C);
type T4 is new T3;
for T3'Size use 2;

type T5 is (A, B, C);
for T5'Size use 2;
type T6 is new T5;
for T6'Size use 3;
```

Suppose the length clauses are legal. State the relationships between the sizes of *T1* and *T2*, between the sizes of *T3* and *T4*, and between the sizes of *T5* and *T6*.

◇◇◇◇◇

T1'Size	=	2	T2'Size	=	2
T3'Size	=	2	T4'Size	=	*implementation dependent*
T5'Size	=	2	T6'Size	=	3

The representation of a derived type is that of its parent type, unless an explicit representation clause is given for the derived type. The following size specification is thus implicit after the derivation of *T2*:

```
for T2'Size use T1'Size;
```

At the point where *T4* is derived, the size of *T3* is implementation dependent. Thus, *T4* derives this implementation-dependent size. After the declaration of *T4*, the size of *T3* is specified. This specification affects the size of *T3*, but not the size of *T4*.

The declaration of *T6* results in an implicit size specification of 2. This implicit specification is then overridden explicitly. To illustrate further the distinction between implicit and explicit representation clauses, consider the following:

```
type X is (A, B, C);
for X use (877, 1601, 3571);
type Y is new X;
type Z is new Y;
```

In this code, an implicit enumeration representation clause is generated for *Y*. This implicit clause is then derived by *Z* as well.

[Ada83]   3.4(10); 13.1(3, 5); 13.2(4 .. 6)
[ARG]   AI-00138/10, 02-23-87

24.6 MACHINE CODE INSERTIONS

Ada defines a means by which machine code instructions can be expressed directly within a program. The package Machine_Code, if provided by an implementation, contains the facilities necessary to construct machine-level instructions. Naming Machine_Code in a context clause will be illegal on implementations that do not support machine code insertions.

A procedure that contains a sequence of statements known as *code statements* provides the Ada user with a means of expressing individual machine instructions within Ada code. The code statements are executed by invocation of the procedure. This section examines the static semantic issues inherent in using machine code insertions on implementations that support this feature of the language.

24.6.1 Static Semantic Issues

difficulty: programmer

Assume that the package Machine_Code defines aggregates for the type Indirect_Address_Load. Is the following program legal?

```
procedure P is
   R1, R2 : Integer;

   procedure Q is
      R3 : constant := 22;
   begin
      R1 := R3;
      Indirect_Address_Load'(From => R1, Into => R2);
   exception
      when others => R2 := -1;
   end Q;
begin
   Q;
end P;
```

◇◇◇◇◇

The program is illegal.

A code statement is syntactically a qualified aggregate and is of a type declared in the predefined package Machine_Code. Code statements may only appear within procedure bodies. If a code statement appears in a procedure body, then

• The package Machine_Code must be named in a context clause that applies to the compilation unit containing the procedure,

• The only declarative items allowed in the declarative part of the procedure are use clauses,

• All statements of the procedure must be code statements, and

• No exception handlers are allowed in the procedure.

Further, an implementation may restrict the use of nonstatic expressions and subprogram formal parameters within code statements.

[Ada83]   13.8

24.6.2 Programming with Code Statements

difficulty: programmer

Consider the following package:

```
package i386_Machine_Status is
   type Io_Privilege_Level is (Low, Medium_Low,
                               Medium_High, High);
```

```
type Status_Data is
    record
        Carry, Parity, Auxiliary_Carry, Zero, Sign,
        Trap, Interrupt_Enable, Direction, Overflow,
        Nested_Task, Resume, Virtual_8086_Mode : Boolean;
        Io_Privilege : Io_Privilege_Level;
    end record;

Status : Status_Data := ( ... );

procedure Update_Status_Object;
end i386_Machine_Status;
```

Give an example of a body for this package that utilizes machine code insertions.

◇◇◇◇◇

The following is an example with the desired properties:

```
with System, Machine_Code;
package body i386_Machine_Status is
    type Compressed_Data is new Status_Data;

    for Compressed_Data use
        record at mod 4;
            Carry              at 0 range  0 ..  0;
            Parity             at 0 range  2 ..  2;
            Auxiliary_Carry    at 0 range  4 ..  4;
            Zero               at 0 range  6 ..  6;
            Sign               at 0 range  7 ..  7;
            Trap               at 0 range  8 ..  8;
            Interrupt_Enable   at 0 range  9 ..  9;
            Direction          at 0 range 10 .. 10;
            Overflow           at 0 range 11 .. 11;
            Io_Privilege       at 0 range 12 .. 13;
            Nested_Task        at 0 range 14 .. 14;
            Resume             at 0 range 16 .. 16;
            Virtual_8086_Mode  at 0 range 17 .. 17;
        end record;

    for Compressed_Data'Size use 32;

    procedure Get_Status (X : out Compressed_Data) is
        use Machine_Code;
    begin
        Mov'(X'Address, Eflags);
    end Get_Status;
```

```
        procedure Update_Status_Object is
        begin
           Get_Status (Compressed_Data (Status));
        end Update_Status_Object;
end i386_Machine_Status;
```

The type *Status_Data* defines the various types of status that can be returned. No representation clause is specified for this type in the hope that the implementation will select the most efficient representation for selecting record components. Then, in the body of the package, *Compressed_Data* is derived from *Status_Data*. A representation is given for *Compressed_Data* so that it has the exact layout defined by the machine. This method of not specifying the representation of a parent type but doing so for a derived type is a common method of reducing the run-time cost often associated with packed representations. That is, selecting components of *Compressed_Data* values is likely to be less efficient than selecting components of *Status_Data* values. The packed representation is then used only at the lowest level, when interfacing with the machine.

The procedure *Get_Status* reads the actual machine register, using a code statement. Note that even for identical target machines, different Ada implementations may have different *Machine_Code* capabilities. For example, one implementation may define an aggregate for each instruction format, including the actual "opcode" as a component, while another implementation may define an aggregate for each instruction, naming the opcode only in the type mark preceding the aggregate. An example of the latter is given in the preceding code. An example of the former is

```
Code_32'(Mov, X'Address, Eflags);
```

The inquisitive reader might wonder why the specification of package *i386_Machine_Status* includes a variable *Status* and a procedure to update that variable. One might rather prefer to export a function that returns a value of the type *Status_Data* instead of using the variable and procedure. The problem with this method, however, is that the selector function would be a user-defined derivable operation of the type *Status_Data*: since the type *Compressed_Data* is derived from *Status_Data*, [Ada83, §13.1(3)] would make the representation clause on *Compressed_Data* illegal. The use of the variable and parameterless procedure work around this language restriction.

[Ada83]   13.6; 13.8

24.7 UNCHECKED PROGRAMMING

Ada provides two generic library units that are used in unchecked programming: Unchecked_Deallocation and Unchecked_Conversion. Both units must be predefined in all implementations; thus, naming either unit in a context clause is always legal. Use of either Unchecked_Deallocation or Unchecked_Conversion necessarily makes code less portable, since not all implementations need support the units at the same level. Note that Ada provides other means of performing unchecked programming. For example, machine code insertions and pragma Interface can have effects similar to Unchecked_Conversion.

Instances of Unchecked_Conversion are used when conversion between values of two unrelated types is required. Unlike other type conversions predefined in the language, an unchecked conversion does not include any constraint checks. This places the onus on the programmer to ensure that such unchecked conversions do not result in erroneous executions. An implementation need not support all forms of unchecked conversions.

Unchecked_Deallocation can be employed when "garbage collection" of a dynamically allocated object is desired. Although an implementation is not required actually to collect and reuse deallocated objects, this is the intent of instances of Unchecked_Deallocation.

This section explores some of the more subtle issues involved in using unchecked programming. In all cases, we assume a reasonable implementation, i.e., one that supports straightforward uses of unchecked programming.

24.7.1 Unchecked Conversion

difficulty: designer

Suppose an implementation supports all forms of representation clauses. What will the following program print?

```
with Text_Io, Unchecked_Conversion;
procedure Unchecked_Axioms is
   type T1 is (A, B, C);
   for T1 use (0, 1, 2);

   type T2 is (D, E, F);
   for T2 use (0, 1, 2);
   for T2'Size use T1'Size;

   type T3 is (G, H, I);
   for T3 use (0, 1, 2);
   for T3'Size use T1'Size;

   function C11 is new Unchecked_Conversion (T1, T1);
   function C12 is new Unchecked_Conversion (T1, T2);
   function C23 is new Unchecked_Conversion (T2, T3);
   function C13 is new Unchecked_Conversion (T1, T3);

   procedure Print (Bool : Boolean) is
   begin
      Text_Io.Put (Boolean'Image (Bool) & ' ');
   end Print;
```

Sec. 24.7   Unchecked Programming   **307**

```
begin
   for X in T1 loop
      Print (B = C11 (B));
      Print (C23 (C12 (B)) = C13 (B));
   end loop;
   Text_Io.New_Line;
end Unchecked_Axioms;
```

◇◇◇◇◇

The program will print *TRUE* six times.

The predefined generic function *Unchecked_Conversion* is used to coerce a value of one type into a value of another type. This coercion is unchecked in that no constraint checks are performed: the bits of the source value are returned as the bits of the target value, uninterpreted. The following is the definition of *Unchecked_Conversion*:

```
generic
   type Source is limited private;
   type Target is limited private;
function Unchecked_Conversion (S : Source) return Target;
```

The behavior of instances of this generic unit are well defined only when the generic actual parameters for *Source* and *Target* are of the same size. If the sizes of these parameters differ, then the behavior of resulting instances will be implementation dependent. Further, an implementation may deem illegal any instantiation of *Unchecked_Conversion* in which the sizes of the actual parameters are unequal, or any instantiations in which the size of the actual parameters cannot be determined at compilation time.

For the purposes of *Unchecked_Conversion*, values of type T are viewed as T'Size bits of memory. It is critical to understand that *Unchecked_Conversion* operates on *values* of a type, not objects of a type. Thus, even if objects of T are represented by more or fewer than T'Size bits, *Unchecked_Conversion* will behave as described here. Consider, for example, the code:

```
type Enum is (A, B, C);
for Enum use (1, 2, 3);
for Enum'Size use 2;

type Arr is array (1 .. 2) of Boolean;
for Arr'Size use 2;
```

Suppose that the representation clauses are legal. Further suppose an implementation in which objects (including subprogram parameters) of both types have a size of 16 bits, and the two "significant" bits of an *Enum* object are the rightmost bits and the two "significant" bits of an *Arr* object are the leftmost bits. In such an implementation, unchecked conversion between these types could not simply return the 16 bits passed to it: the two significant bits must be shifted from one side of the 16-bit word to the other.

A Related Problem: Can a diligent programmer reading [Ada83, §13.10.2(3)] write Ada code that is necessary to check that a value returned by an instance of *Unchecked_Conversion* satisfies the properties of its type without resulting in erroneous executions?

[Ada83]   13.10 (1, 3); 13.10.2
[ARG]   AI-00536/08, 07-06-90; AI-00590/03, 05-22-90

24.7.2 Unconstrained Conversions

difficulty: language lawyer

Suppose an implementation supports all forms of representation clauses. What will the following program print?

```
with Text_Io, Unchecked_Conversion;
procedure Unconstrained_Unchecked is
   subtype Index is Integer range 1 .. 3;
   type Arr is array (Index range <>) of Character;
   for Arr'Size use Index'Last * Character'Size;

   type Rec (C1 : Character := 'A') is
     record
       case C1 is
         when 'A' .. 'Z' => C2, C3 : Character;
         when others     => null;
       end case;
     end record;
   for Rec'Size use Index'Last * Character'Size;

   function R2A is new Unchecked_Conversion (Rec, Arr);
begin
   Text_Io.Put_Line (String (R2A (('C', '+', '+'))) & ' ' &
                     String (R2A ((C1 => '?'))));
end Unconstrained_Unchecked;
```

◇◇◇◇◇

The answer to the question is implementation dependent.

Although the sizes of *Rec* and *Arr* are equal, the Ada Rapporteur Group interpretation of unchecked conversion does not require that values returned by *R2A* be "meaningful" *Arr* values. The Ada Rapporteur Group interpretation simply states which bits are returned, and not how the bits are later interpreted. Specifically, it may be that the bits cannot be interpreted as an array value simply because the conversion failed to produce a meaningful dope vector. If an unchecked conversion yields a value that cannot be interpreted as a meaningful value of the target type, then the execution is erroneous.

[Ada83]   13.10.2
[ARG]   AI-00536/08, 07-06-90; AI-00590/03, 05-22-90; AI-00825/00, 05-15-89

24.7.3 Deallocating Tasks

difficulty: designer

What will the following program print?

```
with Text_Io, Unchecked_Deallocation;
procedure Task_Collecting is
   task type T is
      entry E;
   end T;
   type Acc is access T;

   X, Y : Acc;
   procedure Free is new Unchecked_Deallocation (T, Acc);

   task body T is
   begin
      Text_Io.Put_Line ("Hello.");
      accept E;
      Text_Io.Put_Line ("Goodbye.");
   end T;
begin
   X := new T;
   Y := X;
   Free (X);
   Y.E;
   Text_Io.Put_Line ("No-op.");
exception
   when Tasking_Error => Text_Io.Put_Line ("Tasking_Error.");
   when others        => Text_Io.Put_Line ("others.");
end Task_Collecting;
```

◇◇◇◇◇

What this program will print is implementation dependent, since all executions will be erroneous.

The predefined generic procedure *Unchecked_Deallocation* may be used to reclaim memory of an access type's collection. The generic unit is defined as follows:

```
generic
    type Object is limited private;
    type Name is access Object;
procedure Unchecked_Deallocation (X : in out Name);
```

Although the intended use of the unit is to reclaim memory, an implementation is not required to have this effect. The minimal operational semantics common to all implementations is that upon return from a call to an instance of the unit, the subprogram actual parameter has the value **null**. If an instance is called with a parameter that already has the value **null**, then the call has no effect.

Any attempt to dereference an access value that has been passed to an instance of *Unchecked_Deallocation* is erroneous. In the foregoing program, *X* and *Y* initially have the same value. After the object designated by this value is deallocated, the value is erroneously dereferenced during the execution of the entry call.

Now suppose the entry call were replaced by

```
Text_Io.Put_Line (Boolean'Image (Y = null));
```

This statement does not make an attempt to reference a deallocated object, yet is also erroneous. The Ada Rapporteur Group has decided that if two access objects have the same nonnull value, and one of the objects is passed to an instance of *Unchecked_Deallocation*, then the value of the other object is undefined. Execution of the foregoing statement would therefore be erroneous, since the statement reads an object with an undefined value.

This Ada Rapporteur Group interpretation is needed to reconcile the intended effect of unchecked deallocation with [Ada83, §4.8(7)]. The semantics of [Ada83, §4.8(7)] keeps an allocated object accessible as long as it can be named. In the preceding program, if the object designated by *X* could be named by dereferencing *Y*, then [Ada83, §4.8(7)] would not allow the call to *Free* to deallocate the designated object. [Ada83, §4.8(7)] would, in effect, require an implementation to maintain a complex collection management scheme in order to determine whether an unchecked deallocation could actually deallocate anything. The Ada Rapporteur Group interpretation removes this complexity and thus supports the notion that the deallocation is unchecked.

One may question the effect the call to *Free* has on the task of type *T*. Recall that *X*.**all** is not a task; rather, it is a task object. *X* "designates" a task object and a task object "designates" a task. (It is the task, and not the task object, that is an independent thread of control.) The call to *Free* deallocates the task object, but the deallocation does not affect the task. To further illustrate this distinction, consider the following program:

```
with Text_Io, Unchecked_Deallocation;
procedure Loose_Handle is
    task type T;
    type Acc is access T;

    X : Acc;
```

```
procedure Free is new Unchecked_Deallocation (T, Acc);

task body T is
begin
  delay 10.0;
  Text_Io.Put_Line ("Missed me.");
end T;
begin
  X := new T;
  Free (X);
end Loose_Handle;
```

The program will print *Missed me*, just as if the call to *Free* were simply replaced with

```
X := null;
```

The language provides no means of reclaiming the storage used by a task. It would be reasonable, of course, for an implementation automatically to reclaim the storage used by a task when the task terminated. Specifically, if an access value designates a task object that in turn designates a terminated task, deallocating the task object may have the effect of reclaiming the memory used by the task.

A Related Problem: Where do deallocated objects go?

[Ada83]   4.8(7); 13.10(1 .. 2); 13.10.1
[ARG]   AI-00356/08, 05-23-88

Bibliography

[ACGE85]   Christine N. Ausnit, Norman H. Cohen, John B. Goodenough, and A. Sterling Eanes. *Ada in Practice*, pages 94–127. Springer-Verlag, New York, 1985.

[Ada83]   *Reference Manual for the Ada Programming Language*. U. S. Department of Defense, U. S. Government Printing Office, ANSI/MIL-STD-1815A edition, January 1983.

[ARG]   Ada Rapporteur Group Notes. Internet Electronic Mail Distributions. Available on the Internet host ajpo.sei.cmu.edu in the directory public/ada-comment through anonymous FTP. Some are available in hard copy from Grebyn Corporation, P.O. Box 497, Vienna, VA 22183-0497, (703) 281-2194.
              See also "Approved Ada Language Commentaries." *ACM Ada Letters*, 9(3), Spring 1989.

[Bryan88]   Doug Bryan. Dear Ada. *ACM Ada Letters*, 8(2):19–26, March–April 1988.

[Bryan89]   Doug Bryan. An algebraic specification of the partial orders generated by concurrent Ada computations. In *Proceedings of Tri-Ada '89*, pages 225–241. ACM Press, October 1989.

[BT88a]   Bryce B. Bardin and Christopher J. Thompson. Composable Ada software components and the re-export paradigm. *ACM Ada Letters*, 8(1):58–79, January–February 1988.

[BT88b]   Bryce B. Bardin and Christopher J. Thompson. Using the re-export paradigm to build composable Ada software components. *ACM Ada Letters*, 8(2):39–54, March–April 1988.

[Burns87]   A. Burns. Using large families for handling priority requests. *ACM Ada Letters*, 7(1):97–104, January–February 1987.

[Cohen88]   Norman H. Cohen. Dependence on Ada task scheduling is not "erroneous." *ACM Ada Letters*, 8(2):77–79, March–April 1988.

[Dewar90]   Robert B. K. Dewar. Shared variables and Ada 9X issues. Technical Report
                   SEI–90–SR–1, Software Engineering Institute, Carnegie Mellon University,
                   January 1990.

[Elrad87]   Tzilla Elrad. Letter to the editor. *ACM Ada Letters*, 7(3):14–16, May–June
                   1987.

[Gonzalez90]   Dean W. Gonzalez. Multitasking software components. *ACM Ada Letters*,
                   10(1):92–96, January–February 1990.

[Goodenough86]   John B. Goodenough. *The Ada Compiler Validation Capability Implementors'
                   Guide*. ACVC Maintenance Organization, Wright-Patterson AFB, OH, version
                   1 edition, December 1986. Also available from Defense Technical Information
                   Center or National Technical Information Services, order number ADA189
                   647.

[Hoare81]   C. A. R. Hoare. Response to letters in "ACM Forum." *Communications of the
                   ACM*, 24(7):477–478, July 1981.

[Mendal86]   Geoffrey Mendal. Designing for Ada reuse: A case study. In *IEEE Com-
                   puter Society Second International Conference on Ada Applications and Envi-
                   ronments*, pages 33–42, IEEE Computer Society, Miami Beach, Florida, 8–10
                   April 1986. Also published as a Stanford University Technical Report, June
                   1986, CSL–86–299.

[Mendal88]   Geoffrey O. Mendal. Three reasons to avoid the use clause. *ACM Ada Letters*,
                   8(1):52–57, January–February 1988.

[Rosen87]   J. P. Rosen. In defense of the "use" clause. *ACM Ada Letters*, 7(7):77–81,
                   November–December 1987.

[VMNM85]   Richard A. Volz, Trevor N. Mudge, Arch W. Naylor, and John H. Mayer.
                   Some problems in distributing real-time Ada programs across machines. In
                   John G. P. Barnes and Gerald A. Fisher, Jr., editors, *Ada in Use: Proceedings
                   of the Ada International Conference*, pages 72–84, ACM and Ada Europe,
                   Cambridge University Press, Paris, France, May 14–16, 1985. Also published
                   in *Ada Letters*, 5(2), September–October 1985.

Index

A number of style considerations were used in building this index. First, some page numbers are given in an italic font, e.g., *123*. These entries should be viewed as important references; when many references are provided for an entry, those in the italic font should be examined first. Secondly, due to the format of this book (many small problems), the table of contents, in conjunction with this index, should both be used to locate specific topics. Thus, an effort has been made to minimize the redundancy between these two resources. Lastly, all Ada Rapporteur Group notes, e.g., AI-00594, and problem difficulty levels have been cross referenced here.

<>, *see* box
=, *see* equality

abnormal, *73,* **29, 71**
abort statement, 73, 76
　data type, 122
　derivable, 9
　derived, 7, 9, 13
　extended, 13
　generic unit instance, 121
　renaming, 219
　task vs. package, 20
　visible part, 9
accept statement, 26
　nested, 195
activation, 32, 70
　allocation, 34
　recursive, 36
　versus other states, 37
ACVC, *see* Ada Compiler Validation
　　Capability
ACVC Implementers' Guide, The, xiii
Ada Compiler Validation Capability, 150
Ada Rapporteur Group, xiii, xxi, *xxi,* 68,
　　69, 70, 103, 107, 141, 148, 160,
　　165, 233, 257, 258, 264, 276, 308,
　　310
Ada Reference Manual, xxi, xx, 76
address, *see* System, Address
address clause, 269, 270, 289
　entry, 293
Address, the attribute, 270, 287, 288
AFNOR, xi
AI-00001, 233
AI-00012, 140

AI-00016, 222
AI-00027, 203
AI-00028, 217
AI-00029, 54
AI-00030, 54
AI-00034, 31, 56
AI-00037, 127
AI-00043, 288, 290
AI-00046, 241
AI-00048, 254
AI-00050, 265
AI-00051, 261
AI-00113, 160
AI-00119, 222
AI-00132, 282
AI-00138, 302
AI-00149, 35
AI-00158, 184
AI-00159, 108
AI-00167, 68
AI-00170, 225
AI-00173, 66
AI-00187, 222
AI-00192, 146
AI-00194, 152
AI-00195, 151, 152, 155
AI-00196, 149, 150
AI-00198, 35
AI-00199, 165, 166
AI-00201, 153
AI-00215, 261
AI-00222, 166
AI-00223, 153
AI-00224, 76
AI-00225, 165
AI-00226, 157

AI-00233, 56
AI-00239, 258
AI-00241, 170
AI-00245, 234
AI-00248, 251
AI-00253, 198
AI-00255, 161
AI-00256, 28, 142, 177
AI-00257, 177
AI-00276, 61
AI-00278, 238
AI-00279, 244
AI-00286, 202
AI-00287, 22
AI-00297, 172
AI-00315, 103, 106, 108, 109
AI-00318, 17
AI-00320, 238
AI-00321, 298
AI-00325, 150, 155
AI-00328, 177
AI-00334, 92
AI-00341, 274
AI-00354, 181
AI-00355, 181
AI-00356, 311
AI-00357, 240
AI-00359, 26
AI-00360, 75
AI-00361, 270
AI-00366, 153
AI-00367, 9
AI-00370, 202
AI-00371, 298
AI-00373, 27
AI-00385, 197

AI-00387, 105, 108
AI-00392, 197
AI-00393, 14
AI-00398, 136
AI-00399, 70, 166
AI-00400, 175
AI-00408, 177, 178
AI-00409, 141
AI-00418, 159
AI-00438, 233
AI-00443, 59
AI-00444, 59
AI-00446, 75
AI-00468, 222
AI-00482, 172
AI-00483, 141
AI-00494, 298
AI-00501, 242
AI-00502, 225
AI-00505, 141
AI-00506, 177
AI-00507, 161, 165
AI-00513, 166
AI-00515, 298
AI-00523, 274
AI-00530, 178
AI-00536, 276, 280, 300, 308, 309
AI-00544, 238
AI-00546, 254
AI-00551, 280
AI-00555, 284
AI-00556, 284
AI-00558, 286
AI-00564, 271
AI-00574, 238
AI-00575, 255
AI-00576, 255
AI-00590, 308, 309
AI-00591, 238
AI-00594, 56
AI-00597, 277
AI-00602, 177
AI-00604, 243
AI-00605, 266
AI-00608, 286
AI-00738, 225
AI-00754, 151
AI-00809, 33
AI-00822, 155
AI-00825, 309
AI-00831, 11
AI-00837, 75
AI-00845, 225
AI-00847, 130
AI-00865, 189, 196
AI-00867, 68
AI-00878, 141
amorphism, *see* Owl
ancestor unit, *171*, 169, 171, 173
anonymous type, 3, 5
    task, 21, 25
ANSI, xi
ANSI/MIL-STD-1815A, xi
ARG, *see* Ada Rapporteur Group
Ascii, the package, 156
assignment statement, 106

attribute
    as generic actual subprogram, 130
    derived, 5

Base, the attribute
    derived, 5
basic operation
    derived, 1, 3, 9, 10, 12
    membership, 28
    optimization, 109
    scope, 186
    task type, 27
    visibility, 202
Bell, Alexander Graham, 185
biased type, 277, 282
body stub, *167*, 169
Boolean type, 2
box, 119
busy wait, 56

Calendar, the package, 148
    Clock, 151, 153
    Day_Duration, 148
    Day_Number, 148
    Month_Number, 148
    Time_Error, *149*, 152
    Time_Of, 148
    Year_Number, 148
Callable, the attribute, 29
canonical order, 106
character, literal
    visibility, 203
Character, the type, 272
    derived, 5
Clock, *see* Calendar, the package
Close a file, *see* file, Close
code statement, 302
Cohen, Norman H., 269
collection, 285
Column, *see* Text_Io, Column
compilation, 160
compilation unit, *162*, 146, 164, 168
completion, 29, 70
    library package, 69
    of a master, 65
    of abnormal task, 73
    while updating variables, 75
conditional entry call, *58*, 60
constraint
    in a generic instance, 137, 139
Constraint_Error, 104, 107
    Calendar, 152
    derived subprogram call, 16
    entry call, 42
    entry family, 22
    file operations, 243
    generic parameter association, 129
    hiding, 89
    instantiation, 126, 128
    name evaluation, 218, 223
    optimized, 109
    renaming declaration, 224
    rendezvous, 42
context clause, 204
Count, the attribute, *30*, 50

Crafts, Ralph E., 269
Create a file, *see* file, Create
CREW, 78
Current_Output, *see* Text_Io,
    Current_Output

Data_Error, *247*, 245, 256, 259, 260
    priority, 242
Day_Duration, *see* Calendar, the package
Day_Number, *see* Calendar, the package
deadlock, 72
deadness error, 62, 63, 72
declarative region, 188
default expression
    renaming, 226
default parameter
    task type, 24
delay alternative, *see* selective wait, delay
    alternative
delay statement, 61, 151
delayed binding, 121
Delete a file, *see* file, Delete
Delta, the attribute, 274
derivable subprogram, *11*, 8, 10
derived operations, 1
derived subprogram, 11
    calling, 14
derived type, 1
    collection, 301
    representation, 301, 302, 305
designator
    renaming, 226
designer problem, *xx*
designer problems, 4, 6, 9, 11, 14, 28, 29,
        30, 31, 35, 36, 48, 49, 54, 57, 59,
        61, 64, 67, 68, 72, 75, 77, 80, 82,
        84, 101, 105, 113, 117, 118, 120,
        121, 127, 132, 133, 135, 136, 137,
        138, 142, 148, 149, 150, 151, 152,
        153, 160, 163, 166, 169, 170, 175,
        177, 186, 193, 194, 198, 199, 200,
        203, 205, 207, 213, 215, 219, 225,
        228, 233, 239, 242, 245, 247, 251,
        252, 264, 265, 266, 272, 275, 281,
        287, 290, 293, 297, 298, 306, 309
Device_Error
    priority, 242
Dewar, Robert, 19, 87, 103
Direct_Io
    Index, 238
    Size, 238, 245
discrete range
    entry family, 22
discriminant
    classify tasks, 23
    in generic formal part, 117, 126
dope vector, *290*, 284, 309
Duration, the type, 150
    Small, 153

Elaborate, the pragma, 180, 184
elaboration
    accessing shared variables, 79
    Constraint_Error, 219, 224
    entry family index, 22

erroneous, 218
exception, 98
exception, library package, 99
exception, package, 99
exception, task, 33
exception, task master, 71
generic unit, 134
instance, 91
instantiation, 129, 138, 142, 176, 178, 184
length clause, 285
library unit, 158, 179
main program, 184
order, 180
package, 96
package Calendar, 150
Program_Error, 183
program unit, 179
renaming declaration, 215, 216, 225
subunit, 160, 182
task body, 34
task object, 32
using generic unit, 122
versus other states, 37
End_Error, *268*, 237, 245
   priority, 242
End_Of_File, 238, 267
End_Of_Page, *see* Text_Io, End_Of_Page
entry
   declaration, 21
entry family, 21
   expanded name, 195
   renaming, 229
enumeration representation, 269, 270
Enumeration_Io, 255, 258
environment, 236
environment task, 19, 166
equality
   in a generic formal part, 119
   renaming, 231
   scope, 187
erroneous
   accept statement, 41, 42
   address, 289, 291
   attribute value, 285
   deallocation, 309
   interrupt address, 296
   parameter usage, 85
   reordering, 108
   representation, 280
   shared variable, 39, 78, 79, 80, 81
   task name, 68
   Unchecked_Conversion, 291, 306, 309
   Unchecked_Deallocation, 217
   undefined value, 218
   versus indeterministic, 51
exception, 87
   declaration, 88
   handler, 92
   hiding, 89
   in generic unit, 89
   task elaboration, 33
expanded name, 190, 198, 220
external file, *see* file, external

family index subtype, 22
FIFO, 44
file
   Close, *267*, 237
   Create, 237
   Delete, 237
   external, *237*, 236, 254
   form, 237, 238
   internal, 254
   mode, 238, 240
   name, 238
   Open, 237
   temporary, 240
   terminator, *see* terminator, file
First, the attribute
   derived, 5
First_Bit, the attribute, *283*, 270
Float_Io, 259, 261
   Aft, 262
   Exp, 262
   Fore, 262
forcing occurrence, 298
form of a file, *see* file, form
frame, 92

generic
   compilation, 174, 175, 177
   formal object, 112, 113, 114
   formal parameter, 110
   formal part, 110, 111
   formal subprogram defaults, 119
   formal type template, 114
   instance, *see* instance
   instantiation, *see* instantiation
   parameter matching, *see* instantiation
generic subprogram
   derivable, 18
Gerhardt, Mark, x, 145
Get_Line, *see* Text_Io, Get_Line
Gonzalez, Dean W., 85
Goodenough, John B., 202

Hilfinger, Paul, 103, 250
homograph, *191*, 21, 44, 140, 146, 194, 208
   instance, 140

Ichbiah, Jean, xi
Image, the attribute, 230
immediately, 57, 60
implementation dependent *103-109*
   Address attribute, 290
   address of an entry, 293
   alignment clause, 279
   array size, 284
   character I/O, 257
   collection size, 285
   compilation, 176, 178
   conditional entry call, 58
   conversion, 308
   Enumeration_Io, 258
   external file, 241
   file name, 238
   file read, 245
   I/O of access values, 246

input, 247
internal code, 271
interrupt, 295
memory, 282
program library, 161
real value, 274
record representation, 279
representation clause, 270
shared variable, 78, 81
size, 276, 302
temporary file, 240
termination, 70
Unchecked_Conversion, *307*, 291
Implementers' Guide, *see* ACVC Implementers' Guide
incorrect, 180
indeterminant
   elaboration order, 180
   entry call, 60
   shared variable, 81, 85
   tasking, 37, 52
indeterminism
   selective wait, 50
infinite, 36
instance, 134
   exception, 143
   object constraint, 137, 139
   operations of formal types, 135
   static, 141
   with homograph, 140
instantiation, 123
   Constraint_Error, 126, 128
   default subprogram, 131
   library unit, 162
   Program_Error, 134
   subprogram matching, *132*, 130
   type matching, 127
Integer, the type, 150
Integer_Io, 255, 260
Interface, the pragma, 271
internal code, 271
   noncontiguous, 272
internal file, *see* file, internal
interrupt, 293, 295
Is_Open, 237, 238
ISO, xi

Joy, Bill, 110

language lawyer problems, *xx*, 104, 107, 108, 141, 159, 222, 232, 254, 272, 273, 275, 276, 280, 283, 294, 308
Last, the attribute
   derived, 5
Last_Bit, the attribute, *283*, 270
Lawrence, D. H., 110
Layout_Error, 263
   priority, 242
legal, xxi
length clause, 269, 270
   task type, 26
library task, 166
library unit, 146, 164, 168, 175
limited type
   task type, 24

Line, *see* Text_Io, Line
line terminator, *see* terminator, line
Linton, Mark, 145
logical processor, 77
Luckham, David, 19

machine code insertion, 302
Machine_Code, the package, *303*, 305
main program, *165*, 160, 166
  begins execution, 180
  elaboration, 183
  task, 19
maintainable, 5, 14
master of a task, *62*, 294
  completion, 65
  exceptional elaboration, 71
  library package, *69*, 166
  terminate alternative, 69
McKay, Charles, xi
membership test
  scope, 187
  task type, 28
  visibility, 202
MIL-STD-1815A, xi
misunderstood, *see* [Ada83, §11.6]
mod, 279
mode of a file, *see* file, mode
mode, subprogram parameter
  task type, 24
Mode_Error
  priority, 242
model number, 274
Month_Number, *see* Calendar, the
    package

Name_Error, 236
  priority, 242
New_Page, *see* Text_Io, New_Page
novice problems, *xx*, 22, 26, 50, 88, 89,
    111, 155, 156, 162, 174, 181, 190,
    194, 197, 205, 211
null
  visibility
Numeric_Error, 104, 107
  Calendar, 152
  entry family, 22
  file operations, 243

obsolete unit, 172, 175
Open a file, *see* file, Open
open alternative, *see* selective wait, open
    alternative
optimization, 103
others choice, *96*, 93, 101
overload
  address clause, 289, 294
  compilation unit, 158
  Count, 31
  derived subprogram, 9
  entry, 21
  entry family, 21
  generic formal part, 133
  homograph, 191
  library unit, 162

renaming, 172
  subunit, 171
overload resolution
  renaming declaration, xxx
Owl, Freddy T., 245

Pack, the pragma, *284*, 272
package body
  empty, 175
Page, *see* Text_Io, Page
page terminator, *see* terminator, page
parallel, 77
parent type, *3*, 5, 7, 10
  collection, 301
  in visible part, 4, 7, 8, 12
  representation, 301, 302, 305
  subprogram call, 15
  type conversion, 7
parent unit, *167*, 169, 171, 173
  recompilation, 173
portability
  Numeric_Error, 107
  optimization, 103
  unchecked programming, 306
Pos, the attribute, 230, 271
  derived, 5
position number, 271
Position, the attribute, *283*, 270
potentially affected compilation unit, 173
Pred, the attribute, 230
prefix, 220
priority, 293
Priority, the pragma, 56
Program_Error, *183*, 122, 285
  file operations, 243
  incorrect order dependency, 180
  instantiation, 134
  selective wait, 54
  task activation, 34
program library, 145
program unit
  task, 20
programmer problem, *xx*
programmer problems, 2, 3, 5, 8, 17, 20,
    24, 25, 34, 41, 42, 45, 46, 52, 56,
    62, 66, 71, 89, 90, 92, 93, 94, 95,
    97, 99, 112, 114, 116, 123, 125,
    129, 130, 140, 142, 145, 147, 151,
    157, 161, 165, 167, 168, 172, 179,
    182, 187, 190, 191, 196, 202, 204,
    212, 214, 217, 218, 220, 229, 230,
    231, 232, 236, 238, 240, 241, 243,
    244, 251, 254, 255, 257, 258, 260,
    261, 271, 278, 282, 284, 286, 288,
    291, 299, 300, 301, 302, 303
propagate, 96
  from a declarative part, 98
  from a library package, 99
  from a package, 99
  from an instance, 143
  optimization, 107

raise statement
  with exception name, 95
  without exception name, 94

readable, 14, 214, 250
record representation, 269, 270
record representation clause, 278
Reset, *240*, 253, 265, 267
reuse
  binding time, 121
  generic unit, 110

scope, *185*
  basic operation, 186
  extended, 187
  immediate, 187
secondary unit, 146, 164, 173
selective wait
  delay alternative, 57, 61
  else part, 61
  open alternative, 53
  terminate alternative, 62
selector, 220
Set_Output, *see* Text_Io, Set_Output
Shakespeare, William, xix
shared variable, 78
  file, 238
Size, the attribute, 270, 276
  array type, 283
  biased type, 277
  conversion, 307
  record type, 279
  subtype, 300
  task type, 286
Skip_Line, *see* Text_Io, Skip_Line
slice, 214
Small, the attribute, 270, 274, 275
Socratic, ix, xii, xxii
Standard, the package, 145, 147, 272
Standard_Input, *see* Text_Io,
    Standard_Input
Standard_Output, *see* Text_Io,
    Standard_Output
static
  collection, 284
  derived type, 3
  enumeration representation clause, 271
  expression in a code statement, 303
  generic instance, 141
  length clause, 274
  record component constraint, 282
  record representation clause, 278
  renaming declaration, 233
  task priority, 56
Status_Error, *237*, 242, 254
  priority, 242
Storage_Error, *285*, 286
  file operations, 243
Storage_Size, the attribute, 270
  access type, 285
  task type, 286
string literal
  visibility, 203
String, the type, 272
subprogram
  derivable, *see* derivable subprogram
  derived, *see* derived subprogram
subtype indication
  in a generic formal part, 116

subunit, 167, 171, 173
Succ, the attribute, 230
Suppress, the pragma, 260
synchronization
    transitive, 82
synchronization point, *73*, 39
    shared variable, 78
system dependent, 236
System, the package, 288
    Address, 279, 287, 288, 292
    implementation extensions, 251
    Storage_Unit, 279, 282
    Tick, 153

task
    generic, 23
task state, 70
    abnormal, *see* abnormal
    activation, *see* activation
    completed, *see* completion
    terminated, *see* termination
Tasking_Error, 27, 30
    allocator, 34
    call to abnormal task, 74
    entry call, 47, 54, 67
    file operations, 243
    interrupt, 295
    task activation, 33
temporary file, 240
terminate alternative, *see* selective wait,
        terminate alternative
    with interrupts, 294
Terminated, the attribute, 29
termination, 29, 33, 63, 70
terminator
    file, 266, 267
    line, 252, 259, 264, 266, 267
    page, 259, 266, 267

Text_Io
    buffered, 252
    Close, *see* file, Close
    Column, 238
    Create, *see* file, Create
    Current_Input, 253
    Current_Output, 253, 254
    Delete, *see* file, Delete
    End_Of_File, *see* End_Of_File
    End_Of_Page, 266
    Get_Line, 251, 260, 264
    Is_Open, *see* Is_Open
    Line, 238
    Name, 239
    New_Page, 267
    Open, *see* file, Open
    Page, 238
    Reset, *see* Reset
    Set_Output, 254
    Skip_Line, 259, 264, 266
    Standard_Error, 251
    Standard_Input, 253, 255
    Standard_Output, 253, 255
Text_Io, Enumeration_Io, *see*
        Enumeration_Io
Text_Io, Float_Io, *see* Float_Io
Text_Io, Integer_Io, *see* Integer_Io
Tick, *see* System, the package
Time_Error, *see* Calendar, the package
Time_Of, *see* Calendar, the package
timed entry call, 60
type conversion, 7
    derived subprogram call, 15
    derived type, 6
    explicit, 18

unchecked programming, 305
    omitting checks on I/O, 247

Unchecked_Conversion, *306*, *307*, 247,
    291
    internal code, 271
    unconstrained, 308
Unchecked_Deallocation, *309*, 217, 306
unconstrained
    generic actual type, 126, 128
    generic formal type, 117, 126
    type in a renaming declaration, 214
    variable renaming, *223*, 210
understandable
    derived operation, 14
    derived type, 17
    renaming, 214, 227
usability
    generic unit, 121
    renaming, 227
use clause, 204
Use_Error, 236, 241
    priority, 242

Val, the attribute, 230, 271
Value, the attribute, 230
visibility, *185*
    basic operation, 202
    by selection, 197
    character literal, 203
    direct, 197
    names and labels, 200
    potential, 206

with clause, 155, 180
    circular, 158

**Year_Number, *see* Calendar, the
package**
Young, Michal, 1